TAKING *to* *the* STREETS

ÉTUDES D'HISTOIRE DU QUÉBEC / STUDIES ON THE HISTORY OF QUEBEC
Magda Fahrni et/and Jarrett Rudy
Directeurs de la collection / Series Editors

DAN HORNER

TAKING *to* *the* STREETS

*Crowds, Politics, and the Urban Experience
in Mid-Nineteenth-Century Montreal*

McGill-Queen's University Press
Montreal & Kingston • London • Chicago

ISBN 978-0-2280-0126-3 (cloth)
ISBN 978-0-2280-0127-0 (paper)
ISBN 978-0-2280-0263-5 (ePDF)
ISBN 978-0-2280-0264-2 (ePUB)

Legal deposit second quarter 2020
Bibliothèque nationale du Québec

Printed in Canada on acid-free paper that is 100% ancient forest free (100% post-consumer recycled), processed chlorine free

This publication has been supported by a Faculty of Arts Special Projects Grant from Ryerson University.

Funded by the Government of Canada · Financé par le gouvernement du Canada | Canada

Canada Council for the Arts · Conseil des arts du Canada

We acknowledge the support of the Canada Council for the Arts.
Nous remercions le Conseil des arts du Canada de son soutien.

Library and Archives Canada Cataloguing in Publication

Title: Taking to the streets : crowds, politics, and the urban experience in mid-ninteenth-century Montreal / Dan Horner.
Names: Horner, Daniel, 1979- author.
Series: Studies on the history of Quebec ; 38.
Description: Series statement: Études d'histoire du Québec / Studies on the history of Quebec; 38 | Includes bibliographical references and index.
Identifiers: Canadiana (print) 20200198823 | Canadiana (ebook) 20200198904 | ISBN 9780228001270 (softcover) | ISBN 9780228001263 (hardcover) | ISBN 9780228002635 (PDF) | ISBN 9780228002642 (EPUB)
Subjects: LCSH: Demonstrations—Québec (Province)—Montréal—History—19th century. | LCSH: Montréal (Québec)—History—19th century. | LCSH: Montréal (Québec)—Politics and government—19th century. | LCSH: Sociology, Urban—Québec (Province)—Montréal—History—19th century. | LCSH: Collective behavior.
Classification: LCC FC2947.4 .H67 2020 | DDC 971.4/2802—dc23

Contents

Figures

Maps produced by Gerald Romme, GIS analyst, University of Toronto Map and Data Library.

—m—

Acknowledgments

—m—

I have accumulated a great many debts over the course of seeing this project to fruition, and it is a pleasure to acknowledge these here. *Taking to the Streets* began its existence as my dissertation in the Department of History at York University. It bears the indelible mark of my advisor, Bettina Bradbury, whose guidance and mentorship over the years shaped the way that I approach academic life. I am also grateful for the advice I received from Colin Coates and Nick Rogers, who rounded out my thesis committee, and from Jan Noel, my external examiner. Kristine Alexander, Rebecca Beausaert, Jarett Henderson, Maki Montapayane, and Angela Rooke read early drafts of many of these chapters and provided me with invaluable feedback and encouragement. The years I spent at York were enlivened by the camaraderie of my fellow graduate students in the history department, and I look back upon that time often and with great fondness.

My involvement with the Montreal History Group has provided me with boundless scholarly inspiration and, at some critical junctures, material support. Many thanks are owed to its past and current members, including Denyse Baillargeon, Amélie Bourbeau, Magda Fahrni, Don Fyson, Brian Gettler, Darcy Ingram, Nicolas Kenny, Liz Kirkland, Maude-Emmanuelle Lambert, Andrée Lévesque, Laura Madokoro, Sean Mills, Stéphanie O'Neil, Valérie Poirier, Mary Anne Poutanen, Amanda Ricci, Daniel Ross, Sonya Roy, Jarrett Rudy, and Sylvie Taschereau. In an act of tremendous generosity, Suzanne Morton lent me her apartment in Mile End for two consecutive summers, providing me a home base to do much of the archival work for this project. I first began learning how to become an historian as an undergraduate in Brian Young's classes at McGill, and I am very appreciative of his insights and support over the years.

I was very fortunate to hold three different postdoctoral fellowships where I was given the time and space needed to grow as a scholar and teacher. I spent a very stimulating six months at the Centre for Urban History at the University of Leicester, where Simon Gunn provided wonderful hospitality and scholarly guidance. Viv Nelles welcomed me to McMaster's Wilson Institute, a place that has been such a boon to the entire field of Canadian History. Finally, Michèle Dagenais hosted me in the Département d'histoire at the Université de Montréal, where I benefitted from her expertise in the history of the city. During these years conversations about Montreal and history with Sherry Olson, Patrick Connor, Willie Jenkins, Sebastian Haumann, Dan Malleck, Maxime Dagenais, Ryan George, Robert Sweeny, Elsbeth Heaman, Craig Heron, Ian Radforth and members of the Toronto Labour History Reading Group, and Daniel Samson and his colleagues in the History Department at Brock pushed me to tighten up my arguments. Pamela Swett, Michael Egan, Stephen Heathorn, Sean Kheraj, and Andrew Watson provided invaluable advice during my adventures on the academic job market. Simon Orpana, Megan and Ben Evans, Tarah Brookfield and Dennis Lund, and Ashley and Nathan Hoath-Murray have been the source of much camaraderie during my years in Hamilton.

Marcel Fortin and Gerald Romme from the Map and Data Library at the University of Toronto created the lovely maps found in this book. At McGill-Queen's University Press, Jonathan Crago has been a knowledgeable, diligent, and supremely patient editor, and I am grateful for his years of commitment to this project. Susan Glickman worked miracles as my copyeditor. Comments from the two anonymous reviewers of this manuscript pushed me towards substantive improvements. Thanks as well to Pamela Sugiman and Ryerson's Faculty of Arts for their financial support of this project. Much of this research was carried out with the support of the Social Sciences and Humanities Research Council through doctoral and postdoctoral fellowships. An earlier version of chapter 3 appeared in the *Revue d'histoire urbaine / Urban History Review*.

I owe much appreciation to my wonderful colleagues in the Department of Criminology at Ryerson, including Nadia Aboulhosn, Daniel Alati, Idil Atak, Scott Clark, Kelly De Luca, Graham Hudson, Maria Jung, Zahir Kolia, Kristy Kraemer, Tammy Landau, Alexandra Orlova, Shiri Pasternak, Sharon Ryder-Turner, Ajay Sandhu, Anne-Marie Singh, Jane Sprott, Sara Thompson, Kim Varma, and Emily van der Meulen. Their passion for social justice and zest for life makes the eighth floor of Jorgensen Hall an energizing place to work.

The earliest origins of this work can be traced to the basements of suburban Montreal in the waning days of the last millennium, where I spent many long nights discussing music and politics with Adam Kardos, Blake Evans, Jessie Evans, Paul Cargnello, Karina D'Ermo, and Kurt Houghton. The intervening years have seen some of us scattered around the globe, but even from afar their continued friendship means the world to me.

I am, of course, deeply indebted to my family. My parents, Norm and Beverley, have provided unwavering encouragement to all my unconventional pursuits over the years. Spending my childhood in a home filled with conversations about books and politics shaped who I am more than anything else. Thanks as well to my brother Matthew, sister-in-law Rebecca Hogg, and their kids Madeline and Sam for their support while this project was taking shape. My introduction to history came from talking with my grandparents Stanley and Ray Eccles and Douglas and Frances Horner about their experiences of the twentieth century. It's rotten that these conversations have drawn to a close. My in-laws Bob and Dora Belaskie welcomed me into their family and have been generous in countless ways over the years, especially when it comes to childcare. Thanks to my brother-in-law Paul Belaskie for all of his encouragement.

My daughters Josephine and Winifred are not unlike some of the people whose stories are told in this book. They engage in exuberant celebrations and menacing brawls, spontaneous parades and riotous demonstrations. They always find a way to make their presence known and voices heard. I adore them for that and for so many other reasons. Their arrival in my life has enriched me in ways I am incapable of articulating. Finally, this whole project is inextricable from the life that Cynthia Belaskie and I have forged together. She has lived with these stories and ideas for as long as I have, and her intellectual fingerprints are detectable on many of these pages. She has provided all the necessary encouragement and discouragement over the years, lifting me up off the floor and pulling my head down from out of the clouds. Talking to her every single day is the greatest. This whole endeavour is dedicated to her.

TAKING *to the* STREETS

Introduction

THE CROWD AS AN HISTORICAL ACTOR
AND A LIVED EXPERIENCE

During the spring of 2012, Montrealers took to the streets. They joined marches, they hammered out rickety rhythms on their *casseroles*, they sang and chanted, and they fashioned slogan-laden banners out of old bedsheets. Knots of curious bystanders looked on from sidewalks, terraces, and balconies. This wave of exuberant protests greeted the provincial government's decision to raise university tuition fees. What began as large-scale demonstrations organized in conjunction with a student strike evolved into more loosely organized nocturnal processions through different neighbourhoods of the city. The atmosphere of the marches was at once confrontational and festive, and they quickly widened into a broader critique of the impact liberal economics, with its devotion to fiscal austerity, was having on young people. This became a pivotal moment of community solidarity, when the public seemed to entertain the possibility of a more equitable future. In a world where youth are often pilloried for being apathetic, the protests represented the flowering of a socially engaged political movement.[1]

As spirited as these demonstrations were, there were darker moments as well. Relations between the protestors and the police, who often sported protective riot gear, were strained. The protestors encountered the power of the state in its most aggressive manifestation and violent clashes erupted, with injuries occurring on both sides.

And for every Montrealer participating, there were many more who remained at home, frustrated by stories of snarled traffic and a city and province held hostage by what some dismissed as sanctimonious and naive young adults. The government imposing these tuition hikes, many mainstream commentators insisted, had been elected with a mandate to tackle the province's fiscal deficits. Taxpayers, they argued, could no longer afford to bankroll the studies of its post-secondary students to the degree that it had done in the past. To these observers, the protests were an attack on the democratic process by a privileged minority noisily guarding its interests from the will of the majority.

This wave of protests – what came to be known as Quebec's *printemps érable* – speaks to the vital but contested role that crowds have long played in Montreal's culture and politics. The same collective actions that allow people to forge bonds of solidarity and allow marginalized members of the community a rare opportunity to have their voices heard also raise difficult questions about public order and what constitutes legitimate democratic engagement. While there is an extensive legacy of popular agitation as a cornerstone of Western democracy, there is also a long tradition of hostility towards these same actions. Generations of theorists and social scientists have contemplated the notion that crowd activity represents an abandonment of rational discourse, a turn to something dark, unhinged, and emotional. It has been portrayed as the antithesis of those liberal values that emerged in the nineteenth century valourizing reason, discipline, and one's ability to appear detached and independent in the midst of turmoil. These attributes were assumed by many to be the sole purview of affluent men of European descent. To study attitudes towards crowds necessitates reflection on the process of social and political marginalization. What became clear as the *printemps érable* unfolded was that, more than a decade into the twenty-first century, conflict over the legitimacy of collective action remains unresolved. Taking to the streets remained an integral strategy of those who wished to challenge the legitimacy of a government's project, while hostility towards such actions remained palpable in the public sphere.

What insights can historical inquiry provide on this subject? The spectre of raucous crowds on the streets of Montreal being a driving force of public life in the city was not novel. This experience has been integral to the way that Montrealers express their social, political, and cultural affiliations for the better part of two centuries. *Taking to the Streets* examines one particularly turbulent decade when the streets of Montreal became a politicized space. The 1840s began in the aftermath of a failed uprising against a colonial elite hostile to democratic reform, and conflicts over legitimate political authority would weigh heavily on life in the city throughout the decade. Crowd events like riots, parades, and religious processions not only occurred with great frequency, but played a definitive role in a number of important political, social, and cultural transformations. There is an extensive body of scholarly literature on the role of crowds in driving and contesting social change. This body of literature took shape in the middle of the twentieth century, when a school of left-wing historians began to write ordinary people into historical narratives from which they had previously been erased. Riots provided historians with rare insights into the attitudes and practices of people whose voices were routinely silenced in historical documents widely perceived to be authoritative, like newspapers and government documents.[2] They also shed light on changing practices of authority, as unruly crowds drove innovations in policing and urban regulation. The blossoming of this literature drew attention to the ways that community bonds were formed, asserted, and defended by a palette of rough and rowdy cultural practices that historian Natalie Zemon Davis has referred to as "the social creativity of the inarticulate."[3]

British historian E.P. Thompson was particularly strident in his efforts to reframe collective acts like riots and demonstrations as legitimate and rational forms of political engagement rather than as sporadic outbursts of madness.[4] Thompson's landmark article on the moral economy of the English crowd, part of a broader effort on his part to rethink class as a fluid process rather than as a series of static categories, touched off a wave of scholarship not only by historians but also by anthropologists, sociologists, psychologists, folklorists, and cultural theorists.[5] Thompson was not without his critics. Some argued that he imagined the actions of eighteenth-century English crowds to be more coherent and cohesive than they actually were, and others pointed out that he downplayed the important role that middling sorts of people played in crowd events.[6] These criticisms aside, the work of this first generation of scholars about collective actions opened up a vital and dynamic space to contemplate the roles that women and men from the popular classes played in moments of conflict and the processes of social change. Detailing the actions and reflecting on the motivations of crowds became a defining methodology of those who were writing what became known as "history from below."[7]

Taking a more sociological approach during these years, Charles Tilly published a number of pioneering studies of what he referred to as "contentious politics" in eighteenth- and nineteenth-century Britain and France.[8] He explored how social movements employed a variety of popular demonstrations, including parades and processions, to communicate their vision to a broader community. Like Thompson, Tilly and his collaborators took seriously those acts of popular resistance that previous generations of historians had either dismissed as the irrational clamour of a mob or tried to squeeze into a tidy narrative of class struggle. Instead, he explored the strategies and meanings of their actions, and how they shaped collective identities.[9] The work resonated in the contentious environment of 1960s and 1970s America, where demonstrations and marches were once again seen as driving forces for social change.

Scholarly interest in questions around crowds and collective actions underwent a shift in the 1980s. While many remained engaged in the study of popular protest and the state's response to these actions, others turned their attention to more choreographed events like public celebrations and parades. In some ways, this literature continued to pursue many of the questions first posed by Thompson, Tilly, and their contemporaries a generation earlier regarding the symbolic language of collective action. In an era when the political tone was being set by a reenergized right, scholars critically assessed the complicated relationship between ritual, power, and patriotism.[10] They asked how political, social, and cultural elites from the eighteenth to the twentieth centuries employed public rituals to foster allegiance to their respective regimes.[11] Both the events that historians were examining in this literature and their methodological approach differed from those that interested earlier social historians, yet there was continuity in the fundamental questions they were asking such as: How was authority asserted and resisted through crowd events? How did the popular classes both acquiesce to and resist emerging practices of authority during moments of social, cultural, and political change? What do these crowd events tell us about the politics of race, class, and gender?[12] Both the practitioners of the early literature on crowds and popular resistance and the body of cultural history and theory that emerged around pageantry and ritual were concerned first and foremost with searching out unconventional sites in which to grapple with questions about how power was wielded and resisted.[13]

The most recent writing on collective action has placed these practices in the framework of broader debates around the transformation of democracy in the post-Enlightenment world. Jürgen Habermas' *The Structural Transformation of the Public Sphere* looms heavily over this literature. In this groundbreaking study, Habermas pointed to the turn of the nineteenth century in Western Europe as the time and the place where the public – which he defined as a critical mass of informed citizens actively engaged in civic life through their participation in voluntary associations and their reading of printed material like newspapers and pamphlets – came into being. It was through the expansion of this public sphere that the impetus came for the eventual downfall of political regimes that governed without popular consent.[14] Habermas' work breathed new life into the study of democratic cultures across the North Atlantic World, pushing scholars to explore new lines of inquiry that broadened our understanding of political culture beyond the actions and writings of elites. It also, however, became the target of much scholarly critique, most notably in feminist circles. They noted that Habermas' portrayal of the public sphere paid scant attention to its exclusionary tendencies. During this period of democratic reform only a narrow sliver of the population - namely, relatively affluent white men of European heritage - gained greater access to the privileges of political authority. The bulk of the population, including women, the poor, and racialized communities, found themselves pushed to the margins.[15] The politicization of the urban street through collective actions like riots, parades, and public celebrations became a lens through which historians could grapple with the question of how people on the margins of public life were engaging with this renegotiation of political authority and citizenship.[16] This range of political activity became a site of profound contestation in the middle decades of the nineteenth century. It was at the forefront of discussions and debates about new practices of authority, changing cultural and legal constructions of urban space, and the conceptualization of difference in pluralistic societies.[17] This was where the conflicts that accompanied the cultural and political upheaval of the transition to capitalism were playing out. These studies struck a blow to conventional notions that social and political change occurred primarily on battlefields, in legislatures, and in elite clubs, arguing that the urban street needed to be embraced as a dynamic and complicated site worthy of similar analytical attention.

The middle decades of the nineteenth century thrust the behaviour of urban crowds into the spotlight across the North Atlantic World. In the midst of rapid urbanization, the ability of the authorities to respond effectively to the threat of unruly crowds prompted anxieties that consumed many elite commentators and politicians. It quickly became apparent that fostering an orderly and prosperous society during a time and in places marked by social and cultural upheaval would be the defining political challenge of their public lives. Alongside other bustling port cities in Europe, Britain, and the United States, this became Montreal's story. With its unique demographic composition and its important position in the tumultuous politics of the Victorian British Empire, Montreal is the setting for *Taking to the Streets*. That being said, it is important that we not read the city as a static place but instead recall the sharp increase in the mobility of people during this period, a trend that turned Montreal into a city of migrants. The Montrealers who poured onto the streets to participate in crowd events were therefore not only diverse in their ethnic origins and their position along the spectrum of class but also, just as importantly, in their geographic trajectories and their relationship to the city - in other words, in their lived experiences. The men, women, and children who make appearances in *Taking to the Streets* share one common experience: They lived in a turbulent world, surrounded by people who had been uprooted and stung by the booms and busts of capitalism in the liberal age. Their relationship to their urban surroundings was precarious. Crowd events in all their forms were not just sporadic interruptions of daily life but strategies of community formation and, on many occasions, a balm for social, political, and cultural disappointments.

This dynamic sphere of cultural activity, which included both the stately and imposing parades organized by different factions of the city's elite and the outbreaks of collective violence that occurred on a regular basis throughout the 1840s, played a pivotal role in shaping politics and public life throughout this decade. It offered everyone from the lowly dockworker to the ambitious merchant an opportunity to engage in the politics of community formation. In mid-nineteenth-century Montreal, with its sharp political and sectarian divides, how people used the street as a political space was fiercely contested. Parades and processions were often more than just occasions for celebration and amusement; they were volleys lobbed into conflicts over whose claims to political and cultural authority were legitimate. The ubiquitous outbreaks of popular violence were interpreted in a similar framework, with community leaders on both sides of the city's fault lines casting their opponents as the source of the city's unrest.

If we are to read the 1840s as a transformative moment in the evolution of British North America's democratic culture and institutions, as historians of what came to be the Dominion of Canada have long done, it is essential to grapple with how the contours of public life were being vigorously contested during these years. Thinking about the urban street as a political space provides us with an opportunity to do so. While it reminds us of the dynamic culture that took shape in the colony's largest city during this period, it also demonstrates the exclusionary nature of this development, as women, the poor, and non-whites were consistently pushed to the margins of public life because the political elite insisted on their inability to participate in the world of deliberative politics. These assertions granted legitimacy to the increasingly entrenched concentration of power in the hands of a small elite when the spirit of democratic reform was calling for its wider dissemination. *Taking to the Streets* demonstrates how the rich popular culture that was taking shape in Montreal during this period was targeted for being loud, raucous, and intimidating, and was thus reframed by reform-oriented elites as a series of social problems in need of solutions, a stance that justified the deepening of their political authority in the decades that followed.[18]

While this study is rooted in more than a decade's worth of scholarly reflection and labouring in the archives, personal experiences loom over my interpretive approach, perhaps no more so than when thinking through the motivations of the men and women who took to the streets of mid-nineteenth-century Montreal. Not everyone who lined the streets for a parade or found themselves in the midst of a riot did so for the same reason or with a shared intent. Historians have grown accustomed to interpreting people's engagement in these sorts of events as straightforward statements on the pressing social, cultural, and political conflicts of the age. This assumption, however, sometimes flattens and simplifies the nuances of lived experiences. These crowd events were woven into the fabric of daily life. Election violence was inextricable from interpersonal rivalries that were nurtured in workplaces and on street corners. People filing through the streets in a religious procession may well have decided to participate as a means of enjoying fine weather or to see a neighbour's child decked out in pristine white robes. It is important as an historian working with deeply partisan and biased source material to keep in mind that the subjects of this work were individuals, each nurturing their own jumble of complexities. Similarly, while pondering the political implications of the events and processes I discuss in *Taking to the Streets*, I also try to take into consideration factors that are rarely brought to light in the historical record, namely the emotional impact of these events. In mapping the terrain that overlaps the personal and the political and the deliberate and the spontaneous, this is an attempt to shed some new light on public life in mid-nineteenth-century British North America.

Following a chapter that lays out the context of mid-nineteenth-century Montreal, *Taking to the Streets* explores moments when collective experiences came to the forefront of political life and public debate in ways that highlight the increasing political importance of the urban street during this period. Chapter 2 examines the work of a diffuse group of elites who began to interpret the way that people used the urban street as a subject of reform in the 1840s. While they approached the subject from a variety of different and even contradictory angles, this dynamic group shared the same broadly defined vision of an ideal city – one that was orderly and genteel, where people could circulate without the sorts of hindrances that plagued bustling cities like Montreal. These reformers tapped into a vibrant transnational public sphere debating solutions to the challenges of creating order in the exploding cities of the North Atlantic World. This preoccupation with public order shaped the worldview of those who wielded the powers granted to them through the recently re-established municipal level of government. It also provided the political and intellectual framework through which these elites interpreted urban crowd events of all shapes and sizes. In doing so, they established the street as a pivotal battleground in the conflict between the customary practices of a dynamic popular class and the liberal vision of an orderly city. This is not, however, simply a story about an ambitious elite establishing control over an urban landscape. Court records reveal that the popular classes were also engaged in this process, recording depositions to air their own grievances about the unruly actions of their neighbours. These records also shine a light on the deep veins of resistance to the reforming impulse of the city's elite.

Chapter 3 examines a series of crowd events that unfolded in Montreal, and along the banks of the Lachine Canal on the city's western fringe, during the winter of 1843. The city's commercial elite had been lobbying aggressively for a deepening and widening of the canal for the better part of two decades. They framed the undertaking as being essential to the city's economic competitiveness. Contractors who had made winning bids with the colonial government to carry out the canal's expansion hired crews of Irish migrant labourers. Faced with low wages and dangerous working conditions, these migrants drew on popular customs of protest and resistance to give weight to their demands and drive their competitors away. The string of riots and impromptu nocturnal parades that followed was a major concern to every faction of Montreal for months on end. For engaged Montreal elites, the events occurring along the banks of the Lachine Canal were broadly interpreted as a foreign, anti-modern, and violent attack on their vision of Montreal's orderly, genteel, and prosperous future. These events laid the groundwork for class conflict in the city for decades to come, and revealed that capitalism's growing demand for cheap labour could foster social upheaval. They fuelled doubts about the preparedness of institutions designed to protect the personal safety and secure the property holdings of Montreal's elites from the actions of unruly crowds, with the military, the courts, and the police each receiving stern rebukes from politicians and commentators for their inability to contain the upheaval.

Chapter 4 examines the relationship between popular politics and the public sphere by looking at two different sorts of collective action that took place on the streets of mid-nineteenth-century Montreal. National society parades and election riots became the two most prominent sites where the city's political and sectarian tensions were laid bare. In a rapidly changing and transient urban environment, different manifestations of community solidarity were a powerful draw. Montrealers joined national societies in order to forge bonds with people with whom they shared a cultural background. Parades were important tools for putting the dynamism and aspirations of these national communities on display. But these elaborate and orderly parades did not occur in a vacuum. This chapter reads them as subtle but widely understood interventions into the same conflicts that had been resulting in outbreaks of sectarian violence throughout these years. This range of activity – from spontaneous to deliberate, from rough to serene – highlights the diversity of tactics employed by Montrealers from across the social spectrum to defend their interests and those of their communities. This chapter charts a gradual shift in the city's political culture as the legitimacy of authority became increasingly linked to public displays of physical and emotional restraint.

Chapter 5 examines how the Catholic Church employed increasingly elaborate and public displays of piety to legitimize their growing social power in post-rebellion Montreal. This chapter reflects on how the church's increasing reliance on these popular events marked a number of important cultural and political shifts. First, it demonstrated that being able to command popular support had become a crucial component in defending the legitimacy of their authority. The Catholic Church defended their growing might by pointing to the thousands of Montrealers who took to the streets on a regular basis to make public displays of piety. Secondly, it pointed to the politicization of the urban street. These displays did not occur on a blank canvass or on neutral territory, but in an urban setting that was deeply contested. Montreal was, after all, also home to a dynamic and engaged Protestant community with its own vision regarding what constituted appropriate public behaviour. In this contentious environment, displays of Catholic piety must be read as bold interventions into the city's public life. Drawing on the elaborate symbolic language of ultramontane Catholicism, these events appealed to the popular classes by communicating an alternative model of decorum than that being put forward by the urbane liberal elites of the North Atlantic World, which placed a heavy value on austerity and restraint.

Taking to the Streets concludes with a chapter that brings us to the spring and summer of 1849, when fiercely contested debates about public life, popular violence, and the practice of authority gripped Montreal like never before. The city's British Protestant community, who had successfully taken up arms during the rebellions of the Patriotes just over a decade earlier, were outraged at a series of policy decisions made in quick succession regarding the governance of Canada by the imperial authorities. The adoption of Free Trade policies – long advocated by industrialists in Britain – had thrown Montreal's commercial economy into depression. Then London decided, after a decade of conflict over the matter, to adopt the practice of responsible government in Canada, thereby allowing the Reform majority in parliament to move its agenda forward unhindered by imperial interference. With the stroke of Governor Elgin's pen, the once- powerful British Protestant minority in Montreal saw their special privileges vanish into the ether. Finding themselves suddenly stripped of their power, the city's Tory establishment did what so many disenfranchised communities before them had done: they took to the streets. The city's Catholic majority – both French and Irish – suddenly found themselves thrust into the role of protecting political institutions from violent crowds. It was a conflict steeped in the longstanding passions of sectarian confrontation. While events unfolding on the streets of Montreal raised understandable concerns about public order in the city, efforts to transform the rules of political expression gained momentum. The crisis of 1849 played a crucial role in widening the gulf between popular violence and what constituted legitimate political authority in Montreal and across the colony, a process that would have long-lasting political, social, and cultural implications. This chapter uses the Rebellion Losses Crisis to reflect on how the influence of unruly crowds reached its climax and then began its precipitous decline, permanently reconfiguring the contours of public life in Montreal.

1

A CITY ON THE BRINK: MAKING SENSE OF MID-NINETEENTH-CENTURY MONTREAL

Just as clocks struck noon across Montreal on 10 February 1841, a crowd assembled on the city's parade ground, the Champ de Mars, witnessed a contingent of troops carry out a short procession, perform drills, and fire a twenty-one-gun salute into the air. It appears to have been a straightforward occasion, one not entirely novel in what had long been a garrison town.[1] The press previewed the event but was silent in its aftermath, which suggests that it went off without a hitch. As the sun began to set, Montrealers with connections to the colonial elite made their way to a banquet and levy with the recently appointed Governor Sydenham, where the revelry was likely kicked up a notch behind closed doors.[2]

The seeming banality of the occasion masked the profound and deeply contested significance of what had just occurred. The humble presentation of mid-winter pageantry unfolding on the Champ de Mars commemorated the adoption of the Act of Union. This document was a blatant attempt to entrench the power of English-speaking elites in what had proven to be a contentious outpost of the British Empire.[3] These same elites had long nurtured close relationships with the imperial authorities in London. Amongst other things, this first reworking of the colony's constitution since 1791 dissolved the Province of Lower Canada by orchestrating its merger with the Province of Upper Canada. This had profound implications for the Canadien elite who, from the final decade of the eighteenth century, had harnessed the limited powers of Lower Canada's elected legislative assembly to foster and sustain a dynamic political culture.[4]

Whatever their politics, the Montrealers who gathered on the Champ de Mars that day would have understood the significance of this terse and confident display of British military might. It came on the heels of a conflict over democratic reform that had escalated into armed rebellion in 1837 and 1838 – revolts that had been decisively and bloodily subdued by the colonial authorities and their supporters.[5] The leaders of the militant reform movement had been arrested, exiled, and executed in the months and years that followed.[6] With the colony placed under martial law and its democratic institutions suspended, dissent against British rule had been swept to the margins. The printing presses of Patriote newspapers had been seized by the government. Governor Sydenham made very clear his disdain for democratic reform and his willingness to go to any length – including the use of violence – to derail his political opponents. By the time the twenty-one gun salute was fired on the Champ de Mars, the movement lamenting the political marginalization of Lower Canada's French-speaking Canadien majority was deflated.[7] If any Canadien advocates of reform had decided to take in the festivities on that cool February day, we can imagine them doing so with arms crossed and lips pursed, resigned not only to the survival of the anti-democratic impulses of the British colonial authorities, but to a renewed confidence amongst those who supported this status quo.

Just eight years later, the Champ de Mars would host another decisive moment in the city's political life. Hundreds of English-speaking Montrealers flocked to a hastily organized demonstration on the old parade ground to protest the passage of the Rebellion Losses Act, a piece of legislation that signalled the imperial authorities' acceptance of the principle of responsible government. The colonial authorities would now defer to the elected legislature of the Province of Canada and, more specifically, to the will of the majority that had been cobbled together between Canadiens – including some who had been deeply engaged in the Patriote struggle in the lead-up to the Rebellions of 1837 and 1838 – and English-speakers from the rapidly growing Province of Canada West who supported democratic reform. Political fortunes in the colony, in other words, had been reversed in the eight years since the Act of Union was adopted. While Montreal's Canadien community appear to have greeted the ceremony on the Champ de Mars in February 1841 with muted resignation, the English-speaking Tories who gathered in the same place in April 1849 to hear a series of incendiary speeches on the topic of responsible government took a much more militant stance. Rather than retiring to a stately banquet with the governor, they marched by torchlight down Montreal's main commercial artery and reconvened in front of the public market in the west end that housed the colony's parliamentary institutions. In the midst of a raucous protest that drew thousands of curious onlookers onto the streets, a fire was set that blew quickly through the wooden building, destroying the base of British rule in Montreal in a matter of hours.

What we have here, then, are two very different sorts of crowd events. One a tame midday affair, a cursory display of the colonial establishment's power; the other a menacing nocturnal insurgence – a rebuke to the shifting practices of colonial governance and power. At first glance it might appear to be peculiar to set these events up as bookends to a study of public life in mid-nineteenth-century Montreal. As different as these two gatherings were, however, they highlight the centrality of crowd events in Montreal during a decade marked by disorienting political, social, and economic change. Taking to the streets to engage in public life, whether it was to march in a religious procession, celebrate the arrival of visiting dignitaries, partake in a national society parade, or even to engage in collective violence was a crucial form of political expression.

It was, however, a deeply contested act. Crowd events of every stripe were caught up in a profound cultural and political clash over what constituted legitimate use of public space. For many in the city's swelling popular classes, the streets were the nucleus of social life. They were sites of conviviality, a place in which to partake in raucous celebrations, to share information, to engage in rough conflict. It was where community – the cluster of practices and relationships that made survival in a harsh urban environment possible – was created, fostered and defended. This was also the place where many earned a living and, for quite a few, a place that had to occasionally serve as home.[8] The streets were thus conceptualized as a social space and the tumultuous popular culture found there as an important resource for the broad segment of the community who needed to think strategically about how to make ends meet.

For an increasingly vocal and politically engaged group of elites, however, the way that the popular classes used the streets was seen as unpredictable, an anti-modern impediment to the city's progress and prosperity. Seemingly spontaneous and rough crowd events became one of the most prominent targets of these early urban reformers, who aspired to create a more genteel urban culture by discouraging the raucous practices of Montreal's popular classes. These reformers were motivated by a vision of the streets that placed the utmost value on unimpeded circulation and respectable decorum. These ideas were rooted in a cultural milieu where an increasing emphasis was being placed on restraint and an idealized notion of creating impermeable boundaries between public and private life.[9] It was a culture clash that would make a lasting mark on class relations in Montreal for the better part of the next century.

Meanwhile, many of these same elites were employing crowd events of their own to assert the legitimacy of their aspirations for political authority. Events like the religious processions organized by the Catholic clergy and lay volunteers and the parades organized by different bourgeois national societies were specifically designed to demonstrate the ability of these social groups to bring order and discipline to the unruly streets of mid-nineteenth-century Montreal. Unlike popular crowd events like outbreaks of election violence, these sorts of elite celebrations were conceptualized and defended as fluid events that swept tidily along their preset routes and thus caused minimal interference to the daily business of the city. They were, in other words, eminently modern.[10] National organizations, voluntary associations, and lay societies invested in lavish decorations – ornate uniforms, garlands of cedar branches, bouquets of flowers, and commemorative archways – blanketing parade routes strategically mapped so as to draw the public's attention to their institutional clout and the positive impact that their community was having on the city's built environment. Meanwhile, the composition of the parades delivered a strikingly succinct message about power in the modern city. It articulated how social distinctions and hierarchies were in the midst of being re-ordered in liberal society, with tight boundaries being drawn between those who could access tangible authority – community elites and other publicly engaged men – and those whose presence was intended to be symbolic, namely, women and children.[11]Although there are few mentions of this in official sources, these events also opened up a space for resistance. Civic and clerical figures marching in parades could be mocked and pelted with catcalls and malodorous debris. Occasions deemed by elites to be fit for solemn commemoration could be turned into moments of drunken sociability by residents of the city. The streets, where officials struggled to encourage orderly forms of sociability, were more socially complex and contentious than they were portrayed as being in the elite press.

In order to better understand the contested nature of public life in mid-nineteenth-century Montreal, it is necessary to take a step backwards to trace the origins of the city's social and demographic complexity. Montreal's status as a *carrefour*, a site of cultural and economic exchange, predated the arrival of European merchants and settlers in the region during the sixteenth century. Because of its location near the confluence of the Ottawa and the St Lawrence – two rivers that served as vital trading routes stretching deep into the continent – there is evidence that Indigenous peoples gathered in the area to trade furs and other provisions for centuries.[12] This space, and the nature of the human interactions that occurred within it, was deeply and irrevocably transformed by the European colonial project. The French were quick to tap into this economic world to carve out a piece of the profitable trade in furs. They established a commercial and administrative centre at Montreal, which proved to be an expensive undertaking as they became entangled in sustained military conflicts with Indigenous nations, many of which could be owed to the way that the French positioned themselves in the fur trade.[13] The settlement at Montreal grew slowly through the eighteenth century as a result of repeated outbreaks of hostilities between the settlers and Indigenous peoples present in the area.[14] The ensuing mixture of French settlers, Indigenous traders, and a smattering of African slaves was already giving Montreal a cosmopolitan air during this time. The city's strategic position meant that it was drawn into ongoing imperial confrontations occurring across the Atlantic World, which pitted the French and British empires against each other in the race for geographic and economic expansion.[15] After British victory in the Seven Years War, France ceded their territorial holdings on the North American continent to Britain.[16]

Montreal, which had been one of the commercial and administrative centres of New France, was quickly transformed into a British colonial outpost.[17] During the first decade of British rule, measures were taken to do away with the public remnants of the French regime by, amongst other things, eliminating French civil law and requiring Canadiens to make an oath of allegiance to the British Crown while denouncing their Catholic faith. With unrest growing in the British colonies to the south of Quebec in the lead-up to the American Revolution, however, a more conciliatory strategy was quickly adopted in London. The Quebec Act of 1774 made a series of concessions in an effort to win the allegiance of the Canadien elite. French civil law was reinstated and Catholics were granted the full benefits and privileges of citizenship in the British Empire.[18] These concessions effectively dampened whatever enthusiasm there might have been amongst Canadiens to join the American push for self-government. In the decades that followed, a vocal Canadien political elite emerged in Montreal alongside an increasingly assertive British Protestant elite, whose numbers swelled at the end of the century with the arrival of loyalists fleeing the republican experiment taking shape to the south.[19]

Prior to the massive influx of Irish famine migrants in the 1840s, Canadiens formed, by a significant margin, the majority in the province of Lower Canada, with the minority English-speaking community of merchants and colonial administrators concentrated in Quebec City and the west end of Montreal. The Constitution Act of 1791 established an elected legislative assembly where Canadiens held a majority of the seats. In what came to be the defining political conflict of the next half century, however, this elected body wielded

1.1. The city's culture and public life was shaped by a long history
of colonial encounters, represented here by the depiction of an
interaction between a Canadien and an Indigenous fur trader.
James Duncan, *Montreal, 1847–1850*.

little real political clout, as unelected colonial officials frequently overruled their decisions. To an increasingly dynamic Canadien political elite, well-versed in the politics of democratic reform that was gaining traction across Europe and its settler colonies during this period, this form of disenfranchisement grew more repugnant by the day.[20] The politics of democratic reform drove the emergence of a vibrant Canadien public sphere in the city.[21]

Montreal's English-speaking community, however, was itself a dynamic and highly politicized presence in the city. Like their Canadien peers, they were stirred by the sense that the current political and constitutional arrangements were stifling their ambitions. Among the community's powerful commercial elite, there was widespread opposition towards London's decision to allow the continued use of French civil law and landholding practices in Lower Canada. Community leaders argued that these practices, most notably with regards to property and the seigneurial system, were drains on the prosperity of the colony, whose economy was failing to accelerate at the same rate as those of Upper Canada and the republic to the south. By the 1820s, the English-speaking public sphere in Montreal was rife with calls to "Anglicize" the colony's legal framework, even if that meant partitioning off areas with significant British and Protestant populations from the rest of Lower Canada.[22] These demands might have been rooted in the material preoccupations of the city's merchants, but they were also fuelled by the cultural chauvinism of the period.[23] Montrealers of British descent were tapping into a transnational literature that aggressively portrayed their ethnic community as more progressive, rational, and modern than their European counterparts. These sentiments were bolstered by a strong undercurrent of anti-Catholicism that was emerging in Britain and across North America during this period, in which Catholics were painted as innately superstitious and politically subservient to the clergy and, ultimately, to the Vatican. Their ability to engage as rational individuals in the democratic and deliberative politics that had come to shape the North Atlantic World were thrown into doubt by this rhetoric.[24]

By the 1830s, this conflict between advocates of democratic reform and their Tory foes – which barely masked a strong undercurrent of sectarian tension – had come to preoccupy public life in Montreal.

Parliamentary and municipal elections in the city were not only tightly contested, but were also becoming increasingly infused with rough popular revelry and violence.[25] In 1834, the Parti Patriote, the political faction supported by the overwhelming majority of Canadiens and a scattering of English-speakers who supported the project of democratic reform – most notably, recent Irish Catholic migrants – drafted and sent ninety-two resolutions to the imperial authorities in London. This document outlined their critique of the political and institutional arrangements in the colony, calling forcefully and confidently for reforms that would shift power to the democratically elected legislative assembly. The imperial authorities sat on the resolutions for over two years before tersely rejecting the Parti Patriote's demands in 1837.[26] London's indifference to the 92 Resolutions struck a deep blow against the Canadien elite, who felt that they had made an irrefutable argument that played by the rules of deliberative democracy. The movement soon splintered, with militants under the leadership of the charismatic Louis Joseph Papineau abandoning the more moderate voices in the party, arguing that their approach to social and political change had proven naïve and ineffective. The Patriotes stepped up their actions against the colonial government, organizing boycotts of goods manufactured in Britain and holding increasingly charged public meetings in Montreal and across the colony's rural hinterland.[27]

The colonial authorities immediately clamped down on this blossoming protest movement, arresting prominent Patriote activists and forcing supporters of the movement out of public office. Militant Patriotes established a secret paramilitary organization, dubbed the Société des Fils de la liberté, during the summer of 1837, and outbreaks of collective violence began to escalate on the streets of Montreal. Poor economic conditions provided fertile ground for anti-government rhetoric to gain traction. This was especially true in the city's immediate hinterland, where a stagnating economy fuelled mounting frustration amongst tenant farmers over their obligations under the seigneurial system. Although they frequently portrayed themselves as the loyal defenders of public order in the colony, Lower Canada's English-speaking Protestant minority did not remain above the fray. Young men from the community joined a variety of clubs and secret societies that were deeply implicated in popular violence. During the lead-up to the Rebellions, for example, men flocked to the Doric Club, an organization that targeted supporters of the Patriotes for violence and public intimidation.[28] Armed conflict broke out in November in several locations in the rural areas encircling Montreal, though many of the Patriotes who took up arms were Montrealers who had been driven out of the city by the government crackdown on dissent.[29] Mounting frustration towards the unchecked authority of the ruling elite was frequently expressed in ways that drew on long-standing practices of rural and agrarian protest, such as charivaris and other raucous and intimidating nocturnal processions.[30] This dissent quickly raised concerns amongst British Protestant elites about the government's ability to maintain order, both in the city and in the rural hamlets that fanned out across the St Lawrence River Valley.[31] The Rebellion was quickly and decisively put down by British troops stationed at Montreal's garrison and a militia consisting of local supporters of the colonial establishment, as was a secondary and more radical outbreak the following year.

With the Patriote movement in disarray, the post-rebellion period provided the city's British Protestant merchant elite with an opportunity to push through their agenda of social and economic liberalization with little substantive opposition. Patriote leaders had been jailed, executed, deported, or had fled in exile, and newspapers supporting their cause were censored and shuttered by the colonial government. The colony was governed by a series of Special Councils that were given sweeping powers to undo the political logjam created by the decades-long clash between the Tories and the proponents of democratic reform.[32] Although there was Canadien representation on each of the Special Councils convened by successive Governors General, their reform-oriented agenda owed much to the demands that had been circulating in Montreal's English-speaking commercial elite since the 1820s, particularly through organizations like the virulently anti-Patriote Montreal Constitutionalist Association. The Special Council was focused intently on their vision of liberal modernity; they proposed and approved investments in infrastructure, and incorporated Montreal and Quebec City's municipal governments. They opened a dialogue with the Sulpicians – the Catholic religious order that held property rights over much of the island of Montreal – that would eventually pave the way for the termination of seigneurial tenure in the region. They also approved changes to the criminal code that placed heavy restrictions on popular assemblies, the sorts of collective and communal actions that had done so much to build momentum for the Patriotes during the previous decade.

The social and political project of the city's British Protestant colonial establishment was essentially endorsed by the Governor appointed by the imperial authorities in London in the immediate aftermath of the Rebellions. Lord Durham, who had made his fortune mining coal during Britain's industrial revolution, was known as a supporter of radical causes in parliament. He arrived in Canada in the aftermath of the Rebellions and quickly began keeping company with some of the most viciously anti-French political activists in Montreal, such as newspaper editor Adam Thom. Their influence on Lord Durham was made clear in the report he cobbled together during his altogether brief stay in the colony, whose prescriptions were in keeping with the Special Council's program of capitalist reform while castigating the Canadien community for their sup- posed disengagement from the project of modernity.[33] The fiercely partisan political culture of Montreal had apparently left its mark on the radical parliamentarian's perspective. His report cleared the way for the Act of Union.

Montreal was, by 1840, an important commercial centre and the largest city in British North America. The circulation of people, commodities, and ideas situated it in a network of bustling port cities across the North Atlantic World. The social, cultural, and political turmoil of the previous decades had made it an important laboratory for the exercise of colonial power, as demonstrated most recently by the visit of Lord Durham, and by the political capital expended on both sides of the Atlantic for implementing the Act of Union, which spoke directly to the conflicts rooted in Montreal's diversity. It is at this moment that *Taking to the Streets* picks up the story – when political conflicts steeped in sectarian tension had come to define public life. The same issues that pushed the Patriotes into rebellion against the colonial authorities at the end of the 1830s were not as easily cast aside as Montrealers would have guessed in those early

days of 1841. Supporters of many of the reforms first proposed by the Patriote Party in the decade prior to the Rebellions were taken up by a Reform faction in parliament that knit together Canadiens with English-speaking supporters of democratic reform from Canada West.[34] Despite the formation of this interethnic political party, the conflict over democratic reform remain steeped in ethnic and sectarian tension, and popular violence remained as vital a political expression in the 1840s as it had been in the 1830s. This would not be a decade of resurgent colonial power following the violent interregnum of the Rebellions. It would instead be a decade where the same sectarian and political conflicts that instigated the Rebellions would dominate politics both high and low.

The colonial public sphere that was taking shape across British North America during this period – that dynamic world of newspapers and pamphlets, public meetings and parliamentary debates – was consumed with questions about democratic reform and ethnic and racial difference. While the expansion of Canada's transportation infrastructure provided people in the most remote colonial outposts with opportunities to tap into these public discussions,[35] these

1.2. Images from this period depict Montreal as a bustling commercial port. *Panoramic view of Montreal,* ca. 1845.

conflicts were amplified on the bustling and cosmopolitan streets of Montreal. In this densely populated city where social interaction was firmly rooted in outdoor public spaces, and where fraternal and religious societies were engaged in marking and performing difference on the streets, these debates were not relegated to the confines of the newspaper editorial page but were deeply woven into the fabric of daily experience. This was the framework through which people experienced, contemplated, and debated social change.

In the decade that began with the implementation of the Act of Union, Montreal's evolution from a small colonial administrative and commercial centre to a major city on the brink of industrialization jolted forwards in fits and starts. Montreal, like other closely linked port cities across the North Atlantic World, became an important hub for migration, as the transition to a market economy touched off a period of rapid urbanization. Montreal's population grew from 40,000 in 1842 to just over 50,000 by the end of the decade.[36] Three major ethnic communities made up over ninety percent of the population, with Canadiens making up slightly less than half of the population, and the other half consisting of British Protestants (some of whom were Irish migrants) and Irish Catholics.[37] Smaller communities of Jews, Europeans, Indigenous peoples, and Blacks were highly visible in the city, but formed only a small fraction of the total population. These numbers represent a fairly significant burst of growth and demographic fluidity, yet they tell only a partial story. With the sharp increase in the number of people circulating across the North Atlantic World during these years, thousands took up temporary residence in Montreal in the midst of more extensive migratory journeys. This steady stream of migrants into the city strained the urban infrastructure, especially with regards to public health and sanitation.[38] A considerable segment arrived in a state of destitution and illness, quickly draining the coffers of public and private charities in the process.[39] Hastily erected homes were built on the urban periphery to house these new arrivals. Many of the men, women, and families who migrated to the city found it to be a disorienting and alienating place and especially those who had migrated from the nearby countryside quickly declared the move a failed experiment and returned home. *Taking to the Streets* is thus engaged in the complicated endeavour of thinking through a limited geographic space that was defined by the mobility of the people passing through it. This fluidity left a profound mark on Montreal's culture and politics.

This sense of social upheaval left its mark on Montrealers from across the social spectrum. Many of the city's poorest residents, who struggled to make ends meet working in jobs that were poorly remunerated, physically demanding, and precarious, were new not only to Montreal but to many facets of the urban experience.[40] Negotiating their place in a bustling and chaotic city like mid-nineteenth-century Montreal required a great deal of fortitude and adaptability. In liberalism's golden age, prior to the introduction of much in the way of a social safety net, people leaned heavily on family and national, kinship, and religious connections to survive the economic busts that occurred with considerable frequency.[41] The dynamic popular culture that emerged across Montreal's poor neighbourhoods during this period of rapid urbanization drew heavily on rural cultural practices brought to the city by migrants from places like the Scottish Highlands, the west coast of Ireland, and the rural hamlets of the St

1.3. Map of North America, c. 1840s.

1.4. Montreal in the distance, surrounded by rich agricultural land.
Philip John Bainbrigge, *Montreal from the West*, 1841.

Lawrence River Valley.[42] These practices, which were often rough, spontaneous, and menacing, exerted their influence on politics and public life in the city.[43] Montreal's diversity created a unique and dynamic culture built around exchange and collaboration between its disparate communities. These communities were forged in both formal and informal ways – through voluntary associations that produced a busy slate of cultural events like dances, banquets, and parades, and on street corners, in taverns, on the docks, and in other workplaces where men and women from the popular classes converged.[44] Violence, often fuelled by a vigorous consumption of alcohol, loomed over social life in Montreal. Descriptions of both riotous collective violence and more isolated individual confrontations in newspapers and criminal records reveal that physical conflict was integral to the way that Montrealers negotiated difference and their place in a rapidly changing urban environment. Violence could be the product of spontaneous encounters or a carefully honed political strategy. Either way, it was a vital part of the city's cultural, political, and social fabric.

It was only in public rhetoric that parades and religious processions were ever entirely distinct from the city's popular culture. Both were grounded in the sorts of daily interactions that people experienced on the streets, and both were strategies for negotiating the status of individuals and communities. Just as the city's poorer residents might have participated in a riot or a public demonstration in order to remind the broader community of the clout that they could wield, elites were drawn towards more imposing and restrained events like parades because they demonstrated the power that they could exert. For people from across the spectrum from poverty to privilege, the street became a political space where the interests of their community were asserted and defended from attack.

This tension between the different ways Montrealers used the streets as a political space is at the heart of *Taking to the Streets*. It was a crucial component of a larger process of cultural transformation unfolding during this period. As the values and practices of liberalism and democracy supplanted ancien regime practices of authority across the North Atlantic World, notions of what sort of person was

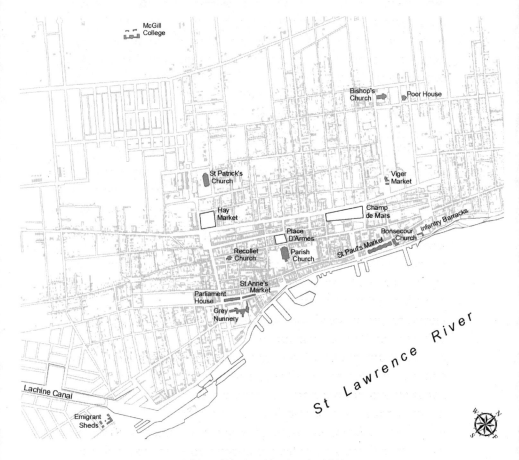

1.5. Map of Montreal landmarks, 1846.

entitled to the full benefits and responsibilities of citizenship became deeply contested. Assertions about how people carried themselves on the urban street were pushed to the frontlines of public debate.[45] The community elites who coordinated and marched in parades were demonstrating their sense of restraint and decorum, and were explicitly drawing attention to their position above the fray of the city's rough popular culture. These events helped legitimize their access to positions of political authority and, in an age where democratic ideas were circulating widely and dynamically, to make their elevated position and all the influence that came with it appear to the broader community as the natural state of affairs.[46]

Meanwhile, those who engaged in the city's rough popular politics were tarred in elite circles as being too irrational to participate in the progressive and deliberative politics of the liberal era. The sort of bodily control and restraint that elite men demonstrated during parades and processions was deemed to be lacking in popular crowd events like riots, charivaris, and impromptu election parades. It is through these events and the range of reactions to them that we can trace how different social groups were being pushed to the margins of the emerging democratic public sphere.[47] It points to the importance of raising questions about gender and class when grappling with the nature of public life during this period.[48] Different factions of the Montreal elite used the pulpit provided to them by the press and other public forums to popularize the idea that the people who engaged in these activities were unfit to participate fully in the democratic process. They employed a rich array of sensory language to achieve this, writing frequently of the deafening noise produced by popular demonstrations, of the menacing scowls of rioters, and noting that the people who participated in these events often did so wearing torn clothes or in various stages of undress. Marginalized groups – be they women, children, the poor, or racialized peoples – were frequently accused of being hysterical, a charge with important cultural implications. Attempts to understand the motivations of people who chose to participate in popular politics were few and far between. Instead, they were seen as moments when people who already had a tenuous grip on their passions and their bodies toppled into a collective frenzy.[49]

1.6. Map of Montreal, 1846.

Not everyone who participated in carefully orchestrated parades and processions were elites. In fact, the city's popular classes embraced these events as a way to assert themselves as being worthy of prospective citizenship. National societies and the Catholic Church welcomed needy Montrealers into these practices as a means of putting forth the idea that their respective communities and organizations were uniquely equipped to lend assistance to people looking to pull themselves out of poverty in an era of harsh economic practices.[50] Likewise, elites were not as removed from popular culture as the rhetoric of their newspapers and community leaders implies. Although such actions are often difficult to discuss with any precision as a result of the biases of the documents that are left to historians to peruse, there is ample evidence to suggest that many elite Montrealers, especially young men, sought out and found pleasure in the city's alcohol-drenched conviviality.[51] We know from reports during the Rebellion Losses Crisis of 1849 that elites were no strangers to the roughest manifestations of the city's popular politics. Many prominent community and political leaders were making eloquent overtures towards public order and emotional restraint while simultaneously nudging their supporters towards violence with language that could be at once subtle and inflammatory. It seems fair to speculate that many Montrealers would have engaged in a diverse array of collective experiences.

Outbreaks of collective violence and lavish parades and processions, despite their obvious differences, would have carried a similar resonance. Both were tied up in people's complicated relationship to the broader community. They occurred on streets that were central to the social interaction of all but the wealthiest Montrealers, thereby knitting them deeply into the fabric of daily life. Working towards an understanding of the significance and interconnectedness of crowd events on the streets of mid-nineteenth-century Montreal requires us to speculate about these complexities and contradictions. Conceptualizing social and cultural change through the lens of rigid and static boundaries and categories largely fabricated by the urbane liberals of the time would only serve to obscure a great deal of the richness here. Instead, we need to think through people's changing relationship to the politics of the urban street as a process whereby innovative ideas about authority and decorum were pressed up against longstanding practices and popular customs. At times this process unfolded in conflict that was rough and boisterous, while at other times it unfolded in far more subtle ways. Either way, there is much to be gained from reminding ourselves that mid-nineteenth-century Montrealers were aware of the political implications of their actions, so much so that this understanding was hardly ever stated explicitly.

The contentious political conflicts of this period helped foster the emergence of a dynamic public sphere in Montreal, with influential newspapers like *La Minerve*, the *Montreal Witness*, the *Montreal Gazette*, *Les Mélanges religieux*, and the *Pilot* being published in the city. Bookstores and reading rooms catered to this politically influential clientele, and newspapers reveal a calendar of political meetings and the existence of dozens of fraternal societies that attracted both the city's elite and middling sorts. Historians have presented a rather one-dimensional portrait of public life in Montreal in this period by focusing their attention on this sphere of elite politics, but the city was also the centre of an equally dynamic and contentious sphere of popular politics. Riots were much more than occasional breaches of public order. They were an extreme manifestation of a raucous sphere of popular actions that was, for many Montrealers from diverse economic, ethnic and cultural backgrounds, an invaluable tool for engaging in public life. Men joined secret societies, like the Still Caps and the Dolphins, whose primary purpose was to disrupt the political process on behalf of their candidate of choice.[52] Others joined fire companies with similarly political orientations and methods. In a charged environment such as this, we must not imagine that politics was strictly a deliberative process where people's allegiances and opinions were shaped by reasoned public debate and carefully-honed editorials.[53] It must instead be remembered that partisan politics were closely entwined in the sectarian conflicts that defined the cultural landscape. Issues were discussed in the city's innumerable taverns and grog shops. The vast majority of Montrealers would have been more familiar with the settling of political conflicts through acts of interpersonal violence rather than through a quiet and respectful exchange of ideas. An audacious group of vocal Montrealers were raising concerns about the rough edges of the city's politics. Their experience of it left an indelible mark on their attitudes towards democratic reform.

Concerns about unruly crowds and disorderly street politics played a critical role in shaping people's attitudes towards democratic reform. Political and cultural elites framed their worldviews around the democratic revolutions (and subsequent counterrevolutions) that had shaken the North Atlantic World at regular intervals since the final decades of the eighteenth century.[54] The legitimacy of political regimes, be they supporters or critics of the status quo, rested largely on their ability to make the case that they could foster an orderly society. The emerging transnational public sphere that linked urban elites in bustling port cities like Montreal with their counterparts across the globe helped fuel the momentum of movements for democratic reform. The tumultuous nature of urban sociability was held up by many supporters of the status quo as undeniable evidence that strong and effective limits needed to be placed on democracy. The actions of the city's swelling popular classes were frequently referenced as evidence of the dangers of giving the broader public a greater say with regards to governance. Competing factions of the urban elite jostled for political power, in part by accusing their foes of attempting to gain position by summoning the passionate and destructive force of crowds. In Montreal, this was how the supporters of the colonial status quo, the Tory faction, and the supporters of democratic reform, known during this period as the Reform faction, were able to accuse each other of threatening to submerge the colony in tyranny. The Reformers did so by suggesting the Tories wanted to maintain their grip on the colony's institutions through the muscular interventions of their young male supporters, while the Tories vigorously responded that the Reformers, in a desperate attempt to gain power, were seeking to stir the passions of the very people who posed a threat to public order. In reality, these two elites shared both a disdain for and a reliance upon the roughest edges of the city's politics.

These discussions occurred at a moment when competing factions of the Montreal elite were thinking through the social, economic, and cultural implications of liberalism. This set of ideas and practices placed a high value on the liberties of the individual – a category shaped and defined by the racial, class, and gender politics of the day to exclude a wide swath of marginalized people, including women, the poor, and people considered to be non-white. Liberalism sought to do away with the seemingly cumbersome knot of reciprocal obligations that knit together ancien-regime societies in favour of codified – and thus transparent – laws and categories.[55] The gradual and contested implementation of this vision saw amorphous collectives re-imagined as quantifiable sets of individuals.[56] Once individuals became quantifiable, it became possible to govern them. This process brought about a transformation in governance. The residents of cities like Montreal were governed to a far greater extent by the mid-nineteenth-century than they would have been just a few decades earlier.[57] They were counted by census-takers, policed by officers, taught by teachers, and prodded by immigration agents determined to impose a liberal public order on a chaotic urban environment. The street politics of the popular classes ruffled the audacious social, cultural, and political project of liberal reform.

The emergence of liberal modernity as the defining political and ideological project of the nineteenth century was not a straightforward transition, but a complicated and contested process that pulled a wide variety of practices into its orbit. The city was in the midst of establishing itself as British North America's leading commercial and mercantile centre, but liberal ideas had been circulating since the end of the eighteenth century. At the heart of these debates was a contested re-conceptualization of the individual's relationship to society. In advocating for the primacy of the individual's liberties they raised questions – and, in many cases, outward hostility – to collective and communal privileges. The liberal perspective certainly made a profound impact on society's core institutions: the state, the family, churches, and civil society. It also left its mark on the way people considered and used urban space.

While these ideas had been circulating in Montreal for decades, events unfolding in the late 1830s and 1840s would have a profound impact on the way that they were put into practice. During this period Montreal was rocked by crises on a number of fronts, including the political deadlock and sectarian sparring caused by the conflict over democratic reform, several outbreaks of epidemic disease that claimed thousands of lives in the city, the social and environmental impact of the city's rapid growth in the years leading up to the onset of industrialization, and the quick succession of economic booms and busts that accompanied Montreal's integration into a market economy operating on a global scale. The arrival of thousands of destitute and diseased migrants – most notably as a result of the famine unfolding in Ireland and, to a lesser degree, the Scottish highlands – profoundly shook the public's faith in the ability of the colonial authorities to maintain an orderly society.[58] The legitimacy of the liberal project was dependent on its assertion that these practices could help communities weather the turbulence of modernity.[59]

The 1840s in Montreal were thus marked by a crisis in liberal governance. The roots of this crisis were varied, complex, and deep, but they manifested themselves and were measured on the urban street.[60] This is where Montrealers from across the social spectrum encountered economic polarization and geographic dislocation. It was on the streets that the shortcomings of efforts to create an orderly city were laid bare. In the cultural climate that this created, different factions of the city's elite asserted themselves as able and legitimate wielders of authority. They did so through the arena of partisan politics and civic governance, lending their support for campaigns for more effective policing and harsher regulations around acts such as vagrancy and public drunkenness. This specifically targeted the sociability of the popular classes.[61] They pursued this reform agenda through the public sphere, tapping into transnational discussions around urbanization and social reform that connected elites from across the North Atlantic World through the press and other publications. As urbanization accelerated on a global scale, the elite citizens of cities that were once relatively stable and contained were forced to grapple with a variety of issues connected to economic polarization and geographic dislocation – most notably around the regulation of migration and public health. This was the context in which elites reconceptualised the city as a space that needed to be ordered and controlled. Some of this was done through the political process. The city's elites made particularly effective use of the powers that had just recently been handed to them through the re-establishment of the municipal government by the colonial authorities.[62] Policing was

ramped up, though due to persistent budgetary shortfalls, this occurred in fits and starts.[63] Regulations were passed around sanitation
and the more raucous aspects of popular sociability. The records of
the lower criminal courts demonstrate a spike in prosecutions for
offences such as petty larceny, vagrancy, and prostitution during this
period.[64] This pursuit of public order could also be traced outside the
sphere of formal politics, such as through campaigns against drinking and the popularity of books, columns, and lectures on etiquette.

Thinking through the draw of street politics in all its forms during this period is an attempt to enrich our understanding of the era's
dizzying social change. *Taking to the Streets* is a study of how mid-
nineteenth-century Montreal was defined by the tension between a
dynamic elite engaged in reforming their urban surroundings and
an equally dynamic (and growing) popular class who relied heavily
on boisterous outdoor, collective, and occasionally violent action to
negotiate their position in a city being rocked by transformations
and conflicts occurring on a global scale. It grapples with a number
of questions that are fundamental to the study of nineteenth-century
cities: How did the rapid growth of Montreal as a result of multiple
and simultaneous waves of migration impact both daily life in the
city and its culture? How did Montreal function as a city of migrants? How was violence employed as a political strategy? How did
mounting concerns about public order and civility fuel innovative
practices of authority? What role did the bourgeoning public sphere
of newspapers, voluntary societies, and public meetings play in shaping people's attitudes towards pluralism, the urban environment, and
social change? Finally, in what ways were the bourgeois visions of an
orderly and modern city contested by the popular classes?

Looking at these events from the distance of nearly two hundred
years, it can be a challenge to remember that the gradual triumph of
this liberal vision of public order was not by any means inevitable.
The cities that most of us live in today are the products of that triumph. The occasional hiccup aside they are, by nineteenth-century
standards, remarkably orderly – people, commodities, and capital
circulate through them with great fluidity. This public culture was
accomplished through a deeply contested attack on a number of
longstanding popular practices of resistance that were engrained in

1.7 Artists painting mid-nineteenth-century Montreal, besides exaggerating
its orderliness, were also keen to depict its heterogeneity.
This depiction of Rue Notre Dame, besides drawing attention to the
parish church in the distance and Nelson's Column in the foreground,
includes images of different ethnic and occupational groups.
John Murray, *North West View, Notre Dame Street, Montreal,* 1843–44.

the rhythms of daily life. The efforts of urban elites to bring about their ideal city was remarkably audacious. In working through the meaning and the impact of a variety of collective acts and experiences in mid-nineteenth-century Montreal, *Taking to the Streets* is an effort to think through the precariousness of both the liberal project of creating orderly urban space as well as the popular efforts to resist, disrupt, and soften the blow of that project. In the course of doing so, it also aims to complicate the conventional narrative of this period in the history of Quebec and Canada by emphasizing the profound cultural importance of urban social interaction in the formation of modern political institutions and processes.[65] Actions that took place on the streets of Montreal were an integral part of the processes of inclusion and exclusion from the public sphere that shaped the conflicts over democratic reform that dominated public life during these years. It was on these bustling streets that people from across the social spectrum – from the migrant labourer struggling to make ends meet to the wealthy property-owner with connections to the colonial power structure – worked through the nuances and implications of pluralism.

The 1840s were a tumultuous decade in Montreal. The political and sectarian turmoil was all-encompassing; it connected elite spaces like the legislature and the press with popular spaces like taverns and the street. The following chapters explore the role that collective experiences played in helping Montrealers from across the city's ethnic, sectarian, and class divides negotiate their place in a rapidly changing city. This study makes no claim to be a definitive inventory of crowd events in Montreal during this period. Instead, it intentionally places a sampling of different events under the microscope to highlight how shifting attitudes reflected changes in the city's political culture. It sets off in this direction with an examination into the broader conflicts over public space, politics, and popular culture in mid-nineteenth-century Montreal.

2

THE RAUCOUS STREET MEETS
THE REFORMER'S GAZE

Josiah Eaton made his living selling muffins on the streets of Montreal. He awoke early each morning, dressed, gathered his inventory of sweet baked goods and hit the streets of the city just as they began to swarm with men, women, and children. Eaton would weave his way through the throng, bellowing his offerings and ringing a bell to attract attention. It was not a highly profitable venture, but it appeared to be Eaton's main source of income in the first half of the 1840s.[1] That he was able to carve out a livelihood on the bustling streets of Montreal with nothing but a bell and a basket of muffins suggests that Eaton possessed the pluck needed to make ends meet in this cutthroat environment.

It was with, in his own words, "shock and dismay," that Eaton discovered that he and his fellow street-vendors had become the targets of a harsh regulatory crackdown by the municipal government in 1844. The Police Commission had been fielding a steady stream of complaints about muffin vendors for several months. Anonymous petitioners stated that the vendors blocked traffic and delayed pedestrians with their antics, and that their relentless bell-ringing disturbed the peace and tranquility of the city.[2] The municipal government sided with the petitioners by passing a motion designed to make it impossible for small-scale pedlars like Eaton to ply their trade effectively.

In order to sell products to pedestrians, vendors would be obligated to purchase a license from the city. Even if they chose to make this investment, which would have no doubt made a significant dent in their narrow profit margin, the bylaw stipulated that they would be barred from employing bells or any other noise-making instrument for commercial purposes.

Montreal's muffin vendors, however, were not about to relinquish their livelihoods without a fight. A number wrote to City Council to make their case. Josiah Eaton wrote the most detailed defence of their practices, arguing strenuously that the bylaw in question "would be his ruin."[3] He maintained that the proposed licensing fee would be beyond the grasp of his peers, and that ringing a bell was the most effective way "to announce to the public the vendors' approach."[4] Eaton's argument did not end there. He made the case that the tactics targeted by the new bylaw were the very essence of Montreal's commercial vitality. He pointed to businesses like Rasco's Hotel – the favoured accommodations of elite visitors to Montreal – and reminded City Council that they made extensive use of bells in their daily operations to summon bellhops and other employees. Likewise, Montreal's harbourfront – the cornerstone of commercial prosperity – vibrated with the continuous blasting of horns from ships arriving and departing from the city. A broad cross-section of Montrealers owed their livelihood to this kind of chaotic bustle. Eaton demanded to know what justified the crackdown on humble street vendors like himself.[5]

It was a question, surprisingly, that the men who sat on the Police Commission were unable to answer. They strongly recommended that City Council reverse their decision, writing "that the inconvenience occasioned by the use of the bell by the persons enumerated in the Bylaw [is] trifling in comparison with the advantages resulting from it," and thereby recommended "the prayer of the petitioners to the favourable consideration of the council, and that the bylaw referred to be repealed."[6] City Council did not protest, and with the stroke of a pen the city's energetic street vendors were able to go on ringing their bells and blowing their trumpets for the foreseeable future.

Josiah Eaton was not a prominent Montrealer, but the sort of character who lurks in the shadows of archival documents for a

2.1. The bustle of daily commerce in the city.
James Duncan, *Wood Market, Montreal, Canada East*, 1849.

moment before disappearing again. Likewise, the municipal government's aborted attempt to place restrictions on muffin vendors failed to garner much attention in the local papers, which were preoccupied with the prolonged conflict over democratic reform. Eaton may have been attempting to contribute to his family's survival by supplying hungry Montrealers with breakfast on the go, but his actions drew him into the sustained and contentious battle over order, decorum, and urban space that simmered throughout the 1840s. A diverse group of reform-oriented elites from across the city's ethnic and sectarian divides joined together in attempts to foster a more genteel and orderly culture on the city's streets: a project that pitted them against the overwhelming majority of Montrealers like Josiah Eaton, who were compelled to defend longstanding uses of public space. These social tensions – anger prompted by having to dodge a muffin vendor clanging a bell on a narrow footpath or panic at having one's business suddenly declared a public menace – played a crucial role in shaping how Montrealers thought about their place in the city. These daily interactions were pivotal to the complicated process of identity formation. It was on the streets that people negotiated difference along the lines of class, race, and gender.[7] Unlike political riots, parades, religious processions, and public celebrations, the issues raised in the complaints about Josiah Eaton were experienced on a daily basis, and encouraged reform-oriented elites to advocate for their agenda.[8] This chapter looks at the interaction between this ethnically heterogeneous community of activists and the popular classes who resisted their efforts to transform the ways people used the city's streets.

It is essential to pause for a moment to remind ourselves of the basic characteristics of Montreal's streets in the middle of the nineteenth century. They were fundamentally dirty and disorderly places where the wind whipped about clouds of dust when the weather was dry and where carriage wheels sunk into thick brown mud when rain and snow fell. They were loud and stinking places where people jostled each other. This was where petty capitalists hawked their wares, where knots of friends and acquaintances stopped to trade gossip and jokes, where soldiers strutted, prostitutes plied their trade, and children played tag. It was where scores were settled with a knockout punch and drunks rested on all fours to steady themselves after long nights out on the town. The streets were, in other words, a vital social space for the vast majority of Montrealers. They were not, however, easy places within which to manoeuvre. Anyone attempting to make their way from one place to another faced a seemingly endless barrage of impediments, from unexpected piles of animal waste to spontaneous crowds gathered to watch a fight.

Faced with chaos every time they stepped out their front doors, urban reformers dreamed that a very different kind of city could be chiselled out of this imperfect slab of marble. We can piece together their vision from the campaigns they engaged in throughout this period: a vision of a genteel city where respectable men and women could make their way through the streets without being jostled by hucksters and carters, where drunken men and women would not be sprawled across the footpaths, and where neither carriages nor pedestrian traffic would become snarled. The intersection of class and gender politics is made evident here. Women who quietly prom-enaded on tree-lined[9] boulevards with their husbands were held up as docile foils to women who peddled, partied, sold their bodies, and fought and yelled on the dark and dusty streets.[10] Reformers expressed an all-encompassing belief in the merits of light, arguing that widening Montreal's narrow streets into broad boulevards[11] lit by gaslight[12] after sundown would not only be aesthetically pleasing but would discourage the criminal activities and vice they associated with darkness. The streets they envisioned would lift the popular classes towards more virtuous and productive pursuits. Theirs was, in other words, an idealized vision that differed dramatically from the realities of life in a port city. Still, local bookstores carried travel literature featuring vivid descriptions of the tree-lined boulevards of European capitals that were snapped up by readers who argued that Montreal ought to aspire to such gentility.[13]

Reformers pursued this project from a number of different angles. Some took up the cause of temperance or efforts to crack down on prostitution. Some pushed for the expansion of schooling as a way to pull idle and rowdy boys off street corners. Some joined campaigns that called for the cessation of commercial pursuits on the Sabbath. Others pursued the push for gentility from a less idealistic position by simply demanding that a group of raucous carters be barred from gathering at the end of their block. Whatever their approach, this elite activism played a significant role in politicizing public space in nineteenth-century Montreal. The street became a laboratory for innovative practices of liberal authority which sought legitimacy from the Enlightenment notions that individuals could be improved and that social problems could be addressed through laws and institutions that resorted to coercion as lightly and infrequently as possible. As this chapter demonstrates, however, these projects encountered sustained resistance, as the vast majority of Montrealers made it clear that they would not abandon longstanding cultural practices that made life in the city sustainable. In keeping with the paradox that lies at the heart of the liberal order, the streets of Montreal became simultaneously the place where the authority of the governing elite was most vigorously practiced and where its shortcomings were most glaringly obvious.[14]

In part because Montreal's elite was fractured along ethnic and sectarian lines, the tactics, language, and preoccupations of reformers frequently diverged. In an era marked by seemingly irresolvable political conflicts, however, the need to reform the city's popular culture gained consensus. This preoccupation with public order was something that Montreal's elites shared with their counterparts across the North Atlantic World.[15] As economic transformations unfolding on a global scale touched off a period of rapid urbanization, civic leaders and commentators grappled with the increasingly daunting challenge of creating orderly cities. The most obvious manifestation of this project was the expansion and professionalization of urban policing that occurred during this period. The social interactions of the urban poor were monitored, regulated, and criminalized to an extent that would have been inconceivable only a few decades earlier.[16]

The transformation of policing, which occurred in fits and starts, was part of a broader effort to expand the state's ability to govern urban society. The police constable walking the beat was part of this, as were efforts to enforce sanitary measures[17] and building codes, and to monitor the settlement of migrants in the city. An ethnically diverse group of urban elites debated reform initiatives at public meetings, shared pamphlets and other tracts on related issues in reading rooms, and sat together on committees devoted to addressing these issues.[18] In a city that had been struck by devastating fires and deadly epidemics with tragic frequency, and where interpersonal violence was woven into the fabric of daily life, there was public support for their undertakings.

Parts of the city were over two centuries old. Its material form, therefore, posed a challenge to emerging notions of what a modern urban landscape ought to resemble and how it should function. In the older parts of the city, nearest the port, the streets did not follow the tidy grid that had come to dominate town-planning in the nineteenth century.[19] With the exception of a handful of major arteries, streets tended to be narrow. During the long winter months, these pinched streets were dark and drab. When it rained, they became submerged in water and mud, trapping the wheels of carriages and making even short journeys difficult. Snow, of course, posed its own set of challenges. The residents of the city often drew on practices that had served them well in rural areas, like pulling materials through the snow on sleds. Bylaws passed by the nascent municipal government in the 1840s reveal the degree to which the urban streets had become a contentious political issue. Bylaws banned a wide array of activities on the street, from skating and playing shinny to using sleds and traineaus to transport people and goods.[20] Also evident here is a substantial power grab: Anyone engaged in a building project or any alteration to the urban landscape had to seek approval from the city surveyor.[21] This was likely an effort to impose a greater sense of order but also expanded the power of the municipal institution.

The widely shared impulse to transform the way that people carried themselves in urban space was the driving force behind the growing reach of the state that occurred during this period.[22] The expansion of the state's authority into nearly every facet of the urban experience was audacious. The efforts of reformers encountered both subtle and explicit resistance on a number of fronts. Many groaned at the burden that these initiatives placed on the public purse. The city's popular classes, meanwhile, rarely embraced campaigns that sought to disrupt longstanding cultural practices, whether alcohol-drenched revelry, using the streets as a social space, or relying on the economic contributions of their children to make ends meet. The tensions that these actions created were no doubt sharpened when public order initiatives came wrapped in the hierarchical language of Christian morality.

A thread connected all the different manifestations of disorder that weighed on reform-oriented elites during this period: spontaneous gatherings of crowds on the city's streets. The tendency towards popular assemblages was part of what made fluid circulation through the city nearly impossible. There were also, however, more abstract yet equally important reasons for singling out crowds for specific attention. When it came to law enforcement, crowds posed a particular challenge. Police forces which, in their present guise, were very recent additions to the urban fray, were poorly funded and thus remained modest in size. While they were capable of breaking up an altercation between two or three people or taking a suspect into custody, dealing with large groups of hostile people quickly brought to light their shortcomings.[23] Even if they were able to make arrests, crowds were frequently able to rescue their prisoners. Legal proceedings against rioters were rarely successful, as such events frequently provided a veil of anonymity for all those involved.[24] That crowds had played a pivotal role in the political unrest of the 1830s only added further to elite hostility. Popular assemblies were carefully targeted in the legal reforms carried out by the Special Council in the immediate aftermath of the Rebellions, not only in explicit sanctions against these actions but also in their commitment to the enhancement of urban policing.[25]

Josiah Eaton was not alone in harnessing the streets in order to make ends meet. In the mid-nineteenth century, urban streets were workplaces for many men, women, and children. Hucksters, carters, vendors, and prostitutes, to name just a few occupations, eked out a living in this environment. Interrupting the flow of pedestrian traffic was the foundation of their strategy. As the petitioners calling for a crackdown on muffin vendors attested, urban entrepreneurs attempted to get attention by making a cacophony of bells, drums, and whistles. They jostled and disturbed passersby. In an effort to attract public support for a regulatory crackdown on such practices, reformers argued that people reported feeling physically intimidated and overwhelmed by the persistent tactics of street vendors. An article on the subject published by the *Times* of London and re-printed in the *Montreal Witness* lamented such "continual molestation" at the hands of street merchants, and noted how everyone from robust young men to elderly women could "neither do their trifling errands, nor get a little fresh air and rest from household occupations" without being "positively driven back by the filthy savages that dodge them wherever they go."[26] They could not move quickly down a city street without people attempting to sell them an impressive inventory of household goods, including "matches, pocket-books, lead pencils, penknives, and key-rings, artificial flowers, and pin-cushions."[27] The *Montreal Witness*, which was directed towards and largely read by Montreal's evangelical Protestants, heartily endorsed the sentiments of the *Times* piece. An editorial appended to it noted happily that the "plague of beggars" on the streets, characterized as one of the most troubling aspects of life in a modern city, appeared to be abating.[28]

Editorials of this sort, which appeared frequently in newspapers across the North Atlantic World during this period, were written to give the impression that the broader community was united by their antipathy towards these practices. If such a consensus did exist, however, the persistence of an unruly popular culture would be confounding. In order to fill in the gaps, we need to take into consideration the targets of this reforming impulse – those who engaged in the popular practices in question. Few people who earned their living on the streets created the sort of documentation that historians are accustomed to working with, like private correspondence or diaries. We are therefore left to rely on the descriptions made by critics of these activities or the records produced by their encounters with the state, such as the municipal government's Police Commission and the lower criminal courts. It is thus necessary to read against the grain of these documents and to consider not only what motivated the targets of the reformer's gaze, but how this culture continued to flourish on the streets of Montreal despite the opposition of those who could draw on wealth and connections to the powerful to further their cause.

Let us take, for example, the *Montreal Witness'* lament about Montreal's "plague of beggars." Because Montreal was a hub of regional and transatlantic migration, and because the liberal approach to urban governance discouraged the creation of an adequate social safety-net, residents of the city regularly encountered destitute people on the street.

This was especially the case during the summer months of the mid-1840s, when migrants fleeing social upheaval in Ireland landed in Montreal's port, and frequently had to resort to begging to get back on their feet.[29] This was not the case, however, with the street vendors that the *Montreal Witness* characterized as beggars. It is clear from reading this piece that these were actually entrepreneurial merchants like Josiah Eaton, who relied on persistent sales techniques to carve out a living. If there were enough men, women, and children engaged in these activities to constitute what the *Montreal Witness* deemed to be "a plague," then it appears that a sufficient number of Montrealers, including, in all likelihood, some readers of the *Montreal Witness*, had grown accustomed to purchasing small items like penknives and pincushions from them.

Why was the *Montreal Witness* bent on blurring the boundaries between the desperate beggar and the canny street vendor? They were engaged in the project of mid-nineteenth-century reform which was, in incremental and quotidian ways, attempting to transform the public's conception of urban decorum. The bustle that Montrealers encountered each time they stepped out their front doors, and which many residents had learned to skilfully negotiate, was in the process of becoming – in the elite imagination at least – something that could be overhauled. Pieces like this helped spread these ideas across the North Atlantic World. They grabbed the attention of the public because they tugged at the anxieties many felt about living in a rapidly growing urban centre on the edge of industrialization where an increasing concentration of people in a relatively confined geographic space combined with a growing polarization between the haves and have-nots. In this tumultuous period, social relations and practices of authority were being re-thought and re-negotiated in the context of urban interaction.

Many expressed their anxiety regarding their place in the urban environment through the language of gender. The masculine ideal that elite men were increasingly engaged with placed an enormous value on their ability to demonstrate restraint and, simultaneously, to protect their female loved ones.[30] The *Montreal Witness* nodded vigorously towards these emerging ideals in their piece on street vendors. "Men," they noted, "can move past a beggar with a hard look or a

2.2 This image of the docks suggests a city more sparsely populated than contemporary Montrealers would have been familiar with. James Duncan, *Montreal Waterfront and Docks*, ca. 1847–50.

scowl, but ladies were more vulnerable to their advances."[31] In other words, Montreal's respectable men might have, after years of living in the city, learned how to brush off unwanted advances by men like Josiah Eaton without a second thought, but this was no excuse to minimize the necessity of curbing them. The project of urban reform had greater ambitions in mind. It sought to foster a city where their supposedly delicate wives, mothers, and sisters could walk with the same sort of confidence. In a rough and tumble port and garrison town, where the vulnerability of women from across the social spectrum was a very real problem, this was an audacious proposition.[32]

Prodding anxieties around the popular use of urban space was one thing, but reformers encountered a daunting challenge when it came to translating their aspirations into action. These elites did have a substantial new political tool at their disposal. In the lead-up to the Act of Union, the Special Council had established a municipal government in Montreal. This institution provided an ethnically heterogeneous cohort of elites with jurisdiction over the regulation of urban space and many of the processes relating to the management of urban growth. This political institution was pivotal in carving out new spheres of authority for liberal elites.[33] As demonstrated by the failed attempt to crack down on the practices of muffin vendors, however, it is clear that efforts to reform the city's popular culture through political means did not always succeed. Why was this the case? For one, it is quite apparent from their actions that many of the men elected to the municipal government did not support the interventionist thrust of urban reformers. While liberalism fostered a spirit of reform, it continuously balanced this impetus with a countervailing animosity towards the expansion of state activity, especially when it interfered with private property and commercial pursuits. These sentiments frequently resulted in both opposition towards measures put forward and supported by reformers and in the persistent underfunding of municipal institutions like the police force, which often made it difficult to enforce regulations that had succeeded in making it onto the books.

This tension was evident in several campaigns that local reformers initiated against other forms of popular street commerce. In 1848, a group of merchants on Great Saint James Street, one of the city's main commercial arteries, presented the municipal government with a petition demanding that they ban the biweekly markets that were held on the street's footpaths. The chief of police's initial response to their petition assured them that he would launch an investigation into the matter "with a view to the abatement of the evil."[34] The petition presented by the merchants did not suggest that the actions of these street vendors were having a negative impact on their bottom-line.[35] Rather, they made the case for a new and genteel popular culture along one of the city's storied thoroughfares. The city's elites, they suggested, should be able to easily circulate on a street that was the very embodiment of the colony's capitalist vitality. There was no place for aggressive hucksters and spontaneous markets in this vision. Despite the initial assurances from the chief of police that he was going to take the advice of the petitioners seriously, there is no evidence that the municipal authorities followed through.

At other times, the municipal government appears to have taken on the role of neutral broker between reformers and shop owners. A wave of petitions landed at City Hall in 1847 calling for a ban on street placards, which many shop owners used to advertise their wares. The petitions complained that this mode of advertising was an increasing eyesore and, most importantly, an impediment to men and women passing unhindered along the city's footpaths. As there were existing bylaws that regulated the dimensions and the placement of these signs, the Police Committee assured the petitioners that they would look into the matter.[36] Following the lead of Josiah Eaton, a group of merchants tabled a response to the original petitioners with the civic government, laying out how these signs played an invaluable role in helping them drum up business.[37] The municipal authorities nudged the two parties towards a compromise: Shop owners would continue being permitted to place signs outside their shops so long as they were elevated ten feet above street level.[38] Like the story of Josiah Eaton, this conflict was not a remarkable occurrence. What it does illustrate, however, is the role that the municipal government had to play in negotiating contradictory visions of how Montreal ought to work, look, and feel.

The opponents of reform campaigns made the case that these sorts of proposals threatened their livelihoods. The reformers had to defend the legitimacy of their vision in more idealistic terms, arguing that the imperative for change went deeper than commercial concerns. Amongst the most vocal advocates for urban reform during this period were the Sabattarians, a coalition of Protestant activists who called for a ban on commercial activity on Sundays. On the surface it would seem that their purpose was to create an environment suitable for spiritual reflection on Sundays, rather than transforming the way people used the streets on a daily basis. It is clear upon reading their petitions to the municipal government, however, that the movement provided a forum for addressing the broader anxieties of a vocal microcosm of Montreal's elite.

The principal target of Montreal's Sabattarians were the city's carters – men and boys who made deliveries and taxied people around the city in horse-drawn carriages.[39] Municipal bylaws already substantively regulated carters through the licensing process, holding them accountable for breaches in conduct and creating a uniform system of fees.[40] That the carters carried out their vocation on Sundays struck Sabattarians as an attack on their vision of public order, the legitimacy of which they supported by biblical allusions. An 1844 petition tabled with the municipal government outlined their position by stating that "such an engagement is not required by the public convenience, that by it the rest of the Sabbath so conducive to health and life is lost, the general quiet of the city seriously disturbed, and disrespect shown to the common Father of us all."[41] The petition continued by outlining the benefits that barring carters from plying their trade on Sundays would bring, arguing that doing so "would essentially promote social order and virtue."[42] This argument drew on one of the core beliefs of urban reformers – that the streets could be transformed into a space that would elevate everyone who spent time there, regardless of their ethnicity, religious beliefs, or position on the spectrum of class.

It is not surprising that carters became the focal point of a campaign to change the way that Montrealers used the city's streets. For elites whose conceptualizations of authority and respectability were increasingly linked to demonstrations of physical and emotional restraint, carters embodied a rough masculinity. Evidence suggests that they had a tendency to be physically aggressive in their efforts to solicit clients, and they competed fiercely amongst themselves for business. Their physical appearance likely had an impact on the Sabattarian assessment of carters. Dealing with horses on the dusty and muddy streets would have made keeping a tidy appearance impossible. Standing in close proximity to working carters would have been a sensory assault. A British traveler visiting the city during the 1840s described descending the plank of the steamboat from Quebec City onto a crowded wharf in Montreal and immediately having both of his arms grabbed with considerable force by an Irish carter, who offered to take him and his luggage to a nearby hotel in exchange for one shilling.[43] An 1843 editorial in *La Minerve* painted a similarly chaotic picture of the wharf where the ferry from La Prairie docked. Unruly knots of carters and other hustlers noisily pushed and fought each other while trying to drum up business from people visiting from villages on the other side of the St Lawrence River. It was a wonder, the editorial mused, that visitors to the city were not more frequently knocked into the water by this reckless behaviour.[44]

While *La Minerve*'s attack on carters demonstrates that these concerns transcended the city's ethnic divide, there is little doubt that in the case of the Sabattarians there may have been a sectarian component. The overwhelming majority of those carters who signed a petition defending their right to work on the Sabbath were Catholics, of both the Canadien and Irish persuasion. Many in their ranks would have interpreted the Sabattarians' demands according to the sectarian tensions that cast a shadow over Montreal. Similarly, the attack on the carters was in keeping with the perspective of many in Protestant elite that viewed the city's struggles with establishing order as the product of its large and growing Catholic population.

The Sabattarians do not appear recognized that carters worked on Sunday because they needed to make ends meet. Nor did they consider placing some of the blame on the wealthier Montrealers who made working on the Sabbath a profitable venture for carters. Montreal remained a bustling place on Sunday not simply because of the labour force, but because merchants demanded that items be transported and people were willing to hire drivers to ferry them through the streets. Carters were simply providing a service that the broader community demanded.

Given the records at our disposal, it is impossible to trace how different interest groups lined up around the Sabattarian campaign. It seems fair to speculate that well-connected Montrealers who employed carters on the Sabbath might have stood cautiously on the sidelines of the debate in hopes that, like so many other battles waged by reformers, it would eventually peter out. Others might well have quietly made their opposition known to those with hands on the levers of authority. The only group vocal in their opposition to the Sabattarians were the carters themselves. They tabled a petition with the municipal government demanding that they abandon plans to pass a bylaw restricting their ability to work on Sundays. In it, they detailed the negative impact that the law would have on their ability to support themselves and their families.[45] This exchange led City Council to vote in favour of what appears to have been an attempt to compromise between the carters and the Sabattarians. In February 1844, after acknowledging that "as many of these persons have formed engagements which it would be impossible for them to fulfill" otherwise, a full ban on carters working on the Sabbath would be delayed for the time being. In the meantime, carters would be permitted to ply their trade until two o'clock in the afternoon on Sundays.[46]

The Sabattarians were not the only group to object to the raucous behaviour of carters during this period. Judicial records reveal that carters were regularly brought before magistrates in the lower criminal courts to face charges for fighting, mistreating their horses, driving carriages recklessly through the streets, and public intoxication.[47] Many of these complaints were initiated by fellow carters or others who laboured on the city's streets. In many cases they might have been rooted in interpersonal conflicts. Still, they demonstrate a willingness on the part of members of the popular classes to engage with the judicial system to address complaints that they had about their peers. Such complaints had more resonance because they tapped into concerns about disorderly behaviour that were circulating amongst the elites. In other words, the longstanding practices of men working in this highly visible occupation were at the heart of the cluster of behaviours that were being criminalized during this period.

Complaints were rarely lodged against men plying their trade in solitude. Most of the petitions had to do with the apparent tendency of carters to gather in large groups between jobs. These complaints remind us of the elite preoccupation with rough and spontaneous crowd events on the city's streets.[48] Hugh Darraugh, who operated a tavern at the corner of Commissioners and St Francis Xavier streets on the city's waterfront, wrote a letter to the authorities in which he complained about a group of "impertinent carters" who had taken to occupying the footpath directly outside the door of his establishment. Darraugh stated that he and his neighbours felt intimidated by their presence, and often had to step out "into the mess and the dirt of the street" in order pass them.[49] The numerous complaints about the tendency of carters to impede circulation suggest that the sorts of exchanges described by Hugh Darraugh had become routine. In keeping with how the municipal government tended to deal with these sorts of complaints, the police committee found temporary solutions. Carters were simply shuffled around the streets to briefly satisfy the concerns of petitioners.

Hostility towards the seemingly spontaneous gatherings of carters also became the subject of editorials in the local press. After an incident in which a horse working on St Joseph Street bolted and ran amok through the neighbourhood, an editorial in *La Minerve* lashed out at the entire community of carters, complaining that they preferred to "tourmenter les passants et s'amuser à se quereller entr'eux, que de prendre soin de leurs voitures."[50] The leap that this editorial takes is telling. *La Minerve* takes an isolated but by no means uncommon occurrence – the escape of a frightened horse – to launch into a diatribe against the city's popular classes. These small groups of idle carters awaiting their next fare were portrayed as a persistent threat to public order. Beneath the surface of these complaints we can see, in the leading organ of the city's Francophone elite, a line of thinking informed by the connections that liberalism drew between virtue and productivity, circulation and modernity, and of the superiority of the restrained individual to the garrulous crowd.[51] These localized exchanges between carters and members of the broader community might appear minor at first glance, but they provide a glimpse into how the city's elite were increasingly seeing popular culture as a subject for reform. They worked with groups like the Sabattarians to exchange and disseminate their opinions and leaned on the judiciary and the municipal government to regulate and police the way that the popular classes used urban space.

It is tempting to read these attacks on carters as an example of elites attempting to assert their authority over the contested space of the street. Upon a closer reading, however, it becomes apparent that a more textured analysis is required. For one, the carters were able to successfully make their voice heard in the bastion of bourgeois authority that was Montreal's civic government, who adopted legislation that did not crack down on carters to the degree that the Sabattarians had demanded. Secondly, the conflict between carters and the broader community did not fall tidily along the fault lines of class. In fact, judicial records reveal that fellow members of the popular classes were amongst their most vocal critics. Furthermore, while it is important to note the way that these sorts of campaigns both reflected and deepened the city's increasingly polarized power structure, this should not be done at the expense of acknowledging the very real vulnerability many felt on the street. During the summer of 1845, for example, a carter by the name of Vincent Lachapelle was arrested after he and some colleagues surrounded an unnamed woman on Notre Dame Street and used threatening language in an effort to "induce her to hire his cab."[52] While this arrest and many others like it can be read as examples of the increased surveillance that occurred during this period, they are also a reminder that we must consider the very real threat such actions posed to Montrealers from all walks of life.

For many commentators, nothing provided better proof of the need for reform than the presence of apparently idle boys on nearly every street corner. Whether at work or at play, boys were a persistent thorn in the side of reformers, public officials, and the police throughout the decade. For the sons of the city's poor families, the streets provided invaluable resources. They were a place where one could escape the domestic drudgery of cramped lodgings to engage in rowdy play. In 1849, however, the police commission banned boys from playing shinny on the streets and on the Champ de Mars.[53] An unidentified member of the commission attached an amendment to the act stating that the ban would be in effect at all times and on every day of the week, which appears to suggest that games of shinny were not an occasional nuisance but were perceived as a persistent menace by the guardians of law and order.[54]

Street commerce also presented boys with an opportunity to make modest yet, at times, vital contributions to their family's economic well-being. Boys were hired to sell newspapers and other consumables on street corners. Local shop owners hired them to make deliveries. Many took to the streets to scavenge for valuable debris – pieces of coal that had fallen from a passing cart or furniture thrown to the kerb by a family departing the city. Others simply begged for handouts from passersby. The records of the lower criminal courts also reveal that boys who engaged in these pursuits regularly drifted outside the confines of the law, shoplifting at the market or attempting to make off with clothes that had been hung outdoors to dry. Whatever activity they were engaged in, boys frequently raised the ire of reformers simply as a result of their tendency to be loud and reckless, and to move in large groups. Few Montrealers would have been surprised by reports made in the aftermath of outbreaks of violence that boys were frequently found at the centre of the tumult.[55]

Boys became targets of the authorities even when they were engaged in lawful pursuits. In August 1848, the Police Commission wrote to the editors of two of Montreal's English-language newspapers, the *Herald* and the *Courier*, to inform them that complaints had been pouring across the desks of local alderman about the flock of young boys employed by both papers to sell their newspapers on street corners. The complaints had to do with the way that the boys made use of an arsenal of noisemakers – including trumpets, horns, and drums – to grab the attention of passersby. This appears, at various moments, to have descended into boisterous games of one-upmanship. The result, many of the complainants argued, was a deafening cacophony that made all other pursuits difficult to carry out.[56] The Police Commission warned the proprietors of the two newspapers that the police had been instructed to focus on the young newspaper vendors. While they would be obligated to keep the noise in check before nine o'clock, a complete ban on the use of instruments for the purpose of selling newspapers would be enforced after that time.[57]

A further complaint addressed to the Police Commission over one year later suggests that this was yet another practice that the authorities had a difficult time curtailing.[58]

While the need to make a contribution to the family economy forced many boys to take jobs as delivery boys and newspaper vendors, evidence suggests that the boundaries between work and play were quite porous, a reality that no doubt prompted consternation amongst their employers. In 1846, a local magistrate heard a case involving a messenger boy who lived in the Quebec suburbs, on the city's eastern periphery. Frank Spranklin had been walking down an unnamed street balancing a basket filled with eggs and other groceries on his head while making a delivery for his employer. To his surprise, a young apprentice tinsmith by the name of William Shannon approached him quickly from behind and leapt on his back. Falling to the ground, Spranklin dropped the basket, causing the eggs and several other items to break on the paving stones.[59]

The boys working on the streets of mid-nineteenth-century Montreal were quickly becoming a leading topic of discussion amongst the reform-oriented elite.[60] In these circles, there was no greater symbol of society's failings than these boys. The *Montreal Witness* printed a long essay on the subject of poor children in the city. The piece described how as soon "as its tiny limbs could carry its stunted body, it is thrown out of its dirty den into the street to beset the doors of the more blessed, or interrupt the passengers on the busy thoroughfares with importunate appeals for charity."[61] A society that was truly engaged in the project of improvement and committed to social progress would set aside the resources necessary to keep these children in school.

Children held a special place in the reform imagination. Reformers supported the expansion of institutions like workhouses, prisons, and hospitals, whose object was to improve adults by preparing them to become productive contributors to society. Children, though, were seen as being particularly malleable to their undertakings.[62] If orderly and regimented schools were a powerful symbol of the process of liberal modernity,[63] then packs of boys idling together on street corners were its very antithesis. In a society that was increasingly placing a high value on public order, sweeping boys off the city's streets became an important gauge of the effectiveness and thus the legitimacy of authority. Concern regarding idle boys became one of the chief arguments employed by education reformers lobbying for the expansion of schooling in the colony. After fielding several complaints about aggressive newsboys who gathered around the entrances to Bonsecours Market, Alderman Jean Larocque proposed schooling as the only permanent solution to the problem.[64] This is a perfect example of how political elites were able to leverage public concern about disorderly acts taking place on the streets of Montreal to build support for a broader social project.

An 1844 address to the Grand Jury attempted to raise concern about the number of boys routinely passing in front of local magistrates. The vast majority of boys arrested on the streets of Montreal and charged with petty criminal offences were between the ages of twelve and sixteen. They appeared, at least to the magistrates who drafted this address, to be "already hardened in iniquity."[65] It was the parents of these wayward youths, the magistrates argued, who deserved much of the blame. They had proven themselves unable to "inculcate with sufficient force those moral lessons which should always be instilled into the mind of youth." The magistrates also suggested that these children had been nudged towards a life of crime by adult criminals that they encountered in the city.[66] Though it continued at length about the troubling number of boys being arrested in the city, this address to the Grand Jury did not attempt to think through what could have been leading so many boys to engage in acts like petty larceny, though the sheer number of cases suggest that many were simply trying to contribute to the economic survival of their families.

When the proponents of educational reform were successful in getting children off the streets and into classrooms, they were eager to display this achievement and thereby cast themselves as effective wielders of authority.[67] Columns of tidily uniformed students were one of the leading attractions in the national society parades and religious processions that became cornerstones of public life during this period. Some institutions went so far as to work these sorts of displays into the rhythm of daily life. The boys who attended the Écoles de la doctrine chrétienne were obligated to model their daily walk to school on these parades. Students wore coloured uniforms to indicate which schools they attended and marched in pairs along a specific route each morning.[68] These parades would have made a stunning visual impact, especially in the midst of the morning rush when many other boys would have been engaged in petty commerce. It demonstrates the Catholic clergy's canny use of public space during this period, as these processions would have been a daily reminder of the church's unique ability to instil discipline in a segment of the population so closely associated with disorder.

Alderman Larocque's assertion that schooling would prove an easy solution to the problems posed by rowdy boys was politically strategic, but did not reflect reality. For one, the children of the popular classes, even if they were enrolled in school, did not necessarily attend classes on a consistent basis. Truancy remained a daunting challenge for school officials for decades to come. Secondly, even when children did attend classes regularly, they continued to engage in rowdy behaviour. In 1846, for example, residents who lived in the vicinity of the British and Canadian Free School, a Protestant institution located on Côté Street, wrote to city council to complain about the "constant noise" emanating from the yard adjacent to the school where the boys congregated on their breaks.[69] Similarly, while they were meant to be powerful assertions of the disciplinary reach of the Écoles de la doctrine chrétienne, those daily processions by students seem to have been periodically interrupted by bursts of rough play. In January 1841, three boys who attended one of the schools appeared in front of a magistrate to testify that they had been attacked on a daily basis as they passed through the Champ de Mars on their way to school from their homes in the suburbs. Eusèbe Archambault, Pierre Pivin, and Théophile Cousineau testified that during the winter months they engaged in daily snowball fights with children who lived adjacent the Champ de Mars. In the preceding days, however, these skirmishes had escalated from a pleasurable diversion before a day of tedious lessons to a violent conflict with sectarian undertones after a group of English-speaking men had entered the fray. The boys sought the assistance of the police after a snowball fight turned into a full-fledged brawl that left Cousineau, who had not yet celebrated his twelfth birthday, with a sizable wound on his torso.[70] In the days that followed the appearance of these children in front of a local magistrate, their mothers filed before the same official, recounting the terror that had struck them upon seeing the wounds of their sons. They demanded that the police put a stop to these confrontations.[71] These two episodes reveal that simply enrolling children in school was not enough to curb their proclivity towards rowdiness. This case is also a reminder of the very real vulnerability of Montreal's youngest residents in a city where these sorts of outbursts were woven into the fabric of daily life.

Given the evidence that children from the popular classes shared urban space with the adult population – sitting in taverns and standing on street corners, to give just two examples – they no doubt would have picked up and even engaged in the political chatter of the day. There were occasions when youthful rowdiness appeared to demonstrate engagement in the rougher edges of the city's politics. In October 1845, for example, a newly constructed Protestant Church in the predominately poor and Catholic neighbourhood of Griffintown had nearly all its windows shattered by rocks. *Les Mélanges Religieux* reported that rumours were circulating that a group of local Catholic children were responsible for the vandalism, which had been carried out after dark.[72] If this was the case, it suggests that young people were already familiar with the tensions that existed in the city between Protestant and Catholic, English and French, and Tory and Reform.

Despite having the support of politicians and other community leaders from across the city, increasing access to schooling proved to be contentious for many of the same reasons that other projects of urban reform were. The boys who engaged noisily in the city's street commerce (or, for that matter, committed acts of petty criminality) were making vital contributions to their families' economies. Even when taking these economic contributions out of the equation, complaints about youthful rowdiness demonstrate an increasing discomfort in some circles for the way that popular sociability spilled out of enclosed and private spaces and into the streets. Increasing access to schooling promised many things to the social and political elite. It was seen as a pathway to a more orderly public culture and a powerful instrument with which to inculcate young minds against the sorts of insurrectionary ideas that had circulated during the

1830s. To the parents and children of the popular classes, however, the promise of education appeared far murkier. Many would have doubtlessly seen it instead as an attack on their strategies – whether social or economic – for surviving in the city.[73]

Boys were not the only Montrealers who were admonished for being a threat to public order. The most visible and persistent challenge to public order throughout the 1840s was, by a wide margin, public drunkenness. Montreal was awash in booze. Drinking was deeply ingrained in the sociability of men and women from all walks of life.[74] Whether one was a recently arrived migrant seeking out precarious work on the waterfront or the member of a well-connected and prosperous family, drink was enjoyed as a social lubricant, a moment of respite, and a balm for a whole slate of tensions and anxieties. There were few city blocks that did not house some sort of drinking establishment, be it a hotel, a tavern, or an unlicensed grog shop. When men and women of the popular classes were arrested and hauled in front of a magistrate, alcohol proved to be an aggravating factor in a sizeable majority of the cases, violent or not. In nearly every instance in which a disruptive and spontaneous crowd assembled, drunkenness was identified by the authorities as a crucial ingredient.

While many imbibed with great vigour, others reacted to this love of alcohol by joining temperance societies and other anti-drinking crusades. Efforts to curb excessive alcohol-consumption prompted people to engage like no other cause during this period. Montrealers from across the city's ethnic and sectarian divide employed public assertions of sobriety in order to cast themselves as committed defenders of public order.[75] Many were no doubt sincere in their concern over the apparently routine sight of drunk men and women slumped to the ground on footpaths across the city. That being said, there was a political angle to these campaigns. For men and women engaged in the temperance cause, public drunkenness was the antithesis of the practice of emotional and physical restraint that was increasingly being pushed to the forefront of their conceptualization of legitimate authority.

The politics of alcohol laid bare the fault-lines around class and privilege in mid-nineteenth-century Montreal. It is evident that alcohol flowed freely in the homes and at the social functions of the city's elites.[76] When the popular classes engaged in similar practices, however, they were far more likely to be seen as a threat to public order. Officials in the police department, the civic government, and the courts harnessed concerns about drunkenness to intervene in the lives of the popular classes to an unprecedented degree.

Temperance activists painted a bleak picture of an urban landscape blighted by the excessive consumption of alcohol. In January 1844, the *Montreal Gazette* published a letter to the editor from the Montreal Victorian Temperance Society that described the city as having "tippling houses at almost every corner," noting that "in some streets four or five may be counted within a distance of about three hundred yards."[77] For the sake of the public good, they demanded seven out of every eight taverns be shut down by the civic authorities, and that efforts be made to eradicate the many vendors who sold liquor without a licence.[78] The Montreal Victorian Temperance Society was not terribly interested in reaching out to Montrealers who had developed addictions to alcohol. They made no mention of personal self-improvement, a theme that would preoccupy temperance activists in the second half of the nineteenth century. They did not propose placing restrictions on people's freedom to drink in their homes, nor did they comment on the way that wine and spirits flowed at the celebrations of the Montreal elite. The focus of their campaign was the raucous outdoor culture of the city's poorest residents. Unlike elites, who had a tendency to tipple in private spaces, Montreal's popular classes routinely spilled out of darkened taverns and grog shops into the streets.

Temperance activism came in many different guises in mid-nineteenth-century Montreal. Voluntary associations like the Montreal Victorian Temperance Society, mentioned above, lobbied elected officials to enforce anti-drinking legislation. They circulated petitions on the matter, held public meetings where medical experts were invited to share research on the dangers of excessive alcohol consumption, and published letters to the editor in elite publications like the *Montreal Gazette*. Not all temperance activism was so staid, however. Other organizations targeted the very people who frequented the city's taverns and grog shops. During the 1840s, thousands of Catholic Montrealers from both the Irish and Canadien communities joined temperance societies that used raucous street celebrations as one of the primary means of disseminating their message to the broader community. As will be discussed in greater detail in Chapter Five, Catholic temperance activists joined brass bands that paraded through the streets and attended huge public meetings where crowds gathered to hear charismatic campaigners deliver their message. This sort of activity was not exclusively Catholic. Protestant temperance campaigners took to delivering sermons on the evils of excessive drinking on street corners.[79] While a wide array of tactics were used, the content remained consistent throughout this period. The focus remained on the threat alcohol consumption posed to public order, a concern that connected temperance activists across the North Atlantic World.[80]

That the temperance movement pulled into its orbit Montrealers from across ethnic and sectarian divides, as well as from across the chasm that separated the poor from the privileged, reminds us how broad the appeal of this vision of a more orderly city could be. When campaigns for public order did not simply attack longstanding social practices that allowed the vast majority of Montrealers to make ends meet – such as engaging in petty capitalism or sending boys out on the streets in search of money-making opportunities – their appeal could be wider, as the monumental success of the temperance movement demonstrates.

This is not to say that the aspirations of the city's temperance activists were in any way less ambitious than their counterparts lobbying to reform other popular uses of public space. One of the largest and most active of the Catholic temperance societies established during the 1840s in Montreal, the St Patrick's Total Abstinence Society, marked their silver anniversary in the final decade of the nineteenth century by publishing a commemorative pamphlet that recalled the state of affairs when Patrick Phelan, a Catholic priest, founded the organization in 1840. Their words echoed those of the Montreal Victorian Temperance Society. "There was," the pamphlet recounted, "a vast amount of open drunkenness to be seen in our city. Men were drunk in the public streets at every hour of the day as well as of the night ... it was not considered a disgrace even for those occupying positions to be seen in that state."[81] Although the St Patrick's Total Abstinence

Society continued their work of rescuing drunkards and lobbying to have taverns closed in 1890, the writers of their anniversary pamphlet argued that their group had significantly, and positively, altered the nature of sociability in Montreal from the conditions that had led to their organization's establishment in 1840. While it is impossible to gauge the accuracy of a ceremonial hagiography of this society, it is intriguing to note the thread that linked these temperance activists to other projects of reform that were flourishing during the same period and in the same problematic environment. By focusing on the public face of drunkenness rather than the private damage and domestic disorder that alcohol created, this became another campaign to transform the way that people used the streets as social space.

Despite their best efforts, these temperance activists found their demands placed firmly on the back-burner by the authorities. The tepidity of the official response to groups like the Montreal Victorian Temperance Society can be read as an acknowledgement that the ability of the authorities to radically and rapidly transform popular behaviour was quite limited. Much of the problematic drinking was taking place on the city's fringe, where police struggled to assert their authority at the best of times. In 1843, the Montreal Victorian Temperance Society alleged that a number of entrepreneurs who had constructed shanties along the banks of the Lachine Canal under the pretence of selling bread and other supplies to the migrants living in the area's sprawling shantytowns were, in fact, making the bulk of their profits through the sale of alcohol. The establishments in question had begun attracting crowds of disreputable people, and "scenes of the most discreditable character have occurred whereby the peace of the neighbourhood has been greatly disturbed."[82]

Seizing upon the letter, City Councillor Adam Ferrie demanded that the police take immediate action, first by tearing down the sheds of the vendors in question and, secondly, by increasing the frequency of police patrols in the area, especially after dark.[83] The violent strike that had broken out amongst the Irish labourers employed by and living in the vicinity of these illicit drinking establishments – the subject of the following chapter – remained at the forefront of the public imagination. Officials like Ferrie took a resolute stand on the issue because it provided them with an opportunity to cast themselves as effective defenders of public order. The Police Commission, however, regretfully informed Ferrie and the Montreal Victorian Temperance Society that the trade in illicit alcohol along the banks of the Lachine Canal was likely the result of their recent decision to curtail their patrols of the area, which had been made as a result of budgetary cutbacks. They recommended that Ferrie direct his energies towards having the police force's funding not only restored but increased, due to the inherent danger of policing the city's periphery.[84]

The reaction of the civic officials to this complaint created a precedent against intervention in such affairs. An 1844 petition drafted by the Montreal Victorian Temperance Society calling on the authorities to shut down unlicensed drinking establishments was dismissed with a terse reply that the matter was outside the jurisdiction of the council.[85] The group persisted, despite the shrugs of officials. They delivered another petition regarding unlicensed taverns three years later, which the Police Commission responded to by stating that the "law would have to take its course" on the issue.[86] After another year passed, there appears to have been a concerted effort to tackle the problem, but it was fumbled just as it began. A letter signed by a Mr Horne was tabled at a meeting of the Police Commission in July 1848. Horne reported on his unsuccessful attempts to shut down a number of unlicensed drinking establishments that had come to the attention of the authorities. For reasons that are not clearly stated, Horne was immediately removed from the municipal payroll. The records of the police commission gently allude to the possibility that Horne had been taking paybacks from the very tavern-keepers he had been hired to shut down. In closing, the chief of police pronounced that efforts to investigate and prosecute these establishments would resume only when it was advisable to do so.[87]

Opposition to temperance campaigners was subtle but well coordinated. The city's tavern keepers organized an emergency meeting at the Nelson Hotel and issued a statement to the local press calling on the civic authorities to focus their attention on the city's unlicensed grog shops rather than on respectable establishments. Again, the class divide looms over these comments. Tavern-keepers were simply reminding the reading public that the sort of unruly revelry that temperance activists were most concerned with was occurring in unlicensed shops frequented by soldiers and itinerant labourers.[88] It is clear that the way that people consumed alcohol during this period became one of the pivotal issues upon which the identity formation around class was negotiated. A sharp and likely exaggerated dichotomy between the way that the poor and the privileged behaved under the influence of alcohol was being constructed in these debates. These cases demonstrate the audacity of these reform campaigns, despite the fact that they were not calling for an outright ban on alcohol consumption. Even their modest demands were met with official indifference, regretful excuses of budgetary restraint, and the invisible hand of corruption.

Despite the failings of activist groups like the Montreal Victorian Temperance Society, it is important not to dismiss their engagement in the city's public life. Their agenda might well have laid their class and ethnic biases bare,[89] but they were expressing a concern shared by a wide cross-section of Montrealers. Much of the nuance of the temperance movement can be obscured by suggesting that this was simply a project of social control being carried out by elites.[90] While it is important to examine the way that narratives put forward by temperance activists became an important component of broader attempts to transform the way that Montrealers behaved in public spaces, it is equally important that we acknowledge the very real sense of vulnerability that people would have felt encountering belligerent or hostile drunkards on dark and narrow streets. In October 1847, Robert Magwood, who listed his occupation as a labourer, was arrested for assaulting and threatening people walking down the footpath along McGill Street. In his deposition before a local magistrate, Constable Michael Lynch reported that Magwood had been seen grabbing hold of and shaking a woman who had been trying to pass him moments before his arrest[91] The reality was that mid-nineteenth-century Montreal could be a rough and threatening place. Soldiers, sailors, and itinerant labourers spent a significant portion of their time outdoors and some, after drinking to excess, behaved in threatening ways. The judicial records from the lower courts teem with cases of drunken men attacking people, jostling pedestrians, and harassing and insulting women. While they were more easily able to escape the police officer's gaze, it is likely that young men from the economic elite also engaged in similar practices. This was, therefore, an environment that accentuated masculine power in a deeply visceral way, and complaints about drunkenness likely reflected this.

Complaints about the intimidating antics of intoxicated Montrealers were not confined to members of the Montreal Victorian Temperance Society. Records from the lower criminal courts reveal that members of the popular classes frequently registered complaints about each other in front of local magistrates. During the winter of 1841, for example, Joseph Cherry and Hugh McLaughlan, both of whom were couriers, appeared in court to record a deposition against Thomas Jackson, a co-worker. The deponents accused Jackson of being "a man of violent habits" who regularly screamed and used threatening language towards them. Cherry and McLaughlan went on to accuse Jackson of being "very often drunk" while on the job, and noted that while traveling the city streets, Jackson "regularly harassed peaceable people" by screaming and swearing at them.[92] In a similar case, Joseph St Aubin and Charles St Germain reported that a fellow carter by the name of François LaPierre was frequently drunk and had lately taken to threatening passersby, in many instances trailing them on the city's footpaths on all fours. On the day that they recorded their deposition with a local magistrate, the deponents reported that LaPierre had been wandering into traffic and pulling people out of their carriages and into the street.[93] Clearly, Montrealers of all classes had reason to be concerned about the sort of intimidating and confrontational behaviour that was often linked to the abuse of alcohol.

The records of the lower criminal courts also remind us that not everybody who was arrested and charged for being intoxicated in public was behaving in these ways. On an August evening in 1844, for example, a labourer named Pierre Bourdon was arrested for drunkenly singing at the top of his lungs in de la Gauchetière Street, thereby disturbing the peace.[94] Six months earlier, a carter named James Cauthorn was arrested in a similar state after a crowd had collected in Dalhousie Square to watch him jumping up and down.[95] The spectre of class looms over these actions. While elite Montrealers could engage in revelry amidst a social calendar replete with private celebrations, the vast majority of the city's residents were accustomed to doing so, at least in part, on the street, which made them increasingly likely to find themselves in front of a magistrate. This culture might have been intimidating in many ways, but it was also part of how community was fostered in the midst of dizzying social change.[96] It provided migrants facing deeply precarious circumstances with altogether rare bursts of joy at its most irreverent.

Efforts to crack down on public drunkenness on the streets were complicated by the reality that police officers were regularly discovered engaging in these unsavoury pursuits themselves.[97] When police raided a gambling den at the corner of St Elizabeth and de la Gauchetière Streets on a Sunday night during the winter of 1840, a number of the men they arrested for betting on illegal cockfights and carousing with prostitutes were fellow officers. Joseph Rousseau, a constable, was identified as one of the ringleaders of the operation, along with Louis Malo, who was employed as the crier of the Court of Quarter Sessions where many of the petty offenses related to public order were tried.[98]

As was the case with the temperance movement, anti-prostitution activists framed their concerns as a public order issue rather than a moral crusade. An 1844 Grand Jury address on prostitution provides a particularly vivid example of this tactic. The presence of prostitutes on the city's streets – an apparently common sight in a bustling commercial and garrison town – was identified as one of the major barriers to the emergence of a more genteel public culture. As was the case with activism around public drunkenness, those calling for the authorities to take a stronger stance on prostitution were not demanding the adoption of new legislation but simply more effective enforcement of laws already on the books. There was a keen sense that prostitution had become a grave problem in the city. "To the more worthy and respectable classes of society," one Grand Jury presentment read, "these polluted females, frequenting our most public thoroughfares, and conducting themselves with all that boldness of demeanour, which distinguishes their caste, must be an eyesore, and the sooner a stop is put to this evil, the more credit, will result to those, in whose hands, lies the government of the city."[99] Prostitution was thus being conceptualized as another troubling manifestation of the city's popular culture.

Like other critiques of popular culture made by reform-oriented elites, advocates of a crackdown on prostitution conceptualized public space as a tool that could be used to elevate the moral character of the city's popular classes. The high visibility of prostitutes in Montreal had, an address by the Grand Jury argued, a corrupting influence on impressionable men and women. They noted that prostitutes "dressed very expensively … in the extreme of fashion" and were permitted to "perambulate the city" without consequence.[100] By doing so, they argued, prostitutes might influence poor women "to depart from the paths of virtue" in order to make ends meet. The order that reformers sought to craft in Montreal would, amongst the many benefits they imagined, provide moral guidance to the underprivileged women of the city. By the same token, the presence of prostitutes plying their trade on the city's streets was amongst the most obvious rebukes of authority.[101] Being associated with a political regime that proved able to curtail prostitution would, the statement by the grand jury made clear, shine a very positive light on their claims of legitimate authority. Like so many other attacks on the city's popular culture by reform-oriented elites, there was no acknowledgement that prostitution was thriving in Montreal as a result of the social and economic conditions that liberalism fostered. Mary Anne Poutanen has demonstrated convincingly that women turned to prostitution at moments of economic precarity.[102]

Further evidence of how prostitution was conceptualized as a threat to public order can be seen in the depositions recorded when men and women were arrested. Louise Vizé was arrested in 1840 on charges that she was operating a brothel in her home "where the youth of the city are in a habit of meeting together to indulge in acts of licentiousness and debauchery." The arresting officer reported that prostitutes were frequently witnessed leaning out of the windows of Vizé's establishment and making provocative remarks to passersby in an effort to lure them into the brothel.[103] While it is important to keep in mind that depositions such as this were tailored in a very specific way to improve the likelihood of a conviction, the description's emphasis on how the activities occurring in the private reaches of Vizé's brothel spilled into the streets is a vivid example of how the authorities understood prostitution as public order issue rather than a moral one. Once again, the reformer's gaze was drawn to the way that the sociability of the popular classes was rooted in gathering and lingering on the streets.

The brothels that police chose to target appear to have been those that had attracted complaints from neighbouring residents. These complaints rarely called moral issues into question. Instead, they argued that the establishments had evolved into hives of disorder and violence that threatened the peace of the neighbourhood. François Dupuis and Robert Laird, both of whom were residents of Amherst Street in the city's east end, visited a local magistrate to record a complaint against a brothel owned by William Church. The brothel, they argued, "had caused scandal throughout the neighbourhood [that] disturbs the peace."[104] Similarly, when Esther Guilbeault was taken into custody and charged with operating a brothel out of her residence at the corner of St Constant and de la Gauchetière Streets, the arresting officers justified their decision to pursue the matter by reporting that upwards of twenty women were living in the residence, and that men came and went at all hours of the night. "All sorts of indecencies occur on neighbouring streets," they continued, "and men often fight and scream there, assaulting the girls."[105]

The judicial records of the lower courts from this period contain hundreds of complaints related to prostitution. With that being said, these complaints were rare enough to justify speculation that in the course of their daily lives, Montrealers were accustomed to turning a blind eye to prostitutes.[106] What appears to have prompted Montrealers to lodge formal complaints with the authorities regarding the existence of a brothel in their neighbourhood was the disorder that spilled out of these establishments and onto the streets. These depositions reveal that men tended to frequent these establishments in large groups. Rather than ducking in and out, they would spend considerable time in these brothels, drinking and fraternizing with the women who lived and worked there. These documents can also be read from another angle. It is possible that complainants were bothered by the existence of these establishments, and were cannily drawing the attention of public officials to manifestations of popular unrest associated with the brothel in order to pique their attention.

Complaints against brothel owners in some instances also drew on other social and cultural rifts to build the case for police intervention. An 1847 deposition recorded by constables William Moore and Louis Bourbon alleged that David Bristler was running a bawdy house out of his residence near Viger Square. The constables wrote that the establishment was open at all house of the day and night, and that it was the site of frequent "balls" thrown by Bristler where "large numbers of men and women of bad fame attend and which [were] invariably followed by fights, noise and disturbances of the peace and annoyance of the neighbourhood."[107] Following the convention of explicitly mentioning the frequent disturbances emanating from the house, the deposition made specific reference to the fact that Bristler was "a coloured man."[108]

That so many of the men who frequented these establishments were soldiers stationed in the garrison in the city's east end served as a persistent reminder of the tension between the project of creating an orderly, genteel, and prosperous city and the reality that Montreal was a colonial outpost where authorities made frequent use of the military to reinforce their hold on power. Although perfunctory efforts had been made by the brass to discipline carousing soldiers, there is no reliable evidence to suggest that soldiers stationed in the city had curbed their customary indulgences.[109] In depositions recorded by the police officers regarding efforts to shut down houses of ill repute, frustration with the antics of soldiers is palpable. One such deposition, relating to the arrest of the proprietor of an alleged bawdy house on Commissioners Street on the city's waterfront, noted that solders were "regularly seen drinking contrary to orders and carousing with known prostitutes like Sarah Walker."[110]

As was the case with drinking, it is important not to assume that efforts to police prostitution in mid-nineteenth-century Montreal were simply a top-down campaign carried out by reform-minded elites. In a number of cases, prostitutes themselves were the ones who launched complaints about the trade in front of local magistrates. In 1844, for example, Rosannah Lewis recorded a deposition against one of her clients that provides a standard description of a brothel riot – the sort of violent commotion that led many in the community to associate these establishments with public disorder. Lewis noted that she and a number of other girls resided at the home in question, which was owned by a Mrs Milligan. At 1:30 in the morning shortly after the Christmas holiday, Lewis was awoken by a loud knock at the door. When she inquired as to who was there, Alexander Cruickshank identified himself, stating that he was alone and begging to be let in. Cruickshank was, apparently, known to Lewis. Upon unlatching the door, Cruickshank and seven other men barged into the home and proceeded to cause "a great tumult … to the great annoyance of the neighbours."[111] The men, two of whom Lewis was able to identify as local "gentlemen," proceeded to make a great deal of noise as they broke several pieces of furniture before throwing the debris into the street.[112] Lewis' deposition neglects to mention whether or not she or any of the other women residing in Mrs Milligan's establishment were injured in the affray. Stories such as this remind us not only of the vulnerability of women who worked as prostitues, but also of the centrality of an alcohol-fuelled masculine camaraderie in the city's popular culture.

As was the case with arrests on charges of public drunkenness, the records of the lower criminal courts reveal that the police were often called to the scene of these establishments in circumstances without the violence described by Rosannah Lewis. While it is important not to lose sight of their significance with regards to sexual politics, brothels appear to have also been sites of exuberant sociability. During the winter of 1840, for example, two police constables appeared before a magistrate to bring charges against Georges Roy, who owned a home at the corner of de la Gauchetière and St Elizabeth streets which, they alleged, was being used as a brothel. The deposition levels the conventional allegations made in cases like this, accusing Roy of running a "common bawdy house where people assemble for illicit purposes."[113] The allegations, however, paint a more vivid picture than we are accustomed to. James Jackson, a sub-constable, alleged that he had long known this establishment as a place where people gathered in varying states of intoxication. On several occasions, Jackson noted, "many danced right up until about seven o'clock in the morning" and, on the day that these depositions were being recorded, he had witnessed Georges Roy on the premises dancing with "two whores."[114] This sort of behaviour was linked, in the imagination of reformers, to a broader pattern where the streets were used as sites of revelry that, given the city's contentious social, political, and economic environment, could easily topple into violence. A crowd of men stumbling out of a brothel and onto the streets was as much of an affront to the vision shared by reform-oriented elites as was an outbreak of election violence.

Mid-nineteenth-century Montreal was a difficult city to police. The presence of soldiers and itinerant labourers helped fuel a raucous culture where drunken revelry and interpersonal violence became deeply engrained in daily life. As the efficacy of authority was increasingly associated with their ability to maintain order on the streets, the city's popular culture provided stark evidence of its limits. In a compact city like Montreal, it was a reminder that would have been nearly impossible to escape. This chapter has outlined some of the ways that politicians and reform-oriented elites took aim at the most visible manifestations of the culture of the street, and points to the audacity of their vision of a more orderly daily life. In reality, enough Montrealers – including, in all likelihood, some who quietly wielded significant power – were either engaged in certain aspects of this culture or, at the very least, willing to turn a blind eye to all but its most dramatic excesses.

The campaigns launched by reformers to crack down on things like public drunkenness, prostitution, and the most raucous aspects of petty capitalism, while not always successful, became crucial sites of identity formation for a diverse segment of Montrealers. The advocates of various manifestations of the reform agenda were actively negotiating their identities in contrast to the Montrealers who engaged in revelry, rowdy commerce, and popular violence. Defining the cultural practices of the popular classes as a social problem in need of reform was a vital part of crafting assertions of respectability and legitimate authority in the mid-nineteenth-century city. This shaped how elite Montrealers – and those who aspired to join their ranks – reacted to outbreaks of popular violence, as we will see in the following chapters. It contributed to the politicization of daily life. While many of the campaigns outlined above met with official indifference or even subtle resistance, they were integral to the emergence of transformations in social relations, attitudes towards urban space, and the scope of the state's authority in the second half of the nineteenth century.

At its very core, the political activism outlined in this chapter was the product of an emerging bourgeois elite grappling with the implications of rapid urbanization. The town that had once been a colonial settlement was quickly growing into a bustling hub of migration and global commerce. In the midst of this period of transformation, social and infrastructural foundations were being laid for the industrial economy that would take shape in the decades that followed. Urban elites were being handed new levers of power and authority as the scope of what the state could do began to expand. For Montrealers living through these processes, however, social change could not be conceptualized from the comfortable distance that historians benefit from. Instead, such changes were evaluated through the prism of daily life. Reactions to the city's rapid growth were frequently expressed in relation to people's physical experience of the city. Those who were most engaged in the politicization of the city's streets – the reform-oriented urban elite – spoke frequently of being jostled by hawkers and threatened by drunkards. These experiences shaped their conceptualization of how the city was changing. They looked to their new tools of political and institutional power to advocate for their vision of an orderly city. While their campaigns took aim at a wide array of popular practices, it was the sociability of street culture and the tendency of crowds to gather that reform-oriented elites kept circling back to. Their vision of order, as was often the case during this period, hinged upon a belief that barriers needed to be put in place between public activity and domestic affairs. The streets had become the canvass upon which the city's elites sketched out their identities, and a laboratory in which to experiment with new levers of political authority.

The patchwork of campaigns established in an effort to create a more orderly street culture in Montreal, however, was met with quiet but sustained resistance from those who found their customary practices targeted as problems. This tension between two dynamic cultures in Montreal – an ambitious cohort of urban elites determined to reshape the city and a rapidly growing working class rooted in the streets – would spar over questions of public life and urban space on numerous fronts in the middle of the nineteenth century. These conflicts would form the lens through which Montrealers conceptualized and debated the city's reorganization to suit the demands of a transatlantic capitalist economy. The next chapter examines how competing factions of the Montreal elite reacted to a series of riots and nocturnal processions carried out by the Irish migrant labourers hired to work on the expansion of the Lachine Canal during the winter of 1843. Concerns about public order that had begun to take shape around daily life in the city came into sharper focus during extraordinary circumstances such as this, when residents grew concerned that unruly crowds threatened to grind Montreal's march towards a prosperous future to a halt.

3

CUSTOM, TUMULT, AND MODERNITY ON THE URBAN FRINGE: THE LACHINE CANAL STRIKE OF 1843

Henry Mason and his foremen arrived at their construction site along the Lachine Canal just after dawn on a cold January morning in 1843 to find an ominous sign nailed to the gate. Written in a careful hand, its message bristled with intimidation and malice: "Any person or persons who works here in the Lachine Canal under 3 shillings and 6 pence per day may have their coffin and bearer [sic]."[1] The project of expanding the Lachine Canal, which Mason was overseeing on behalf of the colonial government's Board of Works, had begun only a few weeks earlier – but already the workers were on strike. The official decision to keep labour costs at an absolute minimum by hiring competing crews of Irish migrant labourers had become a source of conflict not only between the contractors and the men that they employed, but also between different factions of the labourers. The canal workers' strike set the tone for the culture of labour protest that would emerge as industrial capitalism transformed Montreal's economy in the second half of the nineteenth century. The events of 1843 pointed to the profound re-ordering of social relations in the city, a process that had been unfolding since the 1820s.

This chapter examines how the migrant labourers who worked on the expansion of the Lachine Canal drew on customs of agrarian

Notice

My friends; it is now high time that we labourers should
look out for ourselves, and no longer wait on those
unthinking Roten kidnied dogs; that is _has put back
from time to time those publick works, that should
have commenced the first of November last;
we must not hissitae any longer but get to work as soon
as posible; there are plenty of provision store in town
of cuntry, yes & wood yard to, that we can make
subsevant to our presnt wants, why then shoud we be
any longer musing on what we must do at last;
why shall we any longer looking at our little
famylies starving before our faces, rouse yoursel
up; up; & let___ us commence, their calculating will
not fill our belies, n__w let us calculate for ourselve
__e care & do not pull this_____down
__t we see you; and if we do;
__ll exonerate you 1 of 2

3.1 A fragment of the note posted at the entrance to the worksite on the
Lachine Canal demonstrates the language that was used to intimidate both the
contractor and rival work crews. Contained in BA-nQ-M, TL19 S1 SS1, _Depositions to the
Court of Queen's Bench,_ Deposition of Joseph Frobisher McDonald, 5 February 1843.

protest long employed against unscrupulous landlords in their efforts to secure higher wages and better working conditions. These practices were honed over the course of a decade of transient labour along the eastern seaboard of the United States. The chapter also examines the reactions of the city's elites to their actions, which proved a surprising challenge to their project of creating an orderly and prosperous Montreal through ambitious infrastructure projects. The unrest on the Lachine Canal was experienced by the residents of Montreal as a series of intra-ethnic brawls, nocturnal parades, charivaris, and sombre processions which raised serious questions about the ability of the city's institutions, from the courts to the newly-established municipal police force, to deal with acts of resistance to the emerging capitalist order. They serve as an important reminder of the powerful and even transformative role that crowds played during this period of tumultuous social change. This was not simply a clash between labour and capital. The labour force itself was divided into factions. These competing groups attempted to improve their standing by excluding factions of their own community who they felt were jeopardizing negotiations with the contractor employing them. They also used crowd activities like processions to make the case for their inclusion within Montreal's existing Irish community, a group with whom their connections were tenuous and contentious during this period.

The 1843 strike on the Lachine Canal came in multiple waves. Its first stirrings occurred in January, when the two crews of Irish migrant labourers hired by Mason threw down their tools only weeks after work had begun. Although the sign nailed to the gate of the construction site alluded only to their wage demands – the labourers argued that the two shillings they were being paid for a day's work on the canal was not enough to sustain them – this was only part of a broader attack on Mason's practices, which appear to have been subtly endorsed by the Board of Works. The labourers were demanding, for instance, that their wages be paid out in cash at regular intervals, rather than in the form of truck pay at a nearby store owned by Norman Bethune, an associate of Mason's, that charged inflated prices for staples like bread. Other demands suggest that the labourers were bristling under the close surveillance of Mason's foremen. For example, they insisted on having the right to smoke anywhere they pleased on the worksite – a provision that they insisted had not been challenged on any other worksite where they had been employed. The labourers returned to work after several weeks' interruption, but further disruptions occurred at regular intervals in the ensuing months, all related to complaints about low wages and poor working conditions.[2]

The actions of the canal labourers remained at the forefront of public life in Montreal as a result of a series of violent and spectacular events and demonstrations on the city streets and in the hastily erected shantytowns that lined the banks of the canal. Mason had hired two competing crews of labourers who had been working alongside each other on earlier public works projects in the United States, where they had used violence and intimidation to push each other out of areas in order to drive up wages. The two crews hired on at Lachine were built around regional origins and complex kinship networks. The larger and better armed faction were from Cork, on the southern tip of Ireland, and the second crew were from Connaught, on the country's west coast. Drawing on longstanding customs of popular protest, the crew from Cork began conducting torchlight processions in an effort to intimidate their foes who, they feared, would bow to pressure from the contractors to end the strike without having their demands met in full.

These were not the only manifestations of popular protest during the dispute. After having their grievances summarily disparaged and dismissed by Mason and the Board of Works, and after being tarred as disruptive and irrational outsiders in the local press, the canal workers marched in a sombre parade through the streets of Montreal in an effort to create a dialogue with the broader community. They used the street as a platform to put forward the counter-argument that they were not a disorderly mob threatening to disrupt public order but a group of hard-working and respectable labourers, family men, and prospective citizens deserving a fair shake from their employers and their fellow Montrealers. The conflicts – both between the labourers and the contractors linked to the Board of Works and between rival crews of migrant labourers – helped establish the area along the Lachine Canal as a site of persistent upheaval. The events that unfolded in Montreal were part of an emerging pattern of labour strife that had emerged along the eastern seaboard of North America in the previous decade. The same crews of Irish migrants had been hired on large-scale projects of this nature before, and had become deft at protesting the increasingly dire conditions being imposed on them by both state and private contractors.[3] With an economic downturn grinding projects to a halt in the United States, most of these crews of migrant labourers headed north to Canada, where work was underway to improve transportation infrastructure along the St Lawrence River and into the Great Lakes. This was an effort to shore up Montreal's economic position by making sure that agricultural exports from the colony's booming western frontier continued to pass through the city on their way to European markets.[4] The conflict along the banks of the Lachine Canal that spilled onto the streets of Montreal during the 1840s thus demonstrates how the city was an integral part of a restructuring of the North Atlantic economy.[5] This transformation can be traced not only through the way that the network of canals being dug on the eastern seaboard made the Great Lakes region more attuned to the rhythms of the market economy,[6] but also in the social and cultural response to the growing mass of men and women who had no choice but to rely on the precarious, mobile, and dangerous jobs the liberal economic project created.

In interpreting these events, it is important to remember that Montreal had little previous history of mass labour unrest. People participating in and observing the events in Lachine were, therefore, not able to contextualize them in a larger narrative of social relations, nor were they able to conceptualize the unrest as something that would eventually end. The scale of the strike – with several thousand men participating in a city of roughly 40,000 residents – suggests an impact on the city on par with the largest labour disputes of the twentieth century. The magnitude of the strike must be weighed not only by its duration of several months but also by the number of men who threw down their tools and walked off the job. Upwards of 1,100 men had been employed by Mason on the Lachine Canal project. Although we do not possess reliable qualitative data on the itinerant communities that popped up along the Lachine Canal once the project was initiated, as no census material was ever collected at the time, it is evident that many of the labourers were living with wives and children, thereby increasing the size of the community that felt the direct impact of the work stoppage and the ensuing waves of violence.

Whether it was large public works projects like the expansion of the Lachine Canal or simply commercial activity on the city's harbourfront, the capitalist model of economic growth necessitated access to a growing pool of labourers. Only migration – be it of the transatlantic variety or from the city's rural hinterland – could make this model function properly. The continued expansion of the city's economy in the 1840s was, therefore, built on the acceleration of human migration, transforming a colonial outpost into a cosmopolitan hub where connections to networks of kinship and ethnicity had to be continuously asserted.[7] This created a popular culture in Montreal that was vibrant, raucous, and prone to outbreaks of social unrest. Only a small proportion of the violence that the canal labourers engaged in can be described as concerted attacks on Henry Mason or other representatives of the colonial project. Most of the violence during the strike pitted rival crews of migrant labourers against each other. This was evident in the notice nailed to the gate of the construction site noted above, the target of which was rival factions thought to be considering returning to work without obtaining any of the strike demands. Because these crews were organized around Irish regional identities,[8] commentators in the Montreal press assumed that the conflict was centuries in the making, ancient feuds that demonstrated how out of step the migrants were with modern times. This argument belied the facts at hand. Few Montrealers had re-oriented their lives so profoundly in accordance with the demands of liberal capitalist modernity.[9] Their conflicts were not the product of pre-modern grievances but were part of a knot of strategies adopted in response to the transiency and fierce competition that was coming to define the North Atlantic labour market.[10]

Engaging in violence was an important method of maintaining community cohesion amongst the city's poorest residents, but for elite Montrealers, the threat of popular violence confirmed an emerging vision of the city as a subject of regulation and policing. The newly- established municipal police force and the troops stationed at the garrison in Montreal struggled to bring the violence to a halt.

3.2 A rare depiction of the Lachine Canal before industrialization.
James Duncan, *Lachine Canal, Lachine, Quebec*, 1850.

A reform-oriented faction of the city's elite thus increasingly cast themselves as the guardians of public order, and engaged in civil society in ways that reflected this role. Montreal's commercial elite had been lobbying colonial officials for the expansion of the Lachine Canal for years before the project was greenlit in 1842. The canal had originally been dug at the beginning of the 1820s, but improvements had been undertaken on a nearly continuous basis in the intervening years.[11] The commercial class had argued that increasing the capacity of the Lachine Canal was essential, given that the opening of the Erie Canal in upstate New York had made it possible for the farmers of Upper Canada to bypass Montreal while shipping their goods to European markets. Acknowledging the logic in this argument, investing in public works along the St Lawrence River and into the Great Lakes became the centrepiece of the colony's economic agenda during the governorship of Charles Poulett Thomson, the future Lord Sydenham.[12]

As was the case on the original construction of the Lachine Canal, much of the work had to be done manually by poorly remunerated labourers drawn from the local Canadien community, the Mohawk community at Kahnawá:ke, and recent Irish migrants to the colony. In that sense, the experience of the migrant labourers working in the 1840s represented continuity with the past. However, the impact of the liberal approach to governance had deepened in the two decades since the canal was dug. Public works projects had become undertakings driven by risky economic speculation, fostering a competitive environment where contractors like Henry Mason struggled to keep labour costs to an absolute minimum.[13] The solution, Mason and others of his ilk discovered, was to harness the labour power of the geographically uprooted and transient working-class that was being created by the transition to capitalist practices across the North Atlantic World. The labourers hired by Mason were Irish tenant farmers displaced by landlords determined to increase the profitability of their agricultural holdings by increasing the scale of their operations.[14] Although the crews hired by Mason had developed a particular set of skills on large public works projects along the Eastern Seaboard of North America, this was work that was, by definition, transient. It required a mobility that made establishing links to broader communities a near impossibility for the workers, thereby clearing a path for men like Mason to lock them into exploitative relationships.

The funding for the Lachine Canal project came from both public and private sources, with the bulk of the financing coming in the form of a massive loan from the imperial government in London.[15] This investment was framed as an effort to grow the Canadian economy by improving access to the colonial frontier, a direct result of government policies that were in the midst of settling territory torn from Indigenous peoples. To the men hired by Mason, however, the loan's significance lay in the flexibility it gave the Board of Works to double down on their slate of public works projects during the sharp economic downturn that rocked the North Atlantic World during this period. With opportunities drying up in the United States, Irish migrant labourers poured across the border into Canada, where they had few alternatives beyond the dangerous living conditions and wages far below subsistence levels offered by contractors like Henry Mason.[16] This was not merely a happy coincidence for colonial officials. During the summer of 1842, Hamilton Killaly, the president of the Board of Works overseeing the construction of the Welland Canal to connect Lake Erie to Lake Ontario, wrote an urgent letter to Governor Charles Bagot that, because of the emerging labour surplus in the United States "there is no time when [public works projects] can be so economically carried on as at the present."[17] Before plans for the expansion of the Lachine Canal had even been finalized, taking advantage of the continent's turbulent labour market had become a de facto policy.

How Montrealers were thinking through ideas about race and ethnicity forms a vital part of this discussion. As conversations about the outbreaks along the Lachine Canal were often framed around ideas about the Irish character and its propensity for violence, Mason and his associates were able to easily nudge other officials and the broader public into conceptualizing the striking labourers as a foreign menace lurking on the city's physical and social margins.[18] While there were a handful of occasions when the labourers were applauded for being hard workers, or when certain factions of the local elite reached out to them as worthy recipients of public and private charity, there is no evidence of them being considered as community members or prospective citizens.[19] Instead, their presence in the city was understood as threat that had to be managed, be it through coercive measures like policing or by more subtle tools of social control like the guidance of the Catholic clergy.[20] Montreal was at a critical juncture in its evolution from colonial outpost to industrial city. With their prosperity increasingly dependent on serving as a hub of migration, the city's elites had to begin thinking about who would be included or excluded from the public sphere. Reactions to the popular demonstrations taking place during the Lachine Canal Strike demonstrate the first manifestations of this process.

When trouble first began to stir at Lachine, the *Montreal Gazette* was the first newspaper to dispatch a correspondent to the scene. The reporter, identified only as a "gentleman" in the paper, left at dawn, shortly after the first word of the conflict spread to Montreal, reaching the worksite just as 150 troops of the 71st regiment arrived on the scene. The presence of the military, who arrived upon request of Henry Mason and the Board of Works, appears to have prompted the *Montreal Gazette*'s reporter to frame the strike as an armed insurrection and a looming threat to every reader who valued public order. His report went into vivid detail about the raids carried out on lodging houses near the worksite, noting that great quantities of firearms and other weapons had been seized. The most alarming fact offered to readers was that the troops had not been able to quell the escalating violence. The reporter outlined the number and severity of the armed assaults being carried out by marauding gangs of strikers. Emphasis was placed on suggestions that the migrant labourers were sparing neither women or children, presumably to garner sympathy amongst the *Montreal Gazette*'s British Protestant readers.[21] The reporter denied reports that the conflict was the result of protests over low wages or poor working conditions on the canal, arguing instead that the violence could only be understood in the context of longstanding hostility between the Cork and Connaught crews. He outlined how these conflicts had broken out on similar projects in the United States. Freeing Mason and the Board of Works of any responsibility, the correspondent ended his report by lamenting that "it is truly painful to observe these manifestations of hereditary hatred ... imported among us from the various provinces of Ireland."[22]

3.3 Striking labourers gathered along the Lachine Canal.
Henri Julien, *Montreal – The Lachine Canal Labourers' Strike*, 1878.
Although it depicted a later labour revolt on the canal,
Julien's sketch provides a sense of the tense atmosphere
generated by the threat of collective violence.

In short order, this analysis, in content as well as tone, became the primary lens through which Montreal's reading public viewed the strikers and their plight. An editorial in the short-lived *Montreal Transcript* offered its own regret that "one would suppose that in a strange land, in the depth of winter, with want staring them in the face, all local jealousies between persons from the rival counties would have been laid aside, but unfortunately for the labourers the reverse has been the case."[23] *Les Mélanges religieux*, an organ with an unwavering engagement in the project of building a strong and cohesive Catholic community in Montreal, saw the events in a similar light as its British Protestant counterparts, issuing only a terse statement that the inability of the labourers to overcome their internal divisions was "triste."[24] *Le Canadien* pushed this line of argument one step further by suggesting that one of the reasons that military intervention had been necessary was that the behaviour of the troops could act as a positive influence on the labourers, who would see the benefit of harmonious collective action.[25]

This pervasive focus on the violence being the result of factionalism among the striking workers points to the mounting concern amongst urban elites regarding the threat of popular unrest. While the arrival of growing numbers of transient economic migrants was an increasingly crucial component of a variety of commercial projects that formed the basis of their prosperity, the boisterous culture that accompanied them tested the network of institutions, including the courts and the police, founded to maintain public order.

In the opening days of the conflict, the authorities projected an air of confidence. According to sources speaking to the *Montreal Gazette*'s correspondent, much of the violence unfolding near the canal was being carried out by a small group of "ruffianly miscreants" whose actions were plunging the broader community into a state of terror.[26] Much attention was paid to a rumour that an unidentified "Yankee" had been spotted training a group of workers to use firearms in the woods adjoining one of the shantytowns. The same correspondent reported that the troops had been able to ascertain the identities and the whereabouts of the alleged ringleaders and take them into custody in Montreal to await trial. He quoted one of Mason's associates as saying that with these dangerous ringleaders behind bars, work would recommence in short order.[27] At first glance, then, the forces of law and order had marched triumphantly down the turnpike and contained an outbreak that, like the brawls spilling out of the city's taverns on a regular basis, could be staunched once a small group of troublemakers was taken into custody. Government officials appear to have been particularly focused on this idea. From his office in the colonial capital of Kingston, Killaly wrote to his representative in Montreal, asking him to identify "the ringleaders in causing [the] riots" and "transmit a minute description of them to the office, [so] that the direction of other works may be appraised and such disturbers of the peace prevented from getting employment on any of the works."[28]

Public officials were clearly aware that these labourers had engaged in insurrections on worksites in the United States, and hoped to ensure that the unrest did not continue as new works were undertaken further up the St Lawrence River. They were confident, nonetheless, that the authorities would be capable of maintaining order. The state's representatives were determined not to succumb to the pressure being exerted on them by the workers to improve wages and working conditions. This stance would continue throughout the duration of the Lachine Canal project. This does not suggest, however, that the efforts on the part of the contractors and the state were an unmitigated success.

News of the violence being carried out by the Cork faction spread quickly among officials in Montreal and Lachine. Donald Duff, a justice of the peace in Lachine, fired off a letter to one of his counterparts in Montreal, Alexandre Delisle, in which he suggested that "should a conflict take place between so large a crowd of unmanageable persons there is strong reason to apprehend that the inhabitants of this village and vicinity will be greatly exposed both to the loss of life and property, being quite defenceless and unable to protect themselves against so many rioters, some of whom have been walking the street this morning with their arms without the least apparent fear of being reprimanded for their threats."[29] Duff urged Delisle to support the calls emanating from Lachine for a sustained police presence along the canal.[30]

Looming over this judicial process were Henry Mason and other investors, contractors, and public officials with a vested interest in ending the strike. The terms that Mason had agreed to with the Board of Works included a series of penalties to ensure that the canal's expansion would be completed before the shipping season began in the spring. By having a steady stream of witnesses appear before the magistrates providing vivid testimonies of the violent and intimidating tactics being used by the striking labourers, those with an interest in ending the strike quickly and without ceding any significant concessions hoped to pressure the authorities to step up policing at the worksite. It was hoped that a strong, around-the-clock police and military presence would prevent the strikers from continuing to impose their own brand of extra-judicial authority in the area.

After seven arrests were made, witnesses were brought before the magistrates in Montreal to record what they had seen and heard. Although these are problematic documents, given that they were produced in an official setting constructed around a deeply hierarchical power structure, these depositions do provide us with a glimpse into how a diverse group of Montrealers were articulating their experience of the strike. While the voices of Henry Mason, his associates, and other civic officials are overrepresented in the public record, depositions were also recorded by striking labourers and longtime residents of Lachine. In terms of the clashing factions employed on the canal, these records do not tell us the whole story: Only one of the factions made use of the judicial apparatus. The labourers from Connaught, who were on the defensive throughout the strike, took advantage of the judicial process to describe the assaults they had suffered from the more heavily armed Cork faction. It is not clear what motivated these men to lend their assistance to the legal process being carried out against their rivals. Perhaps they hoped that successful convictions would provide them the upper hand in their longstanding conflict. We could also speculate that they traded their testimonies for immunity with regard to their own legal transgressions. Whatever the case, these records provide us with vivid – though distinctly one-sided – accounts of the events.

Reading the depositions they collected makes the concerns of the magistrates explicit. First, they were seeking information on the alleged ringleaders of the violence. Secondly, their line of questioning focused squarely on how the labourers were using violence and spectacle to intimidate both rival factions of the workforce and their employers. While it is important to think through how documents of this nature were constructed around elite biases and agendas, they leave us with some of the most visceral descriptions of what it was like to be on the receiving end of popular customs like the charivari, or what it was like to witness an intimidating nocturnal procession snake its way past a lodging house where labourers resided with their families.

The depositions reinforce the claim repeated in the Montreal press throughout the strike that the area in the vicinity of the construction site became a community under siege shortly after work had begun. The deposition of Edward McGreevy, a labourer connected to the Connaught faction, described in vivid detail one of the parades organized by members of the Cork faction. McGreevy testified that he was able to stand close enough to the parade to serve as a reliable witness and insisted that, from his vantage point, what he witnessed was not a spontaneous brawl but a carefully orchestrated procession designed to display the might of the Cork faction. He described how the workers marched in military formation, with each column three men deep. It appeared to McGreevy that one of the men subsequently taken into custody by the police, Michael Corcoran, was the ringleader, and that he was armed with a scythe that he waved about menacingly. Other marchers were armed, and some waved flags or wore badges that identified them as members of the Cork faction. The parade followed a strategic route that carried it past the shanties and taverns known to be occupied by labourers affiliated with the Connaught faction. At regular intervals, Corcoran and a few other men shouted warnings to their foes that any Connaughtmen who remained in the vicinity of the canal after nine o'clock the next morning would do so at the risk of their life – "there were no two ways about it."[31]

This procession appears to have begun with its destination already determined. The Blue Bonnet tavern was situated near the village of Lachine, at the head of the canal. An extended family of Connaughtmen were boarding in the rooms upstairs. Jeremiah Higgins was part of this group, and described his experience as a target of the charivari that concluded the Corkonian procession. It was just after three o'clock when Thomas Gleason and a tall red-headed man, both prominent figures in the Corkonian faction, walked into the tavern and warned "us to withdraw from this part of the Country, and to cease to labour at the Canal in default of which they would not only have the life of the deponent but of every Connaughtman that remained."[32] As Gleason and the other man delivered this threat, upwards of two hundred of their fellow labourers armed with muskets, pistols, and a variety of other homemade and rudimentary weapons surrounded the tavern. The presence of this crowd lent additional credibility to the threats uttered by Gleason.[33]

This procession was not an isolated occurrence. Actions like this continued regularly throughout the strike. Depositions before the Court of the Queen's Bench frequently observed that the discipline of the Corkonian marchers made these events particularly intimidating to their rivals. These testimonies also provide us with a glimpse into the rich material culture of protest manifested along the Lachine Canal. Besides describing the banners and badges worn by members of the Cork faction, witnesses also emphasize the vital role that music played in these events. The beginning of nocturnal processions was often marked by the sudden clamour of horns and bagpipes.[34] The practice of the charivari, where a crowd would gather around the residence or meeting place of their rivals in order to threaten them with eviction from the community, was inherently musical – pots and pans were banged in a frenzied rhythm, and impromptu songs and chants were hurtled at the targets.[35] It was evident that the Cork faction was not employing these practices for the first time. These were customs rooted in several generations of protest against changing landholding practices in Ireland, sharpened by over a decade of conflict in the United States.[36] While the settings might have varied – from the pastoral landscape of Ireland to North America's urban fringe, the objectives of these actions remained consistent. They were efforts to bind a community together at a transformative moment and make public a particular definition of economic and social justice.

The outnumbered members of the Connaught faction were not the only ones who felt intimidated by the Corkonian actions. Residents of the small parish of Lachine, at the opposite end of the canal from Montreal, were among the first witnesses to record depositions with Montreal magistrates. The prosperity of this small village depended on the shipping trade up and down the St Lawrence River. Merchants in Lachine made heavy use of the turnpike that connected it to Montreal, a road that had become the primary theatre of conflict for clashes between the Cork and Connaught factions. At the outset of the canal expansion project, innkeeper Étienne Courville had been optimistic that the venture would prove profitable for him, as he would be able to rent rooms at his inn to the labourers. In his deposition, he recounts being surprised that every single man renting a room from him was armed, and that they participated in the nightly parades so disruptive to area residents. His community was now under siege, and he noted that his wife was "maintenant très malade de peur."[37] Courville would soon send his wife and children to camp in the woods a fair distance from the village as a precaution. They had reason to be anxious. With the pressure mounting to capture the ringleaders of the violence, representatives of the Cork faction had visited a number of residents, warning them that they would be placing themselves in grave danger should they decide to share information with the authorities.[38]

The meaning and the implications of the unrest on the canal remained fluid and contested throughout the conflict. What prompted the persistent focus on the discipline and cohesion of the labourers from Cork during the strike? After all, the tendency amongst urban elites in the North Atlantic World during this period was to tar the popular classes, especially those who were racially and ethnically marginalized, as being incapable of discipline. Nonetheless, the fact that the violence unleashed by the labourers was conducted with a degree of forethought was consistently emphasized by those who wanted to use the judicial process to instigate a strong and sustained police and military intervention. They hoped that both the authorities and the public would reach the conclusion that this was more than just another example of drunken violence, a phenomenon that Montrealers encountered on a daily basis in the city. These depositions, both in their content and the way in which they were constructed, illustrate how labour relations were being negotiated during this period. Capitalist investors and the state were collaborating against an emerging working class whose ranks were drawn from marginalized communities, and who employed longstanding customs of agrarian protest to resist their vulnerability in the new market economy of the North Atlantic World.[39]

The contractors associated with the project and a number of their associates also recorded depositions. Their explicit aim was to emphasize the threat posed by the migrant labourers, so they made frequent allusions to the violent tendencies found in the Irish character. They provide a glimpse into the way that elites could tap into fears about unruly crowds in order to lobby for the outcome they desired – in this case, police and military intervention into the strike. These men portrayed themselves as disinterested parties who had found themselves threatened with violence rather than as individuals with a stake in the rapid resolution of the conflict. How they constructed their testimonies demonstrates that access to political authority was growing increasingly contingent on assertions of physical and emotional restraint. These representatives of Montreal's British Protestant commercial class glossed over their role in creating conditions at the worksite that pushed the labourers towards confrontation, insisting that they were simply honest brokers who unexpectedly found themselves caught in the middle of longstanding feuds. Despite their best efforts to coax the workers into ending the conflict, events had spun out of their control and they had little alternative but to ask for a greater police and military presence along the canal.[40] The narrative put forward by the representatives of the Board of Works and the contractors was accepted at face value in the Montreal press. It fit comfortably into their biases about mass migration and the Irish character.[41]

The most detailed of these depositions was recorded by Joseph Frobisher McDonald, an employee of the Board of Works who was serving as an assistant engineer on the project. His testimony focused on a confrontation he experienced with a crowd of about 300 Corkonians that had assembled on the Côteau du Pierre, a ridge that overlooked the worksite. McDonald had made his way to the spot with the intention of persuading the Cork faction to lay down their arms. He did so, McDonald testified, despite the Connaught faction warning him of the risk he was taking by confronting the Corkonians without any means of defending himself.[42] Not only did McDonald live to tell his story, he claimed to have succeeded in negotiating a temporary truce between the two parties. The engineer embraced his role as negotiator, describing how during subsequent days he broke up a number of fights in order to preserve the terms of the truce.[43] Of course, because of the silence from the Cork faction in the historical record, it is impossible to corroborate his story. What is clear, however, is McDonald's intent in explicitly portraying himself as the embodiment of rational authority. While the migrant labourers were engaged in violent acts of extra-legal justice, McDonald's measured negotiating tactics succeeded in establishing order, albeit briefly. This type of narrative shows how elites asserted authority in the midst of popular unrest. By making this claim in a public forum, McDonald was playing an important role in maintaining not only his own legitimacy but that of the Board of Works and the contractors associated with it. Interestingly, despite McDonald's assurances that he himself had succeeded in restoring order on the canal, his deposition included a plea for military intervention in order to bring the strike to a decisive conclusion.[44]

Henry Mason's deposition struck a similar note. The contractor, who had the most to gain from the strike's swift conclusion, downplayed the dispute over wages and working conditions that lay at the root of the conflict. Instead, Mason too portrayed himself as a dispassionate observer and kept the focus on the threat that the violence posed to the residents of Lachine. He even suggested that it was not only the residents of Lachine who were living in a state of siege – a number of emissaries from both factions of the migrant community had approached him and, in strictest confidence, informed him that they spoke for a silent majority of labourers who would be willing to work towards a compromise but were terrified of becoming the target of violent reprisals.[45] This claim added further legitimacy to the insistence of elite men like McDonald, Duff, and Mason that only a strong police and military presence would be able to bring about a lasting resolution to the conflict.

Meanwhile, efforts made by public officials to assert their authority were met with continued resistance, thus undermining their theory that tempers would cool once a handful of provocative individuals were arrested. Efforts to successfully prosecute those thought to be responsible repeatedly failed, with magistrates throwing out cases due to a lack of reliable evidence.[46] The threat of popular violence, it seems, made members of the Irish migrant community as well as neighbouring residents unwilling to testify in court. Furthermore, migrants facing allegations of criminal activity were able to slip away from the shantytowns surrounding the worksite and take up residence in Montreal, where neither the authorities nor the broader community would be likely to identify them. As growing numbers of migrants who had arrived in search of work on the canal took up residence in the city, keeping tabs on the alleged ringleaders of the strike became increasingly challenging for the authorities. Rather than being an opportunity to demonstrate the state's capacity for imposing order, the situation quickly grew into the very opposite – a well-publicized demonstration of the limits to their power.

The relationship between migrant labourers and the broader community in Montreal was a complicated one. Although Montreal had long been a hub for regional and transatlantic migration, both the authorities and elite commentators portrayed the economic migrants working on the Lachine Canal as an unprecedented foreign menace. Their use of popular rituals of resistance – the charivaris, the torchlight parades, and other acts of collective violence – played a significant part supporting this narrative. Nonetheless, while the migrant labourers might have been pushed to the social and geographic margins of the city upon their arrival, their circumstances changed quickly. They were, after all, in a city with an Irish expatriate community that had been growing steadily since the beginning of the nineteenth century. It appears that many of the labourers were quickly able to establish contact with friends and kin from their native country upon their arrival in Montreal. Many made the roughly fourteen-kilometre trek from the shantytowns on the Lachine Canal to the city on a frequent basis. The city provided a number of resources, including work in manual labour and domestic service, access to the philanthropic activities of the elite, and social camaraderie.[47] When conflicts erupted on the Lachine Canal, the city became a place of refuge for those fleeing in both material desperation and fear. The two spaces quickly became integrated as the migrants inserted themselves into the city's networks of kin and community.

A number of the depositions recorded by the Connaught faction were made by men who had worked alongside them but had fled the canal worksite and found employment elsewhere. Thomas Fallen, a forty-eight-year-old labourer who had emigrated to Montreal in 1840, testified in front of magistrate Henry Corse that he had heard about the escalating violence on the canal from Bryan Owens, a Connaughtman who he had helped find work breaking rocks on the Molson family's estate. Owens told Fallen that several labourers from the Connaught faction, himself included, had decided to heed the warnings of the Cork faction and flee the vicinity. Most had decided to seek refuge in Montreal, where they blended into the larger Irish community and sought other employment opportunities.[48]

Members of the Cork faction had also sought their kin in and around Montreal. Fallen's deposition stated that emissaries from the Cork faction had visited each of the quarries in the Montreal area, where many of the earlier migrants from that part of Ireland were working, for this purpose.[49] The proximity of the worksite on the Canal to Montreal would come to play a decisive role in the conflict. Not only did the city provide refuge and access to supplies and extended kinship networks, but it also provided anonymity for those looking to escape the rigid divide and interpersonal violence along the canal. Many of the migrant labourers, especially from the outnumbered Connaught faction, went to the city to slip into the broader Irish community and away from a life shaped by material deprivation and conflict.

Even for the other residents of Montreal, the conflict along the canal was not something that could be ignored. This was true not only of the commercial elite, who had much riding on the rapid expansion of the canal. As the strike wore on, violence spilled onto the urban streets. In the city's burgeoning western suburbs, there were regular sightings of heavily armed migrant labourers. These encounters were frequently noted on the turnpike that connected Lachine to Montreal. Michael Murray, a labourer who resided at Lachine, was walking along the road when he rounded a curve and came across a group of approximately fifteen men, whom he knew to be part of the Cork faction, conducting military-style drills in a field. Patrick Quinlan, who Murray identified as one of the ringleaders of the Cork faction, pointed his pistol directly at Murray and threatened his life if "he did not instantly depart."[50] Striking Connaughtmen repeatedly remarked on the dangers that they faced traveling along the turnpike once the conflict began, testifying that they were routinely threatened and accosted by small groups of their foes as they traveled between Montreal and Lachine.[51] What Murray witnessed does not appear to have been an isolated incident: A number of other deponents reported seeing members of the Cork faction taking target practice in the field lining the turnpike.[52] The press used eyewitness accounts like these to build their case that the migrant labourers posed an alarming threat to public order, thereby underplaying the dispute over wages and working conditions that the conflict was rooted in.[53]

While the strike lasted for several weeks, it did not remain at the forefront of public debate, if the local press is a reliable indicator. While there were periodic reports on deteriorating conditions in the shantytowns that lined the canal, they were buried deep in the back pages of the city's French and English newspapers, which were consumed by the partisan divide in parliament, Governor Charles Bagot's declining health, and politically charged debates over the status of the Patriotes exiled in the United States.[54] As violence began to erupt again in the spring, attention returned to the conflict on the canal. As the Cork faction recommenced their nightly parades, the remaining members of the Connaught faction, presumably exhausted by months of violence and material deprivation, fled the area. Reports from Montreal's western suburbs described hundreds of families camped out along the turnpike road. One commentator tellingly referred to these displaced members of the Connaught faction as "refugees," a designation that speaks to the profound dislocation that the labour practices emerging during this period could have on the lives of migrant labourers.[55] Montrealers were warned that they were risking their lives by traveling between the city and Lachine, as there were reports that gangs of "marauding villains" had turned to armed robbery as a means of supporting themselves. Despite the winding down of the conflict on the canal, the migrant community continued to present a daunting challenge to the authorities.[56]

Events took a significant turn in March when the conflict between the two factions spilled onto the streets of Montreal. A violent brawl occurred outside Ste Anne's Market in the west end when, for reasons that were not explained by the press, a group of Corkonians were searching for some Connaughtmen who had taken up residence in that working-class neighbourhood. 200 men poured into the area to take sides in the mêlée. While some of these "rascals" were armed with pistols, many more waged battle with the kinds of rudimentary weapons and tools that had been paraded through the shantytowns only weeks earlier. The police dispersed the crowd that had gathered around the market and arrested two men singled out as ringleaders by witnesses. Two other men identified only by their last names – Hoosick and Ryan – were taken to the General Hospital, where one later succumbed to injuries suffered during the riot.

These sorts of outbreaks were common on the streets of mid-nineteenth-century Montreal, where alcohol-fuelled camaraderie regularly descended into violence, especially during parliamentary and municipal elections. What is noteworthy about this particular riot, however, was that few locals appear to have ventured into the fray. The press reported the incident as another manifestation of the violence that had been occurring at the canal.[57] Whether or not this was accurate is, of course, impossible to gauge. What it does illustrate, however, is that although many of those labourers who had originally migrated to the outskirts of Montreal had now taken up residence amongst their fellow Irish migrants in the city, they were still being pushed to the margins. Their engagement in popular violence linked to the conflict on the canal continued to be used as justification for their exclusion from the broader community.

Aware that their campaign for higher wages and better working conditions would benefit from the moral and financial support of the Irish community already established in the city, in early March labourers who remained in the vicinity of the canal organized an orderly procession into the heart of Montreal's commercial district. It was composed of male representatives of the community marching in neat columns. A small band of fife players led the way, serenading the marchers and curious onlookers with national airs. Despite the fact that their nocturnal parades through the shantytowns had been perceived as a grave threat to public order, this procession was an attempt to win support for the canal workers. In a different spatial and temporal context – during daylight hours, on the streets of Montreal – the rituals once employed to intimidate their rivals provided a way for the canal workers to present themselves as disciplined and virtuous men deserving of the community's sympathy and support.

The procession followed the canal before entering the city on Notre Dame Street. It concluded in front of the imposing head offices of the Bank of Montreal, the most prominent symbol of Anglo-Protestant wealth in the city.[58]

The head offices of the Bank of Montreal held more than just symbolic value for the canal workers. It housed the office of Benjamin Holmes who, in addition to being the bank's head cashier, had recently been elected president of the St Patrick's Benevolent Society. The members of this voluntary society included some of the most prominent figures in the city's emerging Irish elite. Composed of both Protestants and Catholics, these were men who, like Holmes, had established themselves in commerce and professional life after migrating to Montreal in the first three decades of the nineteenth century.[59] The canal workers, who had been smeared as foreign agitators by both the English and French factions of the Montreal elite, were evidently looking to improve their connections to the city's establishment by playing upon the nationalist sentiment of their fellow Irish migrants. Seeing as how their demands for higher wages and better working conditions had largely been ignored by public officials and the local press, this humble pageantry was the most effective means available for forging a relationship with Montreal's Irish elite.

The procession was successful in more ways than one. First, it temporarily transformed the image of the canal workers in the public eye. After months of being portrayed by the authorities and in the press as menacing outsiders capable of wreaking havoc on the city, coverage of the procession portrayed them as respectable men and family patriarchs. An editorial in Les Mélanges Religieux was particularly verbose in its praise for the canal workers' procession. The event revealed that the conditions imposed by the contractors had driven these respectable men to "satanic" excess. Now that the authorities had succeeded in imposing order on the banks of the Lachine Canal, this voice of the Catholic clergy urged them to invite these aggrieved labourers to take refuge in the city.[60] The rhetoric in La Minerve, disdainful of the strikers from the moment they had thrown down their tools in January, failed to reach such lofty heights, but did describe the procession in language that was considerably more neutral than that the canal workers normally elicited on their pages.[61] Only the

English-language newspapers – the organs of the British Protestant commercial elite – continued their aggressive stance against the canal workers. the *Montreal Gazette* downplayed the magnitude of the event, informing readers that the French-language newspapers were misinformed in stating that 500 canal workers had marched on the city and suggesting that 300 was more realistic.[62] The *Montreal Transcript* chimed in with an even lower estimate, suggesting that only 231 men took part in the procession.[63] Furthermore, neither the *Montreal Gazette* nor the *Montreal Transcript* voiced the same sort of approval as was seen in the French press. It is unclear why these Tory newspapers downplayed the scale or the impact of the procession into Montreal. It seems fair to speculate, however, that their dismissive tone speaks to the power that these sorts of crowd events held for groups like the canal workers contesting their marginalization. For newspapers that profited from their close connections to the colonial authorities and the contractors working on the expansion of the canal, no conciliatory gesture towards people who had proven themselves capable of challenging the emerging business model of men like Henry Mason was likely.

What is particularly striking about the canal workers' procession into Montreal is that their voices were almost entirely absent from these discussions. This makes considering what might have motivated them a daunting task for historians. We have no choice but to employ evidence like newspaper reports to piece together what might have been the mood amongst the migrant workforce, and what might have prompted them to adopt the strategies that they did. These reports, however, were constructed around a set of biases that actively pushed the canal workers to the margins of the city's public life.[64] A rare exception is a statement published by the canal workers that was printed in the *Montreal Gazette*. Although it is not the most coherent of documents, this statement demonstrates political acumen on the part of the canal workers. In it, they lashed out at "contractors [who want] to live by the sweat of our brow," and later called out Henry Mason by name.[65] It affirms the spirit of ethnic solidarity that united the canal workers, thrown into doubt following weeks of intra-ethnic conflict between the Cork and Connaught factions. The statement ends with a passionate declaration of loyalty to the Queen, thus framing their demands for higher wages and better working conditions as being in keeping with the traditions of British justice.[66] This clumsy yet forceful declaration suggests that the canal workers put a great deal of thought into how to foster sympathy for their plight. However, it did little to sway the firm anti-strike position of the the *Montreal Gazette*, who likely printed the notice as a matter of public curiosity rather than as an endorsement of the canal workers' stance.

In contrast to the *Montreal Gazette's* readership, the city's Irish elite were inspired to join forces with the Catholic clergy in order to push the labourers towards a resolution. They too employed a crowd event to communicate their message, holding a large open-air mass that drew thousands to the shantytowns. There was little optimism in the press that such efforts could broker an end to the unrest. An editorial in the the *Montreal Transcript* only went so far as to express hope that seeing their respectable brethren on the banks of the canal might influence some of the labourers to denounce their previous actions. In the words of the editorial, because of the failure of the police and military to bring about a lasting return to order, such displays might be the only way to bring "the rioters to a sense of their duty."[67] When the delegation of Irish elites reached Lachine, they were able to arrange a meeting with representatives from both the Cork and Connaught factions. Although much credit was given to Benjamin Holmes for coordinating the event, it was Father Phelan, Montreal's most prominent Irish Catholic cleric, who was hailed for successfully pushing the labourers towards a truce. The charismatic priest delivered a mass and homily that reportedly brought many in the assembled crowd of over 2,000 to tears.[68] At the conclusion of the ceremony, members of the delegation fanned out into the shantytowns lining the canal and into the Parish of Lachine to collect donations to assist the families of men who had either died or sustained serious injuries since the outbreak of hostilities. While making their rounds, they were also able to engage in ad-hoc negotiations with the labourers to lay down their weapons and respect the truce. That the rituals of the Catholic mass and the entreaties of an emerging Irish elite were able to bring the violence to a halt – a feat that the military and the police had not been able to perform – served as a powerful indicator of the increasing social and cultural power of these two factions of the city's elite.[69] The juxtaposition between the restrained masculine authority being asserted by the commercial elites surrounding Henry Mason and the church's assertion of cultural authority, wrapped up as it was in demonstrations of vulnerability and emotion, demonstrates the nuanced and sometimes contradictory ways that Montrealers were thinking through authority and public order during this period.

Of course, it is important to evaluate reports like this with a grain of salt. It was in the interest of newspapers like *Les Mélanges religieux*, which reflected the views of the clergy, to exaggerate the impact of Phelan's encounter with the striking labourers. Suggesting that the church's first substantive effort to reach out to this marginalized group was such a resounding success seems to be a scenario fabricated to lend legitimacy to the church's push for a more authoritative role in the city's post-rebellion public life. But while such claims should be evaluated with a critical eye, dismissing them altogether risks obscuring an important element of the narrative: that events during the winter and spring of 1843 had considerable impact on those migrant communities most impacted by violence and social unrest. While the authority of the church might not have been accepted as simplistically as reports such as this suggest, efforts to reach out to labourers staring down material deprivation, violence, dislocation, marginalization, and loss would likely have been met with some emotion. We must keep such likelihoods in mind, even these narratives betray obvious political and sectarian biases.

Descriptions of the St Patrick's Benevolent Society's visit to the shantytowns reveal that this was a complicated moment of identity formation for both the canal workers and for Benjamin Holmes and other members of the Irish elite. Realizing that their demands for higher wages and better working conditions would continue to be dismissed so long as they were portrayed as a threat to public order, the workers campaigned for support in Montreal, especially from the city's established Irish community. The initial hesitancy of that population to come to the aid of their fellow Irish men and women suggests that they were concerned about the risk of becoming associated with a suspect and marginal group. Being linked in any way to the violence on the canal might undo their efforts to gain a foothold in Montreal's elite circles. As the de-facto spokesman for the city's

Irish elite, Holmes had to choose his words and weigh his actions carefully. In a letter to the editor of the *Montreal Gazette*, Holmes maintained that the St Patrick's Benevolent Society was compelled to come to the assistance of their fellow Irish migrants, but that they had no intention of interfering in the ongoing negotiations between the workers and their employers. In the wake of their successful visit to Lachine and the subsequent end to the hostilities there, he wrote that "the establishment of order on the works was [our] sole object … and this has been secured."[70] In other words, Holmes and those he represented wanted to highlight their philanthropic bona fides without causing friction with non-Irish members of the economic establishment with whom they rubbed shoulders. That they were able to achieve this delicate balance was an important achievement. These same Irish elites had devoted considerable energy to organizing the annual St Patrick's Day parade, which was clearly meant to portray men like Holmes as respectable citizens while drawing attention to the growing prosperity of the Irish community. These undertakings occurred in the context of the community's crowning achievement: the construction of St Patrick's Church, the imposing edifice that wrote this emerging prosperity into the city's built environment.[71]

What motivated the canal workers to engage in negotiations with the city's Irish elites? After all, given the level of material deprivation that had shaped their experience on the canal, the exhortations of any group that refused to unconditionally condemn the practices of their employers must have struck a discordant note. Although their voices are absent in these records, we know from the rare glimpses of their words and sentiments we do have access to that their spokespeople did not hesitate to threaten their foes. Their willingness to bend to the entreaties of the delegation from the St Patrick's Benevolent Society must therefore be read as strategic. Perhaps they realized that their long-term ambitions would be best served by nurturing a relationship with that group. On the other hand, the conciliatory gestures made by the canal workers during the spring of 1843 can also be read as expressing a genuine desire to bring the violence to an end. It had taken a significant toll on the migrant community. Months of violence and intimidation had scattered friends and family, and had not improved the ability of men and women to support their families. By the time Holmes and his delegation arrived, many of the labourers likely felt that they had no alternative beyond migration or picking up their tools and returning to work. On the other hand, the violence that had occurred during the winter had been success-ful in driving much of the Connaught faction off the project, so the remaining labourers had reconfigured the labour market to their benefit. This made their decision to return to work less a product of diplomacy and more the culmination of a successful month of intimidating ritual and collective violence.

As the frequency and intensity of violence receded during the spring of 1843, this slight yet noticeable shift towards greater public sympathy for the canal workers became more visible on the pages the city's English and French language newspapers. Unlike the coverage of the strike's early days, when the complaints of the labourers were dismissed and the conflict was blamed on a violent streak that ran through the Irish character, the press began to hold the actions of the contractors up to greater scrutiny.[72] While they continued to attack the labourers any time they were implicated in a breach of public order, there was an emerging consensus that the more egre-gious practices of the contractors made them partially responsible for the continuing unrest. The practice of paying the canal workers with credit at the store operated by the contractors, rather than in cash, served as a lightning rod for this criticism. Despite repeated assurances that the prices being charged at the store for staples like bread did not vary unreasonably from the prices being charged for similar items in Montreal, the practice struck many observers in Montreal as being fundamentally unfair.[73] This position, expressed in both the English and French language press, suggests that there was an emerging consensus that workers ought to be treated in accordance with basic standards of community justice.[74] The only defence offered for the most exploitative practices of the contractors was that these were the conditions that the canal workers had agreed to upon their arrival in Montreal, and that any subsequent protests were therefore illegitimate.

The strike on the Lachine Canal did not reach a tidy conclusion. Although no formal agreement between Mason and his labourers appears to have been reached, work recommenced on the canal by the end of March and would continue, with sporadic interruptions, for much of the next year. This does not mean, however, that those employed on large public works projects up and down the St Lawrence acquiesced to the model of labour relations that emerged out of the liberal politics of the 1840s. Serious rioting occurred during the summer of 1843 just up the river from Montreal at the village of Beauharnois, where another canal was being expanded to allow larger ships access further into the continent. Similar complaints about wages and working conditions were lodged this time, yet in the Montreal press, the conflict was once again blamed on the violent character of Irish labourers.[75] In this case, a confrontation between striking labourers and the military turned deadly – the troops fired on a crowd and killed six. Although we do not have written confirmation, it seems likely given the time period and the tactics used by the labourers that many of the men at Beauharnois had worked on the Lachine Canal during the previous months. Similar events also occurred later in the decade, as the colonial government undertook large scale public works projects along the St Lawrence River, into Canada West and the Great Lakes region.[76]

Meanwhile, in Montreal, the authorities would spend the remainder of 1843 grappling with what had occurred along the Lachine Canal. In April, a series of reports were tabled that analyzed what had prevented order from being restored at the worksite. Amongst those who contributed to these inquiries were members of the city's commercial elite like John Molson and Charles Tait, prominent politicians like Mayor Joseph Bourret, Pierre Beaubien, and Bartholomew Gugy, and public officials like Charles Atherton, Superintendent of Engineers for the Board of Works.[77] These reports linger over a handful of issues that were considered particularly problematic. First, they highlight the danger of allowing crowds to assemble without any oversight on the part of the authorities, as they did during the strike.[78] It appears that the unrest linked to the canal reinforced official concerns about popular assemblies and insurrection that were raised during the rebellions and subsequently enshrined in the ordinances of the Special Council. These reports proposed different solutions for dealing with any future events. A consensus quickly emerged that large groups of migrant labourers would need to be more carefully managed and contained by the combined efforts of their employers and the state. From the wavering magistrates in Lachine and Montreal who had pulled the 71st Regiment from the area in the midst of the rioting to the inability of the police to provide the courts with sufficient evidence to obtain convictions of the men who were arrested, the strike had proven to be "a burlesque on the inefficiency of the authorities."[79] Historians of nineteenth-century Canada have long pointed to this as the moment when the state began expanding their sphere of activity.[80] The interaction between the migrant labourers employed on the Lachine Canal, the contractors, and the state is a reminder of the limits of authority during this period.

Despite putting forward slightly different interpretations of the strike as the events unfolded, the state and the city's English- and French-language newspapers spoke with a unified voice in its aftermath. They identified mass migration, popular violence, and unruly crowds as barriers to the city's future prosperity. Measures were undertaken quickly, as work had to continue immediately on the canal. The Board of Works and parliament immediately enacted measures to tighten security around public works projects. Among other things, the Act for the Preservation of Public Peace banned the possession of firearms within the proximity of worksites like the Lachine Canal.[81] This measure received across-the-board support in Montreal's elite circles, with prominent Irish Catholic reformer Lewis Drummond being one of its most vigorous supporters. In order to hasten completion of the canal project, the Board of Works successfully pushed to have a permanent force of between thirty and fifty troops stationed within sight of the labourers at all times.[82] When work recommenced on the canal at the end of March, the labourers encountered a very different environment. The contractors with whom they had clashed over wages and working conditions could now draw upon the visible (and armed) support of the state. This no doubt made a significant impact on both the mood of the labourers and their resolve to fight perceived injustices. The relationship between labour, capital, and the colonial state was being hastily re-imagined and re-negotiated in the aftermath of the disturbances at Lachine.

Attempting to trace what happened to the men who participated in the Lachine Canal Strike of 1843 and their families is impossible.

After all, we only have the names of a few men identified as suspected ringleaders or who testified in front of magistrates. It seems likely that some of these migrant families were integrated into the emerging Irish working-class community in Montreal. Others continued their longstanding practice of migrating to the next project, and canals would continue being dug and expanded up the St Lawrence River and into the Great Lakes for the better part of the next decade. That the kinds of popular protests that gripped the western periphery of Montreal during the winter and spring of 1843 occurred at later periods on subsequent public works projects indicates that these customs of resistance and community formation remained an integral part of the process. This was where liberal modernity's reliance on mobility clashed with the customary notions of a moral economy and practices of resistance.

Despite taking steps to nurture an alliance with the established Irish community in Montreal, those who did choose to remain in the city continued to struggle with social and cultural marginalization from the broader community. When Board of Works President Hamilton Killaly suggested that the poorest of canal workers be hired by the city in an effort to provide them with a means of subsistence, Mayor Pierre Beaubien responded that the city was under no obligation to provide employment to migrant labourers when a significant number of Montreal residents required public assistance.[83] The widening gap between the migrants occupying the lowest rungs of the employment ladder and the broader community during this period would continue to make integration problematic.

Meanwhile, the unrest on the banks of the Lachine Canal that began with the strike would become something of a permanent fixture. It was a space where itinerant migrants could settle just beyond the comfortable grasp of the authorities, but in close enough proximity to benefit from the social, cultural, and economic opportunities found in Montreal. During the typhus epidemic of 1847, sheds were erected hastily along the canal to house destitute Irish migrants suspected of being ill.[84] Throughout the decade, there were frequent calls to ramp up the police presence in the area, though budgetary restraints held these in check more often than not.[85] The urban space stretching from the city's expanding harbourfront and westwards along the canal was where the dynamic and destructive impact of global capitalism was felt most viscerally.[86] In the decades that followed the expansion of the canal, its banks, where the shantytowns occupied by migrant labourers and their families had once stood, became the industrial heartland of British North America and, subsequently, Canada. Capitalists built factories in order to benefit from the area's transportation infrastructure and, later, access to energy resources. Just as its earliest backers had insisted, a great deal of wealth was produced as a result of the canal being dug and expanded. This wealth, however, was produced on the backs of labourers who were paid low wages and who faced notoriously dangerous working conditions. It became a magnet for men and, later, women, with few other economic options available to them. The events of the 1840s created a precedent for exploiting the labour of a continuous stream of migrants flocking to the city.

Historians have emphasized the impact that the processes of modernity had on cities like Montreal in the middle decades of the nineteenth century. Industrialization, capitalism, and liberalism transformed the urban landscape, reworked the way that people interacted with each other, and increased the circulation of people, capital, and commodities on both a global and local level. What events like the strike on the Lachine Canal remind us, however, is that customary practices of resistance were an integral part of this process. They provided people with the tools that they needed to negotiate for higher wages and better working conditions. While these efforts were not always successful, they demonstrate that the liberal project being carried out by Montreal's commercial elite did not go uncontested. This was why the city became a laboratory for liberal governance. Infrastructure projects like the work being undertaken to improve access up the St Lawrence River begat broader projects, because of which economic elites and public authorities were forced to grapple with the management of migration, policing, and community cohesion. In order to understand how practices of authority were changing on the ground in mid-nineteenth-century Montreal and, on a broader level, the project of liberal urban governance at various sites across the North Atlantic World during this period, we need to reflect on the way that these measures were resisted by people who stood little prospect of reaping its rewards.

A variety of crowd events played a pivotal role in framing the public's understanding of the unrest along the banks of the Lachine Canal. The Irish migrants employed by Henry Mason drew on longstanding practices of popular resistance to protest their condition. This confrontation occurred in the context of a broader conflict over popular assembly and political legitimacy that loomed over public life in Montreal during this tumultuous decade. The next chapter explores how seemingly very different sorts of crowd events, from the rough popular pageantry that was integral to the election process to the increasingly elegant and choreographed processions of the city's national societies, helped shape the contours of public life during this period.

4

"A VOLUNTARY POWER": MAKING LIBERAL POLITICS ON THE STREETS OF MONTREAL

In May 1844, a brief and curious essay was published on the editorial page of the *Montreal Gazette*. No author was credited, but the piece appears to be the work of a Montrealer writing for the Tory newspaper, as it was not said to be excerpted from another paper as other pieces frequently were. Appearing under the heading "The Look of a Gentleman," the editorial read:

> What it is that constitutes the look of a gentlemen is more easily felt than described. We all know it when we see it, but do not know how to account for it, or to explain in what is consists. Ease, grace and dignity have been given as the exponents and expressive symbols of this look; but, I would rather say that an habitual self-possession determines the appearance of a gentleman. He should have the complete command, not only over his countenance, but over his limbs and motions. In other words, he should discover in his air and manner a voluntary power of his whole body, which, with every inflection of it, should be under the control of his will. It must be evident that he does as he likes, without any restraint, confusion or awkwardness. He is, in

fact, master of his person, as the professor of any art or science is of a particular instrument or theorem."[1]

Taken out of context, this short essay might strike readers as little
more than a stuffy Victorian rumination. But the men and women
who stumbled upon this over breakfast or at one of the city's local
reading rooms were not living in a neutral environment. Montreal
had recently been the site of another in a long line of bloody election
riots. Elite men of every political stripe complained angrily that thugs
hired by their political foes had threatened them with bodily harm
when they set out to vote in a parliamentary by-election. This editorial nudged readers of the *Montreal Gazette* to reflect once more on
the ability of elites to remain above the sort of violence that gripped
public life in Montreal and other cities during this period. Reason,
restraint, and composure were understood to be necessary attributes
for those who wished to achieve legitimate political authority.[2] It was
believed that these attributes of character could be communicated
through the way people carried themselves in public. The idea of
citizenship was embodied by men who marched with sobriety and
purpose in a parade and who never succumbed to the unchecked
passions of an election riot. In a decade when political struggles over
inclusion and exclusion were particularly fraught, crowd events in all
their manifestations became politicized in profoundly contentious
ways. These were cultural practices and political assertions that could
simultaneously empower – as was the case with ambitious members
of the Canadien and Irish Catholic political elites – and disenfran-
chise – as was the case with women, the urban poor, and migrant
labourers. In Montreal, as in other cities across the North Atlantic
World during this period, the contours of a liberal and democratic
public sphere were being negotiated.[3]

This chapter explores the impact that cultural practices on the
urban street had on public life in mid-nineteenth-century Montreal.
It will examine how crowd events were employed by a variety of
different communities for the purpose of seeking access to political
influence and authority and, conversely, to exclude certain groups
from the same. Election riots, national society parades, public celebrations, and funeral processions occurred against the backdrop

of tumultuous conflicts over power and privilege. As British North American society grappled with the impact of democratic discourse and the transformation in economic and social relations that marked this period, the bourgeois elites who wished to legitimize their asser-tions of authority employed public displays of restraint, rationality, and composure to do so.[4] With collective violence conceptualized as a pressing social problem, the leadership abilities of competing factions often hinged on their ability to portray themselves as capable of standing apart from popular unrest.

What we know about these crowd events has, in most cases, been filtered through the lens of the cultural and economic elite. While the press and various voluntary associations marked the emergence of a democratic public sphere across British North America, these institutions tended to privilege that elite perspective.[5] In order to en-gage critically with the politics of the street, we must speculate about the likely gulf that existed between how these events were described and how they were woven into the lived experience of ordinary Montrealers. The streets were a messy and contentious space where the popular classes had more opportunities to engage in politics and where elites were obliged to vigorously defend their authority. How people employed the streets was central to the dramatic renegotia-tion of social relations that occurred during this period, providing us with evidence of processes of exclusion.[6]

Local elites, Protestant or Catholic, French or English, became enthusiastic organizers of crowd events during the 1840s. Voluntary and fraternal societies played a prominent role in coordinating these events. Dignitaries from the Société St Jean Baptiste, the St Patrick's Benevolent Society, the St George's Society, and the St Andrew's Society were consistently on hand to celebrate events like the arrival and departure of dignitaries from Montreal's harbour, commemora-tions of the British victory at Waterloo, and the Queen's birthday. A symbolic language of public celebration took shape as streets were garlanded with cedar branches and bisected with floral archways to lend them a festive air. Colourful flags were frequently hoisted up the masts of ships in the harbour. Public celebrations both large and small required a significant amount of anonymous labour, much of which was undertaken by women. Banners and uniforms were sewn, streets and homes were decorated, processions of schoolchildren were rehearsed, and voluntary associations had special meetings. These sorts of occasions took place with regularity in mid-nineteenth-century Montreal. Whether one engaged as an organizer, a participant, a volunteer worker, or an observer, these dynamic crowd events became integral to the way that Montrealers negotiated their place as citizens (or prospective citizens).

While it is important to interpret these events as a form of political activity, Montrealers integrated them into their daily experience in ways that did not relate directly to sectarian politics. Men, women, and children did not engage in these activities only to make a political statement but also because they were exciting and pleasurable. Parades, celebrations, and even riots drew people onto the streets with a variety of motivations. They might have attended a celebration to welcome a new governor to the city out of curiosity, out of a desire to spend time with friends and relatives, or because, as was noted in chapter 1, they were already there working and socializing. Furthermore, while elites might have coordinated such events in order to make assertions about their relationship to political and cultural authority, these events did not always unfold the way their organizers had envisioned. By putting themselves on display in front of the broader community, they made themselves vulnerable to acts of popular resistance. It was not always easy to hold the attention of Montrealers. When the new governor, Charles Bagot, arrived in the city in August 1843, those who had lined the streets to catch a glimpse of his carriage winding its way from the docks to his hotel gradually lost interest after seemingly interminable delays and teeming rain. When Bagot finally did arrive, he did so to the eerie quiet of empty streets.[7] On other occasions, the official message of an event could be hijacked. Charles Metcalfe's arrival in the immediate aftermath of the 1844 election rioting provided a platform for the city's Orange Order, who reportedly hung banners and flags in windows along the route of the procession welcoming the new governor to the city.[8]

The political implications of crowd events became increasingly contentious in the first half of the 1840s. This followed moves by the Special Council to restrict popular assemblies. The desire to place restrictions on crowd activities crossed partisan lines. It was made evident with the passage of the Party Processions Act of 1843 by the Reform-dominated ministry. This legislation, championed by Upper Canadian reformer Robert Baldwin, placed heavy restrictions on sectarian processions and secret societies. It was widely interpreted as a thinly veiled attack on the Orange Order and their rowdy annual commemoration of the Protestant victory at the Battle of The Boyne, held every 12th of July. The act mandated justices of the peace to keep a careful eye on these processions and to impose fines and prison sentences on anyone who displayed provocative sectarian symbols.[9] It was virulently opposed by Tories across Canada. What angered them most was that the bill was worded in such a way that Catholic religious processions like the commemoration of Fête-Dieu fell outside its purview, thus giving the Catholic supporters of the Reform faction unfettered access to public space. These debates played a prominent role in shaping public life across the province during this period, especially after the ministry that drafted and passed the bill resigned en masse to protest the governor's reluctance to defend the principle of responsible government in late 1843.[10] How officials addressed concerns about crowd events became a crucial battleground during this period.

Because of its vague wording, the Party Processions Act was only enforced sporadically, yet remained deeply contested throughout its brief existence.[11] While often understood through the lens of sectarian conflict, it says much about the negotiation of social relations along the lines of class during this period. This was part of an effort waged by reform-minded elites to provide greater legal ammunition to address the raucous and often violent sphere of popular politics across the province.[12] The Orange Order relied on the muscle of young men from the popular classes, many of whom were deeply engaged in election rioting and other outbreaks of collective violence.[13] This was also part of a broader attack on the clandestine world of secret societies, which advocates of democratic reform argued helped foster networks of illegitimate authority and riled the passions that fuelled such violence.[14]

The middle decades of the nineteenth century witnessed nearly continuous debates over the fundamental structure of democratic cultures and institutions across the North Atlantic World and other outposts of the British Empire.[15] These debates manifested themselves in British North America around the issue of responsible government. To what degree would men elected to the legislative assembly be able to effectively wield power, especially with regard to the public purse? This question had been the main thrust of Canadien politics for more than two decades, and the conflicts of the 1840s revolved around the details of democratic reform.[16] The Reform faction in parliament were committed to the principle that the authority to govern ought to rest with elected officials. The Tory faction were just as committed in their opposition to any plan that, in the words of an editorial published in the *Montreal Gazette*, would render the governor a nullity. They accused the Reform faction of wavering in their loyalty to the crown. Reform leaders like Lafontaine, their argument went, were essentially only committed to maintaining Canada's connection to the British Empire if the imperial authorities handed them unhindered access to the levers of colonial power.[17] Only the *Rouge* faction in parliament actually advocated for a decisive break with the British Empire through their continued opposition to the Act of Union and the political manoeuvring that came with it.[18] Their republicanism, however, combined with a vigorous anti-clerical stance, failed to gain traction over the course of the 1840s. The moderate reform agenda of Lafontaine and the broad coalition he knit together with Upper Canadian reformer Robert Baldwin was gaining broad public support through initiatives around the practice of responsible government and lobbying for amnesty for exiled Patriotes.[19]

Historians have long pointed to this jockeying over responsible government as a transformative moment in the evolution of Canada's political culture and institutions.[20] The number of newspapers and political tracts circulating to the furthest reaches of the colony expanded rapidly, as did other political activities like public meetings and debates.[21] On the pages of newspapers published in Montreal and across British North America, these discussions were wrapped up in lofty rhetoric. The heated discussions that marked the 1840s were driven by two fiercely opposed factions attempting to rally support for their vision of how a democratic colony ought to be governed. Tories insisted that they were open to the process of reforming the colony's political institutions, and that their concerns about giving the legislative assembly, with its strong Canadien contingent of representatives, too much political power was a testament to their commitment to preserving the British connection. For the Reform faction, the struggle for effective political representation was couched in their commitment to the democratic impulses of the British Constitution.[22] Both factions, in other words, ostensibly supported some form of democratic reform. Like many extended political conflicts, these debates over responsible government tended to pull other issues and debates into their orbit. Concerns about disorderly behaviour at popular assemblies are a poignant example of this phenomenon. Whether boasting about the success of a national society parade or condemning the participation of political foes in an election riot, community leaders in Montreal defended their position with regard to responsible government.

Crowds events could also be used to justify the inclusion or exclusion of different actors and communities. As much as responsible government expanded access to real power, it was accompanied by simultaneous processes of exclusion. This would be keenly felt by all those who were not white men of property. Women, people of colour, the poor, the Indigenous, and certain immigrant groups saw the legitimacy of their presence in the public sphere systematically attacked during the post-rebellion period. Public life in a society that imagined itself to be in the process of democratizing was carefully constructed as the preserve of elite white men.[23] The gradual and highly contested move towards responsible government is often portrayed as the flowering of colonial democracy, but at its core it simply sought to enlarge the sphere of elite men who had access to the public purse. This is made evident in studies of the state formation process, which demonstrate how bourgeois elites were able to harness their expanding access to political power to further their own commercial and cultural interests.[24] Meanwhile, steps to marginalize women, certain racial and ethnic groups, and the urban poor accelerated during this period.[25] How people carried themselves on the urban street became an important means of defending these acts of inclusion and exclusion.

Many of the same Montreal elites advocating for the principle of responsible government were also engaged in campaigns to foster a more genteel public culture as outlined in previous chapters. For example, as the sphere of what was considered legitimate politics narrowed, the spontaneous and raucous popular rituals that surrounded the election process were increasingly seen as incongruous with how elites wished to portray themselves to their constituents, to each other, and to the broader community.[26] Similarly, the growing popularity of highly choreographed events like the St Jean Baptiste Day Parade was partially due to the fact that they represented a model of social order demonstrating the ability of those elites to wield authority.

Historians of nineteenth-century politics, in Montreal and across the North Atlantic World, have long acknowledged that popular violence loomed over elections, especially those held in urban settings. Elections were conceptualized as public undertakings inextricable from the contentious culture of the streets.[27] Election violence is frequently held up as an example of how fraught difference along the lines of ethnicity and class could be in these communities. This violence is often conceptualized as sporadic, thus downplaying the degree to which it was rooted in popular culture during this period.[28] Political campaigns were drenched in alcohol and bawdy customs. Roughly one month before property-owning men and, before 1849, some property-owning women made their way to the polling station, partisan meetings began to convene in hotels and taverns across the city, after which many of those present would take to the streets. Candidates who delivered rousing speeches and greeted supporters at these meetings were frequently paraded home afterwards by their supporters, who whooped and cheered as they made their way through the city. These impromptu – and usually nocturnal – parades were couched in a symbolic language of electioneering: songs were sung; noisemakers were liberally employed, and pins and ribbons were affixed to lapels. Strategic routes through the streets passed by the offices of competing newspapers and the homes of opposition politicians. In a city where urban elites were moving towards a consensus on the connection between decorum and legitimate authority, this brand of activism was increasingly seen as problematic.

Election riots occurred on a regular basis throughout the 1840s in Montreal, which suggests that a significant proportion of Montrealers had come to expect them. None of these violent confrontations, however, prompted the level of sustained and polarizing debate produced by the 1844 parliamentary by-election in the western ward of Montreal pitting the Tory brewing magnate William Molson against Reformer Lewis Drummond, an Irish Catholic who had risen to prominence in liberal political circles after serving as the defence attorney of several Patriotes in 1838. Held in the midst of heated debates over responsible government across the colony, this by-election was invested with great significance by supporters of both parties, who approached it as a referendum on the issue. Their persistent focus on crowd-related issues demonstrates just how pivotal a role concerns about popular engagement in the democratic process played in larger debates about reform. The atmosphere in the weeks leading up to election day was tense, with large partisan meetings spilling out into the streets, and reports of nocturnal brawls between the supporters of Molson and Drummond. Tension reached a crescendo on the day the polls opened. There were violent confrontations between young male supporters of the rival factions, and troops were summoned to patrol the streets. In attempting to break up one particularly bloody skirmish in Haymarket Square, a soldier stabbed Julien Champeau, a bystander who had been drawn into the brawl, with his bayonet. Champeau succumbed to his injuries, and his death sparked an intense war of words between Tories and Reformers that began with trading accusations over who was responsible for the man's death, but quickly evolved into an extended and heated reflection on ethnic politics, the meaning of citizenship, and the nature of the democratic process.

The actions of the crowds during the election were interpreted through the lens of partisan politics. This became evident as soon as the by-election was called and public meetings in support of the two candidates began to convene in local taverns. The *Montreal Gazette*, a vociferous defender of the Tory cause and of Metcalfe's decision to undo the steps that his predecessor had taken towards acknowledging the principle of responsible government, described Molson's supporters as "the great majority of the opulent and intelligent inhabitants of Montreal."[29] This took on obvious class and ethnic overtones as the campaign progressed, with Molson's supporters in the Tory press accusing Drummond of recruiting the Irish migrant labourers employed on the Lachine Canal to intimidate prospective Tory voters.

This was part of a larger strategy, the *Montreal Gazette*'s editorialist continued, which demonstrated the willingness of the Reform faction to usurp the democratic process. Attendance at rallies for Molson might have been sparser, the *Montreal Gazette* conceded, but all of the men present were real voters. Drummond, on the other hand, had taken to addressing large crowds of "canal-men and strangers enlisted … to act the part of citizens of Montreal."[30]

According to his opponents, by failing to disassociate himself from the rough culture of his supporters, Drummond was endorsing their behaviour. Minor incidents were used to bolster these charges. After a British Protestant doctor accused a crowd of Drummond supporters of assaulting him as he made his way home from a house-call, the *Montreal Gazette* thundered that the city was under siege from a "ferocious anarchical party struggling for political supremacy."[31] In another editorial, the *Montreal Gazette* accused Drummond and his supporters of "descending to the dirty work of an election."[32] The debates over responsible government were dominated by the contentious politics of inclusion in and exclusion from the public sphere. Molson's supporters in the Montreal press harnessed ongoing concern about the disorderly practices of the migrant labourers employed on the Lachine Canal to buttress their claims that only the conventional Tory elite was capable of wielding authority in a legitimate manner.

That Montreal's newspapers took liberties with the truth is evident in the cultural gulf that they imagined between Molson and Drummond during the 1844 by-election. While Drummond's supporters were portrayed as wild-eyed canal workers prone to acts of wanton violence, Molson's were portrayed in the Tory press as the embodiment of rational deliberation. After a public meeting in support of Molson's candidacy was stormed by a crowd of Drummond's supporters, the *Montreal Gazette* reported that bloodshed was only averted because the Tories in the room were so calm and composed that they could not be baited into violence.[33] It is often clear that supporters of the rival candidates engaged in very similar acts. When Molson's supporters escorted their candidate home after a public meeting, it was described in the Tory press as a respectable procession, the fitting conclusion to an evening of rational debate.[34] When Drummond's supporters did the same, however, comparisons were quickly drawn between the practice of parading politicians home from a public meetings and the disreputable spectacle of the charivari, where people who breached community norms would be intimidated with boisterous and bawdy nocturnal demonstrations. Numerous allusions were made to the shabby attire of the crowd alongside vivid descriptions of the sorts of noises that they made during their processions, referred to as "roars" and "groans."[35] In one instance, a gathering of Drummond supporters at a public meeting was described as "bellowing like so many traveling mountebanks out of the windows of a tavern," an image that, in all likelihood, would have been just as apt if used to describe a similar gathering of Molson supporters. It is a useful reminder that efforts to portray a given community as inherently more rational were, more than anything else, works of fiction. These persistent assertions that Molson voters were cut from a different cloth than those of Drummond were made to justify the larger Tory claim that only they were capable of maintaining public order.

These assertions did not go unchallenged in Reform circles. *La Minerve*, the leading French-language newspaper in the city and a loyal backer of the Reform faction, embraced reports that Drummond was consistently attracting more supporters to his meetings than was Molson. This was evidence, they argued throughout the campaign, that Molson's public support was dissipating: proof that democratic reform was an inevitability. When Molson did attempt to stage the sort of raucous outdoor meeting adopted by Drummond, an eyewitness account the Reform mouthpiece published compared the Tory rally to a "pygmée à côté d'un géant."[36] Rather than being seen as a discrediting factor, as in the Tory press, Drummond's supporters presented their candidate's ability to inspire support from a broad cross-section of Montreal as a mark of legitimacy in the Reform press.

La Minerve also attacked their rivals' party line by reminding their readers that critics of democratic reform were not above inciting their young male supporters into acts of violence. Frequent references were made to the connections that many prominent Molson supporters had to the Doric Club, the armed militia that lashed out at suspected Patriotes on the streets of Montreal during the rebellions.[37] Evidence of these connections was frequently presented to supporters of Papineau and the *Rouge* faction, some of whom were contemplating voting for Molson in exchange for the promise that they would be given a voice in the ministry that would be formed by Metcalfe following the by-election. The Reform faction did not hesitate to employ the same brand of discourse that the Tories used against them to tar their *Rouge* foes, arguing in one editorial that the only Canadien support Molson retained was from the ward's carters and couriers, many of whom were so impoverished that their support could easily be purchased.[38] These attacks appear to have been successful, with reports in the press and the subsequent election results suggesting that Canadien support for Molson evaporated. Beyond the partisan lens, however, these exchanges suggest a consensus among supporters of both factions that engaging in violence threatened the legitimacy of authority.

The Reform press also noted the contradiction between their rivals' claims that the Tories were the voice of law, order, and public decorum with the reality that their candidate in the by-election had accumulated his personal fortune in brewing. The temperance cause, an editorial in *La Minerve* noted, had gained nearly 10,000 loyal adherents in the first half of the 1840s alone. How then could the Tories justify running a candidate who was deeply engaged in the campaign to fight temperance reform? They reported on a number of visits Molson had made to the provincial capital at Kingston in which he forcefully lobbied the ministry against voting in favour of the tax hikes on liquor that had been proposed by temperance activists.[39] While the Tory press lobbed accusations about connections between Drummond and the violence on the Lachine Canal, Reform newspapers like *La Minerve* were able to make a convincing case that it was the sober and lawyerly Drummond who was the true public-order candidate.

Longstanding residents of Montreal would not have been surprised by the scenes they encountered on the day that polling opened. Crowds lingered on the streets, songs and chants drifted through the air, jostling and intimidation occurred, and gossip about preliminary results reverberated on street corners and taverns. Men and women making their way to the polling station to register their votes were engaged in this political revelry. Eyewitness accounts published in both the Tory and Reform press suggests that on the first day of voting the atmosphere of the streets was equal parts festive and menacing. While a handful of activists undertook campaigns to reform the practice of voting, most appear to have accepted the popular pageantry of politics. Thousands took to the streets with supporters of each political faction taking part in fisticuffs and brawling, despite vehement assertions that their side did not engage in such practices. Tory and Reform newspapers accused their rivals of threatening the legitimacy of the by-election by hiring thugs armed with sticks and sections of iron pipe to intimidate prospective voters.

The violence that unfolded across the city, and particularly on Haymarket Square in the west end where Champeau met his demise, was particularly jarring. It brought back visceral memories of the rioting that occurred during an 1832 by-election in the same ward, when troops fired on a crowd and three men with connections to the emerging Patriote party were killed.[40] The use of lethal force by troops stationed in this garrison town was replete with implications regarding the ongoing struggle between the colonial authorities and the advocates of democratic reform. The subsequent inquest into Champeau's death garnered a great deal of public attention.[41] Discussions of the rioting during this by-election can help us piece together just how couched in popular revelry the act of voting had become in Montreal.

Acts of violence were part of a range of activities that Montrealers engaged in, sometimes by choice and sometimes not. These actions, like raising toasts and singing songs at public meetings, or punching the supporters of a rival candidate during a street brawl, were increasingly construed as problematic. They were, however, often the only opportunities available to Montrealers who, as a result of their race, class, or gender, were disenfranchised from the formal aspect of institutional politics.[42] Although there are no explicit references to women in accounts of the 1844 by-election riots, this is likely because contemporary observers would have assumed their presence.[43] Evidence suggests that women were canny participants in public life. Politics played out in spaces where women were present – in taverns that they owned or were employed in, or on streets that were important sites of sociability. The pageantry surrounding elections provided women, most of whom could not vote, with an opportunity to engage in public life.

A similar tendency is visible with regards to how Irish migrant labourers were treated during the campaign. The accusation that thousands of armed labourers forced potential Molson voters from making their way to the polling station became the chief rallying cry of the *Montreal Gazette* and other Tory newspapers throughout the campaign and in the aftermath of the rioting. It was a charge that the newspapers backing Drummond and the Reform faction were not eager to deal with at length, because they too wanted to portray themselves as above the fray. The threat to the voting process posed by the labourers even prompted an official response from the colonial government. Hamilton Killaly, the head of the Board of Works, wrote a letter to the contractors of the canal project, encouraging them to take whatever measures necessary to prevent labourers from leaving the worksite and making their way to Montreal to interfere in the election. With their reputation for engaging in acts of collective violence already established by the strikes described in chapter 3, Killaly was convinced that some attempt to exert their influence during the by election was inevitable. He wrote that he had been "assured that a quantity of bludgeons have been prepared with the object of unduly influencing this election by intimidating voters."[44]

The by-election was, for all intents and purposes, over only hours after it had begun. At the first sign of violence Molson resigned from the contest, citing reported attempts to obstruct his supporters from voting. The Tory press published vivid descriptions of the streets surrounding the polling station in Place d'Armes being filled with "ragged desperados" who would not hesitate to grab a well-dressed gentleman by the throat and pull him away from a polling station.[45] The language used to describe the labourers did much to discredit them. During the coroner's inquest into Champeau's death, for instance, the *Montreal Gazette* drew attention to an excerpt of Police Chief Alexandre Comeau's testimony, in which he recalled making his way through the western ward surrounded by men "naked to the waist" and brawling.[46] Then, in the days following Molson's resignation from the race, the Tory press launched an informal campaign to discredit the decisive Reform victory. One editorial argued that urban election results simply could not be trusted. Montreal's "dense and labouring population" was especially vulnerable to succumbing to political demagoguery, because it "in times of excitement ... throws its weight into the scale of the party which appeals to its passions."[47] Their position with regards to responsible government hardened and took on a virulently ethnic tinge. They claimed that by being obstructed from voting by Irish migrants, Montreal's Tory gentlemen were being robbed of their rights as British subjects.[48] What had occurred during the by-election, they argued, was a scenario that a *Montreal Gazette* editorial had warned of shortly after the writ had dropped: The city's respectable residents had become, despite the "flag of England still [waving] over [them] ... slaves of the mob."[49] The combination of an emergent migrant working-class in Montreal with the persistence of popular practices around the electoral process was used by the Tory press to fan fears that responsible government would bring about the same turbulent political culture that defined American cities during this period.

The descent of the by-election into violence was presented by the Tory faction as evidence that the Reform faction's advocacy for responsible government was nothing more than a ruse. What the Reformers actually aspired to was unhindered access to political power through the elimination of the stabilizing oversight of the crown. That the Reformers defended the legitimacy of the by-election results despite the widespread violence that marred voting in the western ward was, the Tories argued, further proof that they were willing to play fast and loose with democratic principles. Perhaps because they appeared to have been suffering from a decline in support, prominent Tories used the riot to peddle the idea that they were not the enemies of democratic reform, but that the Reformers could not be trusted with the reins of power. With controversy swirling around the riot, the *Montreal Gazette* published an editorial in which they denounced Montreal's Reform press for dismissing their arguments as mere Tory posturing. The *Montreal Gazette*, the editorial continued, was not steadfastly opposed to responsible government, and its editor actually held liberal views on the subject. What it opposed was a transition to responsible government that amounted to little more than handing over power to Reformers without any sort of check on how they wielded it. These "pseudo-disciples of Durham," the *Montreal Gazette* suggested, demonstrated that they did not know the slightest thing about liberality by their failure to denounce the actions of those who prevented British citizens from casting their ballots for Molson.[50]

It is hardly surprising that the Reform press offered a very different interpretation of the rioting. While the Tories focused on suggestions that Drummond had hired canal workers to intimidate Molson's supporters, the Reform press focused on the actions of the 89th Regiment during the election. Like the coverage of the riot in the *Montreal Gazette*, *La Minerve's* unwavering defence of the actions of Drummond's supporters drifted frequently towards the disingenuous. They repeatedly suggested that Drummond's supporters were drawn into the streets and towards the polling station by their own naïve curiosity. The Reform press insisted that it was the military and young thugs connected to the Orange Order who instigated the violence. *La Minerve* carefully laid out the parallels between the 1832 by-election in the western ward when troops opened fire on a retreating crowd of Patriote supporters and the killing of Julien Champeau. This violence, they argued, was how the Tories wielded power when their authority was under threat. They demanded an independent investigation into the shooting, insisting that either Thomas d'Arcy, the soldier who delivered the fatal blow, or John Dyde, the magistrate who ordered the troops onto Haymarket Square, ought to be held responsible for the young man's death. To emphasize the connection between 1832 and 1844, dignitaries including Lafontaine, Francis Hincks, the Nelson brothers, Augustin-Norbert Morin, and Pierre Beaubien led a massive funeral procession from Champeau's residence at 42 Sanguinet through the streets of Montreal, stopping for mass at the parish church before arriving at the Catholic cemetery where the young man was buried beside those who had been shot during the 1832 by-election.[51] This was a way of using both ritual and public space to assist in the construction of a narrative about the persistent abuse of power by the Tories who governed the colony.

The Reform faction defended the principle of democratic reform by persistently raising doubts about the decisions Tories made about public order. Could their authority be legitimate if it was only made possible by their monopoly on force? The tone of Tory coverage of the by-election, *La Minerve* argued, was evidence of their increasing desperation. Molson and his supporters realized that their only chance of maintaining the status quo was to convince those who wielded authority in both the colonial and imperial governments that democratic reform posed a threat to public order. The question of Drummond's alliance with the canal workers, they argued, was moot. The results of the by-election were so disproportionately in favour of Reform that this form of interference would not have been necessary. Molson did not drop out of the race because he was outraged that his supporters were being jostled on their way to the polling stations but because he had little hope of victory.[52] In a letter written to Robert Baldwin, his counterpart in Canada West, Reform leader Louis Hippolyte Lafontaine interpreted Molson's resignation as sign that the Tories would never be able to elect a candidate in a Montreal riding again. "Quelle déconfiture," he wrote, "pour notre insolent parti tory, dans la même ville où il se vantait toujours de posséder, en exclusivité, l'intelligence, le talent, la richesse, l'influence, etc."

It is worth noting that *La Minerve* made no attempt to justify the behaviour of the canal workers. In fact, they applauded Hamilton Killaly and the Board of Works for attempting to prevent them from leaving the worksite for the duration of the election. Despite the profoundly partisan divide in the city, a consensus was clearly emerging about who had a legitimate claim to political citizenship. This process was pushing women, the poor, and the racialized to the margins of public life. This is not to say that the two factions did not clash over details. The Reform press did take issue with the suggestion that the labourers were to blame for the rioting, when they were armed only with sticks and paving stones while a number of Tory supporters were flashing pistols. The Reform press used these events to unpack how unchecked Tory power was during moments of crisis. Magistrates with connections to the Tories were quick to summon the troops of the 89th Regiment, stationed at the garrison in Montreal's east end. It had long been rumoured that many of these heavily armed troops had sympathy – if not solid connections – to the Orange Order, long a source of muscle for the Tory faction during elections.[53] Although less preoccupied by street violence than their counterparts, when the Reform press did report on the rioting they focused on moments when Molson supporters were the aggressors. During a scuffle when one of Molson's supporters drew a gun, for example, *La Minerve* reported that a bullet whizzed by the head of a young boy by the name of Régnier, who came within inches of a fatal injury. The incident was held up as an example of how brazen the Tories had become in their efforts to cling to power.[54] The Tories were working hard to fan outrage about the violent actions of a few migrant labourers, but it was their own attempts to suppress the will of the majority that were truly to blame, the Reformers argued.[55]

A number of incidents were reported in which prominent Tory politicians lost their composure in public when it became evident that Drummond would easily carry the election. Bartholomew Gugy, a prominent Tory politician and one of the rare French-speakers who had backed the colonial authorities during the rebellions, received a great deal of press when he was accused of attacking a twelve-year-old boy selling copies of an unnamed Reform newspaper on a street corner. The courthouse was packed on the day that Gugy appeared on charges of assault. Although the case was dismissed, the incident provided the Reform press with further evidence that the Tory elite was so shaken by their declining political fortunes that they were no longer able to remain composed on the city's streets.[56] A similar analysis was made in the Reform press with regards to rumours that distraught Tories were firing their Irish and Canadien servants, and that the contractors on the Lachine Canal were considering taking similar action. Throwing the city's most vulnerable residents out of work at a time of public unrest, an editorial published in *La Minerve* argued, threatened to unleash even more ethnic conflict on the city.[57]

The emerging consensus on the need to reform the city's political culture is most visible in the broad support amongst elites loyal to both political factions for proposals to transform the voting process. Representatives of both parties began to explore long-term solutions to address the aftermath of the 1844 riots. In the spring of 1846, the fruits of their labour appeared in the form of a petition circulating through the city's reading rooms and bookshops. The anonymous document proposed that voting be moved indoors to a specially reserved room at the courthouse, and that individuals be given a fifteen-day period in which they could discretely record their vote with a magistrate.[58] The act of voting would thereby be removed from the streets, a contentious space where the popular classes socialized, worked, and outnumbered elites, and placed in a building that was designed to communicate social, cultural, and political power.[59] The courthouse was a location that the poor would have little reason to enter unless they had they been charged with a criminal offence or been the victim of one. It was designed to legitimize hierarchy and authority. When voting took place on the street, it was infused with partisan energy and the very real threat of violence. The proposal to move it into the courthouse re-imagined the act as contemplative, physically ensconced in a space set aside from the messiest aspects of urban life.

Advocates of these proposals aimed to protect the rights of voters. Many, they argued, met the minimal threshold of property ownership but, under the current arrangement, had avoided voting out of fear that they would be intimidated on the way to the polling station.[60] By doing so, however, they eliminated some of the informal means that those too poor to participate in the political process had to engage in public life. Through their presence on the streets during election campaigns, those who did not qualify for the franchise were able to assert a collective voice. The labourers working on the Lachine Canal, for example, could support their fellow Irish migrants over the issue of democratic reform by taking to the streets. The same could be said of the young men affiliated with the Orange Order, many of whom might not have yet acquired the property required to vote, but who wanted to vigorously support the Tory cause.[61] For those who were not rich but still managed to meet the property requirement, the plan envisaged by the drafters and signers of this petition still signalled an important cultural shift. A quarter century before the adoption of the secret ballot in Canada, a message was being sent that the colony's democratic institutions were the purview of the elite, and that the broader public needed to approach them in a restrained manner. This petition provides insight into the gender politics of this period as well. Three years before legislation supported by political leaders of all stripes stripped women of the right to vote even if they did meet the property-holding requirements, there was support for moving the electoral process into a space that resonated with male authority.

In a city that had grown weary of elections descending into bloody sectarian violence, a diverse chorus applauded the proposals put forward in this petition.[62] Two editorials in *Les Mélanges religieux* praised Montrealers for signing the petition in great numbers.[63] They expressed their utmost confidence in the proposals, suggesting that "cette mesure qui fera sans doute disparaître les scènes tumultueuses et les meurtres qui ont eu lieu dans les dernières élections."[64] The editors of the *Montreal Gazette* also warmly backed the petition, although they took issue with some of its details. Having all voting take place in one location would allow any ruffians who wished to interfere with voting to collect there, and having the polls stay open for up to fifteen days would leave a huge window of opportunity for fraudulent activity. The *Montreal Gazette* also expressed reservations about involving magistrates in the process, seeing as how the same officials could be called upon to review the results of a contested election.[65] These objections aside, a consensus was clearly emerging that measures needed to be taken to make voting more orderly.[66]

Support for this petition did not occur in a vacuum. Elites of every political stripe in 1840s Montreal were, in both overt and subtle ways, drawing boundaries between respectable politics and popular politics. This is a thread that can be traced back to the immediate aftermath of the rebellions, when the Special Council placed restrictions on the sorts of popular assemblies that advocates of democratic reform had used to organize opposition to the colonial authorities. These policies were entrenched by the government of Canada following the adoption of the Act of Union.[67] Such measures were pitched as efforts to curtail popular violence and the threat of insurrection, but they did so by narrowing access to the public sphere.

Petitions and other attempts to regulate how people engaged in politics on the streets of Montreal were not the only means elites had at their disposal in their efforts to foster a more orderly public culture. During the decade that followed the rebellions, in the midst of a great deal of handwringing about the danger of popular assemblies, a sharp increase occurred in the size and frequency of national society parades. Montrealers by the thousands participated in these events. They marched in orderly columns, they lined the streets as spectators, and they crafted banners and other decorations. During a decade where assertions about decorum and ethnic conflict weighed heavily on public life, parades became an important site of cultural formation. These crowd events worked on multiple levels. They provided a venue for aspirational community leaders to make assertions about their legitimacy. Parades also allowed Montrealers from all walks of life to create and foster community bonds and to share moments of awe and levity with neighbours, friends, and relatives. They became a means of establishing a connection to place in a city that was undergoing rapid economic and demographic change.

National society parades were a common occurrence on the streets of mid-nineteenth-century Montreal, but the city's four major ethnic communities did not celebrate their respective patron saints with equal degrees of enthusiasm. There are no traces in the public record of the Scottish community, for example, celebrating St Andrew's Day on the streets; instead, they expressed their nationalist sentiments through private banquets. The English celebrated St George's Day sporadically. In 1844, the *Montreal Gazette* mentioned that there had been no effort to organize a celebration in Montreal, although there had been a successful parade featuring one hundred children waving Union Jacks down the river in Quebec City.[68] As parading became an increasingly integral component of Montreal's public life, the English embraced the practice. In 1849, at the height of the tense debates over the Rebellion Losses Act that would soon explode into bloody sectarian violence, "the national festival of 'Merrie England'" was celebrated with drinks at Orr's Hotel on Notre Dame Street – a hotbed of Tory organizing – followed by a short procession to St George's Anglican Church. After the service the celebrants returned to Orr's, "whose table was filled with every delicacy which the season affords" where a long series of toasts were made with "national enthusiasm."[69]

This celebration might well have been prompted by the political turmoil that gripped Montreal during the spring of 1849. It was, however, a more subdued affair than other national society celebrations that took place on an annual basis throughout the post-Rebellion period. This reflects a pattern: elites from communities that felt they were being marginalized by the British Protestant Tory elite celebrated these occasions with the most vigour. Canadien and Irish elites used grand and carefully choreographed parades, moving national celebrations from banquet halls and taverns out onto the streets. These parades were more than simply festive occasions. They were pulled into the same contentious political debates that swirled around election violence.

The Société St Jean Baptiste employed these tactics extremely effectively. Established in 1832 by publisher Ludger Duvernay, it quickly became the focal point of Patriote organizing. Like other national societies operating during this period, they focused much of their energy on lavish annual banquets. In the years leading up to the Rebellions, these celebrations became the highlight of the social calendar for bourgeois Canadiens. They were characterized by rousing speeches delivered in rooms laden with national symbols, including maple leaf centrepieces, banners, and the tricolour flag of the Patriote movement.[70] There was a crackdown on Canadien public life after the colonial authorities suspended Lower Canada's elected assembly and censored publications and organizations they felt had been encouraging dissent during the political conflicts of the late 1830s. The organization lay dormant through the Special Council period and into the first years of the 1840s. But when the Société St Jean Baptiste was re-established in 1843, it was a different creature. While it still served as the national society of the Canadiens, the second incarnation of the society largely shed the liberal rhetoric that had characterized it during the previous decade. The organization continued to foster links between Canadiens with differing ideological perspectives, but the tone of its public statements reflected the more conservative orientation of the 1840s.

The announcement published in the French-language press in Montreal regarding the re-establishment of the society bore the signatures of a diverse cross-section of Canadien politicians, some of whom had established their reputations during the struggles of the previous decade, like Benjamin Viger and Ludger Duvernay, as well as the next generation of leaders, including George Étienne Cartier.[71] The society forged links with Catholic temperance organizations, the popularity of which was spiking. This alliance allowed the society to tap into the energy of the city's street-based politics while communicating the sobriety and legitimacy of the Canadien elite who were gathering under its banners.[72] They also reached out to the city's popular classes by establishing an early prototype of a mutual aid society. Those who joined the society were required to pay an annual subscription fee, and the funds collected were disseminated amongst members who had fallen upon hard times as a result of illness or injury.[73] The most politically astute and audacious strategy undertaken by the Société St Jean Baptiste in its second incarnation, however, was to pull the annual celebration out of the city's banquet halls and onto the streets in the form of increasingly lively and elegant parades.[74]

Bringing the political and cultural project of the Société St Jean Baptiste onto the streets of Montreal speaks volumes about the nature of public life during this period. It was no longer sufficient to have a relatively small group of community leaders gather for a boozy and self-congratulatory banquet as a way of marking a national holiday. In the context of heated political skirmishes over democratic reform and the challenges that came with rapid urbanization, these same community elites wanted to demonstrate their mastery over the physical and cultural landscape of the city. Parades provided them a forum to do just that. It was the absence of an annual public celebration of St Jean Baptiste Day on the 24th of June that appears to have prompted efforts to revitalize the society in 1843. Montreal, an editorial in *La Minerve* noted, was the largest French-speaking community in North America, and yet there was no parade to mark the occasion. This was especially galling, the editorial continued, seeing as how smaller national communities in Montreal hosted celebrations in honour of their patron saints.[75] That so many notable figures in the city's Canadien elite devoted their attention to the re-establishment of the society likely speaks to the political capital they sought to gain from involving themselves in these celebrations.

Pressure in the Canadien community to mark St Jean Baptiste Day was no doubt inspired by witnessing the annual celebration of St Patrick's Day by Montreal's Irish community. These parades became increasingly elaborate during this period, with the city's main thoroughfares decorated by banners and other decorations. Brass bands played thunderous version of "God Save the Queen" and temperance societies marched in all their finery. The imposing

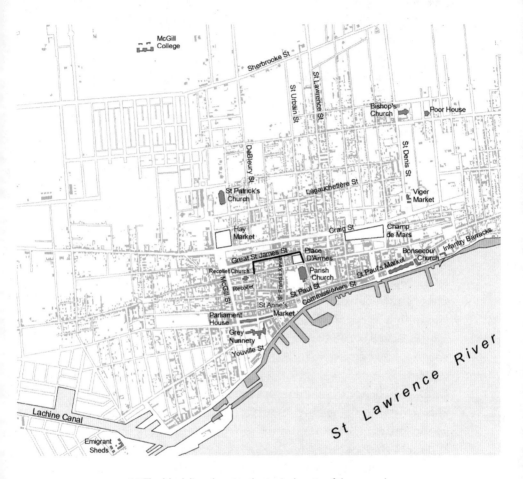

4.1 The black line denotes the typical route of the annual
St Patrick's Day parade, based on newspaper reports.
Note how it made its way from the Recollet Catholic Church to
the parish church on Place d'Armes along Great St James Street.
This incorporates two of the city's main Catholic institutions
and powerful symbols of the financial elite.

procession of several hundred community members filed down the city's main commercial arteries and past institutions – like churches and schools – that were leaving a distinctly Irish mark on the city.[76] The parade was fuelled by the political aspirations of the Irish elite. It was clearly designed to communicate an image of these men as capable wielders of social and political authority to the broader community.[77]

It is clear that these parades were sharing a script. They were processions of a specific community's economic and cultural elites, organized along the lines of professional or associational membership. They made very explicit and specific interventions in the city's spatial politics in their routes and the landmarks they encompassed.[78] Unlike parades of the late nineteenth and twentieth centuries, which reflected and celebrated a political culture built around universal male suffrage by celebrating the idea of a "common man" with columns of regular citizens marching in formation, elites in mid-nineteenth-century Montreal used parades to legitimize the process of limiting access to the public sphere. They were demonstrations of how the organizers of the event envisioned the project of governing a modern city. They emphasized voluntary engagement, public order, restraint, and a transparent social hierarchy. Parading was a public performance of elite authority.[79] When non-elites did march in parades, it was as representatives of how the project of governance worked – students and members of a temperance society, for example, demonstrated how community leaders were ordering the tumultuous popular culture of the city. That parading became such a common tool for elites during this period is hardly a coincidence. A political culture was emerging that increasingly linked access to legitimate political authority to one's ability to convey physical restraint and respectability through physical performance.[80] Parades were an ideal place to display these sorts of traits – marching in a parade lent itself to ruminations on one's posture and decorum. Crafting, asserting, and defending multiple layers of identity was a continuous process, and parades became a valuable way to negotiate one's standing.[81]

In a city where national celebrations were once marked with boozy banquets during which community leaders worked their way through dozens of toasts, the prominent role that temperance societies came to play in the parades of the 1840s might appear to be a dramatic cultural transformation. Both the St Patrick's Day and St Jean Baptiste Day parades featured temperance societies and their marching bands in prominent positions.[82] This was a means of connecting these national communities to a social movement that was rapidly gaining momentum. Parade organizers were eager to tap into this energy, and temperance societies saw these events as a perfect opportunity to engage in community outreach.[83] The two were a good fit. National society parades were not jubilant or entertaining affairs. There was a solemnity to them that suited pointed messages about sobriety and restraint.[84] The inclusion of temperance activists in parades provided organizers the opportunity to present an image of themselves exerting leadership over society's most orderly elements. The vice of excessive drinking was highly visible, and reform-oriented activists were successfully pushing the public to re-conceptualize alcohol consumption as a social problem. In this context, highlighting one's connections to the temperance movement was a canny move.

With that being said, it would be simplistic to conceptualize these crowd events solely as tools of social control. They would not have been politically effective had the residents of Montreal not enjoyed participating in them. We must therefore consider how these carefully orchestrated parades, which aspired to solemnity, could be a source of pleasure for a diverse cross-section of Montrealers. Emotions like joy are not always easy to trace through the historical record, and taking them into consideration entails speculation. With that caveat in mind, the community leaders who organized these events had no means at their disposal to compel people to line the streets to watch these parades go by. Yet they did so by the thousands throughout this period. National society parades quickly became an integral component in the festive calendar of the mid-nineteenth-century city.

Because of the deeply polarized nature of Montreal's public sphere in the 1840s, newspaper reports focused on the political messages of these events rather than the experience of spectators. The newspapers were dedicated to rallying citizens around a partisan cause, and thus saw no need to report on things like the public's behaviour during a parade. This leaves us with blanks that we need to fill in. Did spectators heckle? Was their attention rapt, or did they treat the occasion like a street festival, with the procession serving as little more than background noise? The crowds lining the streets of Montreal to watch a parade go by were themselves a social space where people interacted. There may well have been moments of solemnity in the midst of a parade, but also opportunities for cheering, laughing, and hurling bawdy remarks.

For residents from the popular and middling classes, who did not have access to the balls and banquets thrown by the city's elites, these parades became a welcome source of conviviality. Some groups used parades as an opportunity to put themselves on display. A report on the budget of the Union Fire Company noted that a significant expenditure was "parade dress." Much of this cost was related to the replacement of their old felt hats with new leather ones, which they justified with the remark that "there is nothing like leather."[85] That a volunteer fire company had earmarked so much of its discretionary budget on costumes for parading speaks to the importance placed on these events. Fire companies, which were deeply implicated in the city's rough sectarian politics, understood parades to be crucial opportunities to assert the status of their organization and their entire ethnic community. They were also likely a great source of enjoyment for the young firefighters, and marching in uniform in these parades would have been a boon to their personal reputations. To paraphrase two seminal works on American parades during this period, these were events that had nearly as many meanings as they did participants and spectators.[86] For the aspirational community leader marching at the head of an orderly procession, parading might have filled the heart with pride, while for a young migrant day labourer standing to observe the same parade on a crowded footpath, the event might have been embraced as an opportunity to skip out of work for a few hours to mock the pompous spectacles of their social betters.

The parades owed much of their popularity to their increasingly dramatic and ornate symbolic language. By the middle of the 1840s, events like the St Patrick's Day Parade and the celebration of St Jean Baptiste Day had become imposing affairs that were described as "breathtaking"[87] in the way that they transformed the dark and narrow streets of Montreal into a celebratory space. Organizers of the St Jean Baptiste Day Parade, for example, draped the parade route with decorations laden with national symbolism, including garlands

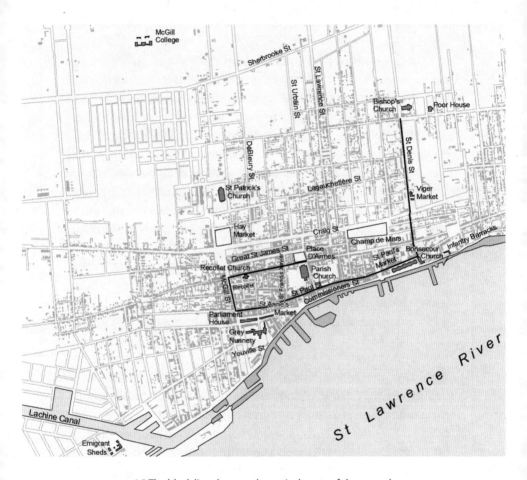

4.2 The black line denotes the typical route of the annual
St Jean Baptiste procession. Beginning on Rue St Denis in the city's northern
suburbs, the procession made its way to the waterfront, then along
St Paul and Notre Dame via McGill Street, thereby encircling the city centre.
The procession ended at the parish church on Place d'Armes.

composed of maple leaves and cedar branches. Such actions altered the atmosphere of the space and helped break the rhythm of daily routines. These parades delivered political messages to the broader community, some of which were explicit, and some of which were implicit. Take the St Patrick's Day Parade, for example. The stated purpose of the event was to celebrate the patron saint of the Irish people and to remind Montrealers of the steady progress towards prosperity – and thus respectability – of the city's Irish community. In the context of heated debates over responsible government and the social challenges that came with the mass migration touched off by the famine crisis in Ireland, the parade became an important means by which the Irish elite could distinguish themselves from the thousands of transient Irish migrants pouring into the city each summer. Again, this is a likely explanation for why organizers of the parade were so eager to place temperance societies at the forefront of the procession. During the 1843 St Patrick's Day Parade, nearly all the men marching in the procession wore two emblems pinned to their lapels: A pin or a ribbon featuring an Irish symbol like the harp or clover, and a temperance medal. The presence of immaculately dressed children marching in neat columns was meant to communicate not only the promise of the next generation of Irish Montrealers, but also the success that elites were achieving in improving access to education amongst the popular classes.[88] The prosperity of the city's emerging Irish elite was also celebrated, with numerous mentions in newspaper coverage of the "fine dress" of prominent Montreal Irishmen like Lewis Drummond.[89] With so much attention being paid to Irish migrants and the proclivity of migrants towards public drunkenness, this became a means of issuing a rebuttal and creating a distinct Irish identity.[90]

This message was also delivered via the route of the parade, which was clearly constructed as a geographic manifestation of the ambitions of the Irish community leaders. It passed from the Recollects Catholic Church in the west end of the city along the city's most prominent and prosperous thoroughfares – McGill and St James Streets, past the homes and businesses of Montreal's wealthiest residents – before spilling out onto Place d'Armes in the shadow of the imposing parish church.[91] The press reported that seven thousand men marched in the parade, a startling and perhaps exaggerated number given the population of Montreal at the time, but an indicator of the scale upon which the event unfolded all the same.[92] While a significant portion of Montreal's population was transient during this period, the popularity of these events demonstrates that there was a shared understanding of the spatial politics of parades. They knew what it implied for Canadiens to transform thoroughfares that represented the commercial and political might of the English-speaking community – like McGill, St Paul, and St James Streets – into parade routes laden with symbols of their national identity. These were political acts that reinforced the streets of Montreal as a dynamic and contested site in the broader struggles over responsible government.

The annual Jean Baptiste Day Parade was clearly aiming to hit many of the same notes. An account of the festivities from 1846 paid particular attention to the highly disciplined columns of over one thousand children from the city's Catholic schools who marched, under a sea of patriotic banners, at the head of the parade. These children captured the public's attention, but they were also symbols of a larger struggle to preserve the French and Catholic presence in Montreal in the face of British Protestant chauvinism and hostility. The presence of children on the streets of the city also struck an emotional chord with adult spectators. One observer wrote a letter to *La Minerve* describing how, walking past the courtyard of a local Catholic school where boys were rehearsing for the parade, he was engulfed by joy that brought him to tears. Their rousing brass band playing martial music and their colourful banners waving in the air reminded the man that the prospects of Montreal's Canadien popula-tion did much to compensate for the defeats that they had suffered in recent memory.[93]

Such sentiments were no doubt further reinforced when spectators had a personal connection to the children marching in the parade because they were the sons and daughters of friends, neighbours, and relatives. This was how these events, steeped as they were in the language of national solidarity, ultimately gained traction at the local level. People lined the sidewalks of Montreal not necessarily because they wanted to see community leaders but because they had personal connections to the people marching. Reform-oriented elites were increasingly troubled by the engagement of children on the urban street, where they hawked newspapers and participated in petty capitalism, often in a very raucous manner. By associating themselves with disciplined schoolchildren neatly dressed in their finest attire, community leaders were demonstrating that their cultural projects could play an important role in creating a more orderly city. This was a crucial means of asserting the legitimacy of their claims on political authority.

What is particularly compelling about these parades is that they employed a symbolic language designed to lend an air of timelessness to the occasion, so as to craft a narrative about current political debates rooted in the very recent past. This was particularly evident in the St Jean Baptiste Day celebrations, where the representation of Canadien history figured prominently. In their report on the 1848 parade, for example, *Les Mélanges religieux* urged readers to use the celebration as an opportunity to reflect on "nos longues années de luttes pour obtenir les droits de notre pays."[94] The parade occupied the same cultural milieu as the work being done to popularize Canadien history during this period by writers like François Xavier Garneau.[95] Coverage of the St Jean Baptiste Day parade in the French language press was marked by ruminations about the state of the Canadien nation. This was often expressed in language that was particularly sentimental. Nationalism, *Les Mélanges religieux* noted in one editorial, was a mysterious feeling that the annual parade could conjure more effectively than words alone. The sounds and sights of the parade prompted people to reflect on their lineage and fostered a sense of fraternity that cut across lines of politics and class.[96] The emergence of parades during this period demonstrates the importance of emotion in the dissemination of political ideas and the formation of communities in modern political culture.[97]

The political messages being conveyed by these parades were not necessarily forthcoming when it came to the actual state of the community. Organizers of both the St Jean Baptiste and St Patrick's Day celebrations used the symbolic language of these events to suggest that these communities were speaking with a single voice. In reality, however, these events were attempts to paper over schisms within the community. The moderate *La Minerve* and the aggressively liberal

L'Avenir each used the occasion of the parade to assert themselves as the true voice of the community.[98] Meanwhile, the willingness of Protestant and Catholic Irish to temporarily ignore sectarian conflicts in order to celebrate St Patrick's Day together was already waning during the 1840s. By the next decade, the event would become exclusively Catholic.

Nonetheless, these parades were widely embraced in newspapers of all political stripes in the city. This suggests that, beneath the political divide, there was an emerging consensus with regards to legitimate authority. Elites of both the Tory and Reform persuasion concurred that crowd events like this were a desirable alternative to the raucous practices seen, for example, during elections. Coverage of the annual St Jean Baptiste Day Parade in the *Montreal Gazette* was generally positive, though perfunctory. Each year, the *Montreal Gazette* published a succinct report detailing the order of the procession and its route through the city. Their editorial comments were limited to complimenting the quality of the music and the discipline demonstrated by the schoolchildren in the parade.[99] Parades were the ideal way to communicate emerging notions of political legitimacy to the broader community. This explains why organs that might have been hostile to the political aspirations of the Canadien elite, like the *Montreal Gazette*, gave a pass to parades. Even the *Montreal Witness*, whose editor launched heated attacks on Catholic religious processions during this period, which will be discussed in chapter 5, simply ignored national society parades.

The 1840s were a turbulent and transformative decade in Montreal, as they were across British North America. The colonial public sphere was consumed by debates on the subject of democratic reform. Dynamic urban elites attacked the legitimacy of the political authority wielded by a small circle of Tory loyalists with close ties to the colonial establishment. Tories returned the charge, arguing that these advocates of reform lacked the character traits necessary to govern effectively. These debates were steeped in ethnic and sectarian conflict – the vast majority of reformers were either Irish Catholics or Canadien while the Tory establishment was soundly British and Protestant. Discussions of democratic reform were thus not confined to the realm of ideas. They spilled out onto the streets.

Competing assertions of legitimate authority made by both the Tory and Reform factions leaned heavily on how they and their political foes carried themselves in public, as the anonymous author of "A Look of a Gentleman" understood so well. Prospective civic leaders were eager to present themselves as restrained and respectable. They used words and actions to distance themselves and their allies from the rough popular culture. Sweeping assertions about how Montrealers carried themselves on the streets thus came to play a decisive, albeit contested, role in negotiating the contours of the city's public sphere during this decade. Local elites could use parades to cast themselves as legitimate wielders of authority, while assumptions about the composure and restraint of women, racialized people, and the poor were used to legitimize their relegation to the margins of public life.[100]

Rioting and parading can, in some ways, be construed as polar opposites of each other. One is furious and seemingly spontaneous, the other carefully choreographed. Their differences aside, these two common crowd events were elements of a broader spectrum of political acts carried out on the streets of mid-nineteenth-century Montreal. They were crucial sites of social, cultural, and political negotiation as Montrealers thought through the contours of community, citizenship, and legitimate authority. Yet not all Montrealers who took to the streets during this decade shared this same symbolic vocabulary. As the next chapter demonstrates, the 1840s also witnessed an escalation in the public presence of the Catholic Church in the city. Much of this was due to an outreach strategy that leaned heavily on acts of popular piety in the form of religious processions and other public celebrations. By taking this approach, the Catholic Church communicated a vision of respectability that differed significantly from those that were communicated to the public in national society parades. This became the subject of significant rancour that had important implications with regards to the politics of power and authority in nineteenth-century Montreal.

5

CACOPHONY AND AWE:
POPULAR PIETY AND PUBLIC ORDER
IN AN AGE OF SECTARIAN CONFLICT

In August 1843, an announcement in Montreal's French-language newspapers invited readers to attend a celebration in Place d'Armes, the public square that faced the city's imposing parish church. They were being called to witness an impressive feat of engineering. Massive bells, forged at a British foundry and shipped across the Atlantic Ocean, were set to be installed in the recently constructed church towers – named Persévérance and Tempérance – that dominated the city's skyline. First, though, a construction team headed by a man named Poitras – who had established a reputation for pulling off these sorts of challenging tasks – had set up scaffolding and pulleys to bring the existing bell in the older of the two towers down to the ground. The Catholic Church, headed by the energetic and politically shrewd Bishop Ignace Bourget, decided to turn this event into a celebration of the prominent role that the church was increasingly playing in Montreal society. This event took place three years into a decade in which the clergy had begun using popular rituals to draw people into a deeper engagement with institutional Catholicism. Montrealers who participated in religious processions and other rituals and commemorations were inundated with rhetoric and visual cues that communicated the growing social and cultural authority of the church. These sorts of events must be read as audacious rebukes of the cultural chauvinism of Montreal's British Protestant minority, many of whom believed that the assimilation of the city's French and Catholic community was inevitable.[1]

In a raucous environment like Montreal, however, these occasions did not always turn out the way their organizers had in mind. This one quickly began to unravel, thus providing us with a rare glimpse into the delicate and socially constructed boundaries between order and disorder. Word had fanned out across the city that the removal of the bell would begin just after four o'clock. The crowd of curious onlookers grew so large that several police officers arrived on the scene to keep them at a safe distance. As the labourers shifted the weight of the bell onto the scaffold it immediately became apparent that Poitras had miscalculated its weight. The scaffolding groaned under the pressure and planks of wood began snapping in two. Within seconds the scaffolding collapsed, and the bell, supported by a single cable, swung perilously over the church and its adjoining buildings. When the cable eventually snapped and the bell plunged to the ground "avec un fracas qui fait trembler la terre," it narrowly missed both the buildings and the stunned crowd. Seemingly frozen in shock for several instants, according to an eyewitness account published in *La Minerve*, the crowd soon burst into frantic activity and "un espèce de culte se manifeste bientôt." Some people even overwhelmed the police barrier, swarming the collapsed debris from which they pulled off shards of wood and handfuls of nails to keep as relics.[2]

The scene on Place d'Armes was spontaneous, but it speaks to the demonstrative brand of religiosity that the church fostered during these years. This chapter examines how the Catholic Church began placing a stronger emphasis on longstanding rituals like religious processions to communicate the legitimacy of their authority. As the events on Place d'Armes suggest, by encouraging this popular and emotive brand of religiosity, the church risked becoming associated by its most vigorous critics with manifestations of social unrest.

In the aftermath of the rebellions, the Catholic Church had begun to assert itself as the most legitimate and capable defender of the interests of the Canadien community. They drew on methods that they had seen successfully implemented in Europe, where efforts

FRENCH CHURCH, PLACE D'ARMES, MONTREAL.

5.1 Krieghoff's depiction of Place d'Armes and the parish church captures its expansion and modernization during the first half of the 1840s. The image suggests a genteel calm on the streets that likely had more to do with the ideals of the artist than reality. Cornelius Krieghoff, *French Church, Place d'Armes, Montreal*, after 1845.

to expand lay activism and an emphasis on the sublime aspects of Catholic pageantry were drawing people – particularly women – into the pews in greater numbers. The crowd that had flocked to Place d'Armes to watch the bell being gently lowered down from the church tower consisted of people whose social calendar was increasingly filled with ceremonies and demonstrations designed to bolster their religiosity. They marched in religious processions, attended massive temperance rallies, celebrated the building of new churches, made pilgrimages, and descended to the harbourfront to greet clergymen returning from Europe tours. The Catholic Church used this popular engagement to bolster the legitimacy of the increasingly prominent role it was playing in public life, which would eventually include everything from interventions in electoral politics to being, in the absence of an interventionist state, the single greatest provider of social services in the city.[3]

In their efforts to communicate their vision to the broader community, the Catholic Church drew upon cultural practices that were an increasingly integral component to the experience of modern urban life. Parades, processions, and public celebrations frequently drew on customs that dated back centuries, but which were being re-imagined in cities that, like Montreal, were seeing their size, scale, and demographic composition rapidly transformed by changing patterns of global migration and the industrial revolution. Crowd events carried with them a political resonance that worked on multiple levels. First, as was the case with the celebration around the installation of the new bells, they had the potential to serve as a powerful representation to the broader community of a groundswell of public support for a given political or cultural project. During a period marked by contentious debates over democratic reform, that an institution like the Catholic Church was able to summon hundreds of Montrealers onto the streets was portrayed as evidence of popular consent to their endeavours. Secondly, these crowd events spoke to the political project that resonated most with urban elites during this period, which was the challenge of fostering public order. As a cursory glance at the Montreal press will attest, urban elites expended considerable energy discussing the threat of popular violence and disorderly behaviour. Making an orderly city was understood to be not only a political project, but also a cultural one. A diverse cross-section of elites harnessed the power available to them in institutions like the municipal government to impose their vision of public order on the streets of Montreal.[4] Similarly, crowd events by different organizations and institutions, be they national societies, political factions, or religious institutions, were explicitly designed as demonstrations of each body's ability to create orderly displays in the midst of the tumultuous realities of daily life. When events were described in newspapers aligned with the organizers of a crowd event, much was made of how respectable the people who lined the streets were. In the deeply partisan public sphere of mid-nineteenth-century Montreal, there was little rhetorical space for nuance on this front.[5] What one segment of the community celebrated as a harmonious display of support for their social vision was held up by their foes as an example of their disregard for order. Competing factions of the city's elite – French and English, Protestant and Catholic – vigorously defended their interpretation of these events in the editorial columns of the press and at civic meetings.[6] This reminds us that the streets served as a vital social and political space in the negotiation of social relations in the mid-nineteenth-century city.[7]

Crowd events were reported in ways that could be either salacious or banal, depending on the ideological perspective of the newspaper doing the reporting. The sectarian press of mid-nineteenth-century Montreal depicts these events as either occasions of genteel solemnity or dangerous breaches of public order in order to advance a broader political agenda. What becomes apparent when reading these conflicting reports was that the elites who organized them did so at considerable risk. Conflict was woven into the fabric of daily life in the city. Efforts to attract Montrealers by the hundreds or even by the thousands for the purpose of commemoration or religious observance did not occur without the strong possibility of igniting tempers. Simply put, the very events that were meant to communicate the social power of the body that organized them frequently risked igniting the sort of popular upheaval from which they were attempting to disassociate themselves.

The brand of Catholic religiosity that emerged during these years was highly demonstrative. Engaging in processions and other public rituals became central to the practice of the faith. These practices, while unique in their connection to the church, resembled the broader sphere of voluntary association that provided the foundation for the political culture emerging across the North Atlantic World during this period.[8] By engaging in this public culture, it would appear that the Catholic Church was working within the cultural framework of mid-nineteenth-century liberalism. The vision of public order being communicated by the church through these popular rituals, however, challenged liberal notions of authority, decorum, and restraint in important ways. In particular, the church's use of crowd events that were ornate and emotional differed from a liberal elite culture that was increasingly banishing such expressions to the private sphere of domestic space.[9]

This increased emphasis on popular celebration by the Catholic Church was a crucial part of the institution's renewed focus on public outreach. Frustrated by the secular tone that permeated the 1820s and 1830s, the local clergy had set out to deepen the public's engagement with the church. First under the leadership of Bishop Lartigue and, most prominently under the leadership of his successor, Bishop Bourget, the church drew on strategies that had been employed successfully in Europe since the Counter-Reformation of the sixteenth and seventeenth centuries. Strategies to expand lay activism and place a greater emphasis on the sublime aspects of ritual and pageantry had been put into practice by advocates of Ultramontane Catholicism.[10] It is clear that many Catholic Montrealers found these practices fulfilling on multiple levels. There was also, however, an important political assertion being made here. As consensus emerged that the urban landscape was in need of reform, the Catholic Church was carving out an important institutional niche for itself, vigorously building on its longstanding interventions in areas such as education, health care, and assisting the underprivileged.[11] In order to carry out this expansion, Bishops Lartigue and Bourget oversaw a rapid increase in the number of clerics and religious orders throughout Lower Canada.[12] Popular rituals were thus part of a larger project of asserting the Catholic character of Montreal.

When Ignace Bourget took up his position as bishop, he grasped that events that had recently unfolded in Lower Canada had created a political vacuum which a dynamic and populist Catholic Church could fill. Historians of Catholicism in nineteenth-century Quebec have long debated the intricacies of the religious revival that occurred amongst French-speaking Catholics during this period.[13] What seems apparent is that for the first decades of the nineteenth century, many in Montreal had a rather limited engagement with the church. They observed major life events including christenings, marriages, and funerals in an institutional setting, but those who wove the church and its rituals more deeply into the fabric of their lives were a minority. Bourget and the clergy surrounding him understood that drawing Montrealers into a deeper relationship with the church would expand their social, political, and cultural influence. Crowd events became an important part of this strategy. Bourget frequently placed himself at the centre of these ceremonies. In May 1847, for example, a huge crowd gathered on the docks to greet the bishop upon his return from Rome. Surrounded by an entourage of priests and prominent lay activists, Bourget was paraded to the parish church in Place d'Armes, where a special mass was held to commemorate the occasion. The event was clearly meant to communicate to the broader community how devout the city's Catholics had become.[14] The men, women, and children who lined the streets to catch a glimpse of the bishop would no doubt have been reminded of similar events marking the arrival and departure of British governors, and may well have drawn connections between the powerful institutions that these men represented and their own challenging experiences of urban life.[15]

The church's growing use of crowd events drew on longstanding Catholic customs and rituals. This was a contentious and audacious strategy. In a city shaped by ethnic diversity, and where sectarian violence had become a defining feature of public life, this use of public space opened the Catholic Church to further attack from their detractors. The Church's emphasis on crowd events was seen by some as a rebuke of the restrictions that the Special Council had placed on public assemblies in the aftermath of the Rebellions, as well as the limitations placed on the Orange Order through the Party Procession Act of 1843. Amidst widespread concerns about the menacing potential of crowds, these sorts of assemblies tested the parameters of elite authority.[16] In an effort to discredit the growing influence of the Catholic Church, evangelical Protestants persistently raised doubts about the church's claims that these events were orderly and restrained. They put forth a counter-narrative that these events were intimidating, raucous, and a breach of longstanding agreements about the use of public space.

Bourget seized upon the 1840 visit of a popular French priest, Monseignor de Forbin-Janson, the Bishop of Nancy, as an opportunity to reach out to the broader Catholic community. Bourget invited him to make a prolonged visit to Montreal and conduct a religious retreat. Forbin-Janson's retreat was the earliest example of the strategies of popular outreach being put into practice on a large scale in Montreal. His method relied on drawing attention to the rituals of Catholicism and their emotional impact.[17] The city, it was reported, was overtaken by a "pompe sacrée."[18] Catholic churches were draped in garlands of flowers and glowed with the flickering lights from hundreds of candles.[19] Practicing a more demonstrative brand of Catholicism was framed as a means of contesting Anglo-Protestant efforts to brand Montreal as a distinctly British city in the aftermath of the failed rebellions.[20]

This retreat, essentially a series of special masses presided over by Forbin-Janson, was declared a resounding success in the city's Catholic press. For many Montrealers, especially those from the swelling ranks of the popular classes, Forbin-Janson's retreat marked a dramatic break from their quotidian routines. In the press, participants described being woken before dawn by the church bells ringing out across the city and feeling compelled to quickly dress and make their way to mass.[21] One enthusiastic Catholic wrote an emotional letter published in *Les Mélanges religieux*, in which he exclaimed "Oh vraiment! Ce spectacle était si beau, que je me croyais transporté aux portes du Ciel, et à la source de la lumière céleste dont jouissent les bienheureux!"[22] On the basis of testamonies such as this, it appears that the retreat's success can be attributed to the focus that it placed on collective ritual. In his homilies, Forbin-Janson called on his audience to dedicate their lives to pious ends, to ensconce themselves in the rhythms of Catholic ritual, and to do all of this with sobriety and discipline. There was a strong political undercurrent to these statements. Leaders like Bourget and Forbin-Janson were consciously crafting a Canadien identity that eschewed the secular values that had come to define public life across North America throughout the eighteenth and nineteenth centuries.[23]

Catholic commentators celebrated not only the number of people filling the pews during the retreat, but the diversity of the bishop's audience. The events were attended by young and old, men and women, rich and poor. The retreat, like the popular Catholic celebrations that would occur in its aftermath, was widely embraced by the city's Catholics, many of whom might have drifted away from this sort of demonstrative religiosity in previous decades. "Personne", exclaimed one writer, "ne voulait être étranger aux graces extraordinaires de la retraite."[24] As the retreat drew to a close in January 1841, a special address noted that upwards of 17,000 Montrealers – approximately two thirds of the city's Catholic population – had participated in the events. *Les Mélanges religieux* noted that absenteeism and tardiness had been rare.[25] While it might be tempting to note the source's bias and consider that these numbers were exaggerated, it is clear that the retreat did encourage popular interest in Catholic ritual.

Another characteristic of the retreat observers remarked upon was the degree to which its focus on emotive rituals resonated with women. One of the largest outdoor events occurred on Christmas Eve 1840, when Forbin-Janson performed a special mass for women at the parish church. Women began gathering on Place d'Armes hours before the mass was scheduled to begin. The crowd grew so large that four additional priests needed to be summoned at the last minute to serve communion, a process that ended up taking several hours.[26] Why were women amongst the most enthusiastic supporters of the Catholic Church's outreach efforts during the 1840s? There is no definitive answer to this question, but the lives of the majority of the city's women during this period were marked by the challenges that came with poverty and migration and the physical toll extracted by both waged and unwaged work.[27] Meanwhile, the legal regime that marginalized their status as citizens had implications on their material experience.[28] Participating in the rituals of the Catholic Church was, in this context, a welcome reprieve from their daily routine – the source of a much-needed jolt of camaraderie as well as an opportunity for silent reflection. In a culture where reminders of their subservience to men was woven into the fabric of daily life, the emotive rituals of the Catholic Church would have felt empowering.[29]

The popular embrace of Forbin-Janson's Montreal retreat was not an isolated phenomenon. It was part of a broader Catholic revival that occurred across the southwestern corner of Lower Canada in the decade following the rebellions.[30] Organizing this slate of cultural events created an opportunity for the church to assert itself as a force for public order. It was no coincidence that the one of the most prominent topics of Forbin-Janson's addresses during the retreat was temperance.[31] With its large population of garrulous soldiers, a significant number of women who relied at various intervals in their lives on prostitution to make ends meet, and transient labourers in the midst of extended migratory journeys, men and women in drunken stupors were a routine feature of the urban landscape. Speaking to a congregation of Irish Catholics during the retreat, Forbin-Janson painted an unforgiving portrait of the typical drunkard, with "les yeux égarés, le langage incertain, n'articulant que des sons entrecoupés, pouvant à peine avancer quelques pas et bientôt étendu là sur le pavé de la rue … rejetté même de ses compagnons."[32]

Forbin-Janson's discussion of the toll of alcoholism on their community appears to have struck a chord with the city's Catholics. Membership swelled in the Catholic temperance societies founded during the retreat. These organizations became the dynamic cornerstones of the lay activism that propelled the upturn in religiosity that occurred during this period.[33] Given the rapid emergence of temperance activism as a driving force in Montreal's public life in the aftermath of Forbin-Janson's retreat, it is important to note the way that drunkenness was constructed as a social problem rather than as a private vice. Later temperance advocates focused on the damage that drinking could do to domestic life, but Forbin-Janson remained focused on the threat that it posed to public order.[34] How people carried themselves on the street was central to temperance activism during this period, with the church asserting its ability to foster public order through the success of these groups. In doing so, the Bishop of Nancy was connecting with an audience that was increasingly conceptualizing the city's popular culture as a social problem in need of reform.

Over the course of the 1840s, tens of thousands of Canadien and Irish Catholics signed the temperance pledge in Montreal, thereby committing themselves to either total abstinence or, at the very least, a significant moderation in their alcohol consumption.[35] Signing and upholding the temperance pledge was, no doubt, a matter of great personal significance. For those accustomed to the city's alcohol-drenched popular culture, this shift in behaviour would have made a transformative impact on personal relationships, the family economy, and one's reputation in their community. It was, however, a private commitment that was wrapped up in emotive public demonstrations. This began with signing the temperance pledge in a public ceremony and continued through the calendar of processions and mass meetings designed to keep Montrealers committed to the cause. Many joined brass bands that marched in parades and greeted visiting dignitaries. In marking their sobriety in such a performative way, the men and women engaged in the temperance movement were continuously marking assertions about their relationship to the broader community.[36]

There is an extensive historical literature on how the temperance movement came to carve out such a significant place in the global public sphere of the nineteenth century. It was surely the product of this era's staggering social change.[37] With the intertwined shift towards a market economy, industrialization, and urbanization, elites became particularly sensitive to what they viewed as hindrances to productivity and threats to public order. The temperance movement, however, would have been a mere shadow of itself if it had only been the preserve of social and cultural elites. In fact, the movement gained traction because it was widely embraced by the popular classes. At the same time, the movement was characterized by great diversity in both ideas and approach. These tensions would eventually come to weaken the cause. The most divisive issue was the more emotional aspects of the temperance experience.[38] While some temperance activists favoured quiet coercion and restrained language, others encouraged an approach that included street-corner evangelizing, raucous public meetings, and even violent confrontations with those involved in the sale of spirits.[39]

In a city where public drinking was a way to forge relationships, Catholic leaders were forced to think strategically in their efforts to broaden temperance's appeal. They did so by building a movement infused with the energy of the collective experience. The temperance movement in Montreal was anchored by a lively and rich material culture of banners, medals, and pins that differentiated their bearers from their fellow citizens. The ability to mark difference on the streets was significant in a city small enough that webs of affiliation and kinship played an important role in shaping how people conceived of their place within it.[40] The widespread embrace of the movement suggests that it was not simply a mechanism of exerting control over the popular classes. In many ways, it was an understandable reaction in an urban landscape where the negative consequences of excessive drinking were highly visible. The movement's public face, and particularly its bold use of the city's streets, made it a source of camaraderie and a crucial site of identity formation during a period of urbanization and social change.

The temperance movement enjoyed immediate and sustained success in Montreal and its surroundings because its appeal cut across political divides. For the clergy and the city's devout Catholics, it was an indicator of a broader embrace of the social, moral, and spiritual project of the church. Catholic Montrealers who participated in the movement were organizing their lives around the tenets of the church and its lay activism, something that would not have been imaginable on such a scale only a decade earlier. The temperance movement, however, was not the sole preserve of devout Catholics. For secular-minded Canadiens who supported the *Rouge* political faction of Papineau and the Viger family, read *L'Avenir*, and increasingly found themselves in conflict with the clergy, temperance was a hallmark of progressive reform. Drunkenness, especially in its public manifestations, was ill-suited to the modern society that secular liberals wished to foster.[41] Both Catholics and anti-clerical Montrealers frequently framed the temperance movement in the language of nascent nationalism, arguing that sobriety was essential to the survival of a French-Canadian society under British rule. With that being said, that a parallel temperance movement was flourishing in the city's English-speaking Protestant community points to an emerging consensus around temperance and public order being forged across sectarian lines during this period.[42]

As successful as Montreal's Catholic temperance movement was in mobilizing men and women to reconsider their relationship to alcohol, it was not without its complexities and contradictions. Just as Montreal elites appeared to be reaching a consensus around a vision of public order, the raucous nature of certain Catholic temperance events raised concerns in clerical circles and heckles from the city's vocal Evangelical Protestant community. This tension was most evident in the treatment of Catholic priest and temperance crusader Charles Chiniquy. Chiniquy disseminated his message through open-air rallies that drew thousands across the St Lawrence River Valley. While many Catholic leaders celebrated Chiniquy's following as evidence that Catholics were increasingly committed to creating a more orderly society, observers could not help but compare his oratorical gifts and popular appeal to the rabble-rousing Patriote leaders of the previous decade.[43] Chiniquy's *Manuel des sociétés de tempérance* was reprinted numerous times throughout the 1840s, becoming the most widely read pamphlet on the subject in French Canada. In it, the priest boasted of the massive crowds that gathered to hear him. Perhaps in reaction to those who had misgivings about these charismatic demonstrations, Chiniquy argued that the zeal of these crowds was proof of the inherent might of a temperate people. This is another example of how the politics around public order was linked with mid-nineteenth-century nationalism in French Canada.[44] In his speeches, Chiniquy argued that signing the temperance pledge was more than a simple commitment to curtail one's own indulgent impulses. With rhetoric that leaned heavily on military metaphors, Chiniquy maintained that he was assembling an army of sober men determined to overthrow the forces of drunkenness.[45] As he traveled up and down the St Lawrence River Valley, he framed his temperance crusade as a successful military campaign that had led to entire parishes choosing to go dry, and had left once flourishing inns and taverns suddenly vacant.[46] For many of Chiniquy's supporters, the widespread embrace of temperance campaigns connected the dots between public order, piety, authority, and the political aspirations of the Canadien political elite.

But these sentiments were not universally shared, even in the highest echelons of the Catholic Church. Bishop Bourget, whose strategy for expanding the social grasp of the church during this period was by no means averse to popular demonstrations of piety, tried on a number of occasions to rein Chiniquy in.[47] Bourget's deepening discomfort with Chiniquy's charismatic public performances landed the bishop some strange bedfellows. The secularly minded editors of *L'Avenir* were Chiniquy's most vociferous critics. Like many liberal activists of this period, they valued reasoned debate, and therefore raised concerns about his ability to stir the passions of large crowds. An incident in Sainte-Hyacinthe, a small town south of Montreal, served as a rallying point for Chiniquy's critics. After hearing the cleric give an impassioned address at an open-air temperance rally, a crowd descended on a local tavern and tore it down board by board.[48] Bishop Bourget also voiced concerns about the power that Chiniquy appeared to hold over young women who, it was assumed, were more easily captivated by the cleric's striking good looks and impassioned delivery.[49] Such practices could easily push the boundaries of what some considered to be proper behaviour.

The popular culture fostered by the Catholic Church in the 1840s was distinct from that of the economic elite, which placed an enormous value on restraint and decorum. The shifting gender politics of this period were visible in this distinction. Economic and other cultural elites were placing an increased emphasis on public life as an intrinsically masculine sphere of activity, where women could only intervene under a carefully policed set of circumstances.[50] In contrast, the Catholic culture emerging in the 1840s saw women pushed to the forefront of public endeavours. Women filled the pews of parish churches, embarked on pilgrimages, and flocked to religious orders.[51] The church's emphasis on introducing ritual into the quotidian experience appears to have been particularly successful at drawing women into a deeper engagement.[52] Thus while the crowd events orchestrated by other Montreal elites, like parades and celebrations held to honour the arrival of a new colonial governor, were celebrated in the English-language press for being demonstrations of restrained respectability, Catholic celebrations were characterized as being emotive, impassioned, and, in the eyes of some Protestant observers, even feminine.

Much of the social and philanthropic work that women were engaged with during this period occurred behind closed doors and was rarely discussed in the public sphere. A few exceptions to this tendency were produced by the dynamic popular celebrations of the Catholic Church. For example, in 1843 twelve hundred Montrealers were reported to have lined the streets to watch a procession of female students to the parish church, where they attended a special mass celebrating the Virgin Mary. The event garnered vociferous praise for the nuns overseeing their educations. Reporting like this legitimized not only the Catholic Church's social project but the role that women played in it.[53]

The contrast between an emerging Catholic popular culture and the more secular liberal politics articulated in other public events were often drawn during the annual celebration of Fête-Dieu, an annual religious festival marked by an elaborate procession.[54] Coverage of the 1848 Fête-Dieu procession in the Catholic press notes that it passed by an orphanage run by Mélanie Quesnel, the wife of Côme-Séraphin Cherrier, a prominent Patriote lawyer. Quesnel took the opportunity to dress her charges in their finest clothes and line them up in front of the institution, which had been decorated in the spectacular fashion that had come to mark the occasion. The impressive appearance and decorum of the children was praised. One commentator noted that they could be seen mouthing the words of the hymns being sung as the procession passed by, which was seen as a testament to the success of Quesnel's labours.[55] At first glance, there were limited opportunities for female engagement in public life in mid-nineteenth-century Montreal. Women like Mélanie Quesnel were working in areas that were understood to be particularly well-suited to them according to the gender politics of the day because of their maternal impulses. However, being recognized for supporting the church's social project may have contributed to the deepening religiosity many women expressed during this period. Catholic events regularly pushed women into the centre of public life to a degree that would have been less likely in the city's English-speaking Protestant community.

In many ways, the Fête-Dieu procession resembled the ethnic society parades that marked the city's social calendar. Columns of community members carrying banners were organized to communicate a sense of cohesion to the broader public. The presence of well-behaved schoolchildren, dressed in their finest clothes, was a nod to widely understood indicators of progress and the promise of a prosperous future. The city's residents, whether motivated by piety, curiosity, or the bonds of kinship and community, lined streets sumptuously decorated with garlands, cedar saplings, and commemorative archways.[56] The clergy and the lay activists who decorated the route drew on the symbolic language of both the secular parade and the Catholic mass to heighten each procession's emotional impact. The emphasis placed on order and discipline was explicit and persistent: men, women, and children marched in a tightly choreographed sequence, and cues to sing specific hymns at carefully selected intervals came frequently.[57] The procession was clearly planned in the context of the city's spatial dynamics. The route rarely altered from year to year. It began at the end of mass in the parish church on Place d'Armes, turned onto Commissioners Street along the bustling waterfront, then up McGill Street, where it passed the Grey Nuns' church and the newly constructed St Patrick's Church. It subsequently wound its way back to Place d'Armes along De La Gauchetière, Bleury, and Craig Streets.[58] This route circled the city along its major thoroughfares in a way that drew attention to the centrality of Catholic institutions, both with regards to public life and the built environment.

Similarly, the manner in which the procession was composed expressed the Catholic clergy's vision of the social order.[59] The procession began with members of the St Patrick Society and the Société St Jean Baptiste, respectively the fraternal organizations of the Irish and Canadien communities. They were followed by representatives of Catholic temperance societies and Catholic lawyers. Next came members of the city's male religious orders accompanied by their students, who were routinely described in the press as "little angels,"[60] and boys being educated at the Catholic college. The parade culminated with the appearance of the city's clergy, nuns being followed by priests. This order was an expression of the church's social, cultural, and institutional presence. It communicated their social vision more than words could have. The Fête-Dieu procession wove the expanding authority of the church into the urban landscape in a way that felt timeless and natural to Catholic Montrealers. This impression lent these events an undeniable political resonance during this period.[61]

Why did these rituals prove to be so popular amongst Catholic Montrealers in the decade that followed the rebellions? First, they could be easily integrated into existing webs of social interaction and affection. An eyewitness account of the 1843 procession of children enrolled in the schools operated by the Frères des Écoles chrétiennes remarked that "larmes douces coulèrent des yeux de bien des mères spectatrices d'une cérémonie qui répondait si parfaitement au voeu le plus cher de leurs coeurs."[62] For these misty-eyed women, the political and cultural implications of the procession were likely beside the point. In a city where liberal economics made daily survival a persistent challenge, the sight of their children and the children of their relatives and neighbours marching in their tidy school uniforms was powerful.

Commentators in the city's Catholic press, many of whom were priests writing anonymously, used the splendour of the Fête-Dieu procession to make assertions about the cohesion of the Catholic community. It was, an editorial on the 1846 procession argued, a dynamic testament to the power of collective acts of piety.[63] Elites were drawn to these sorts of rituals because they communicated the idea that they possessed the authority required to grind the bustle of the nineteenth-century street to a halt.[64] This feat was experienced and expressed in sensory terms. Commentators noted the visual impact of the decorations and even the distinct odours given off by the cedar saplings and incense.[65] As one 1841 correspondent remarked in poetry, the procession brought the city to a standstill and "prend soudain cet aspect enchanteur / d'une ville qui s'ouvre à son libérateur."[66] By placing an emphasis on crowd events held on the city's streets, they were consciously targeting an audience beyond those already attending mass on a regular basis. During a period when Montreal's Evangelical Protestants funded efforts to convert Canadien and Irish Catholics, this was an important intervention in the city's heated sectarian politics. In their report on the 1843 procession, *Les Mélanges religieux* called the event "un spectacle majestueux et étonnant *même* pour ceux dont l'admiration n'était pas inspirée par des idées de foi."[67] While the ritual shared some symbolic aspects

5.2 An artist's depiction of the annual Fête-Dieu procession that gives an idea of the event's scale, though it suggests that it took place on empty streets. *Place d'Armes et la cathédrale pendant le défilé de la Fête-Dieu, Montreal 1840.*

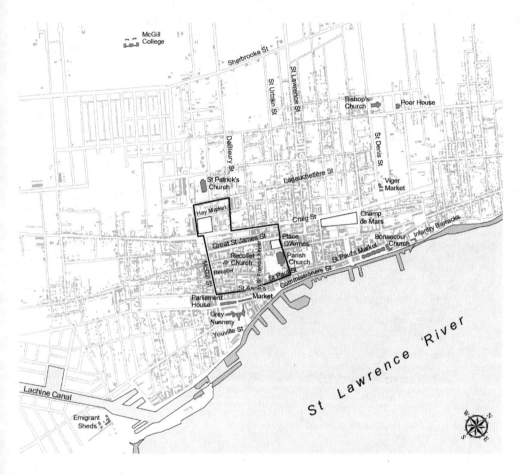

5.3 The black line denotes the typical route of a Fête-Dieu procession, designed to assert that Montreal was a Catholic city.

with secular parades, the Fête-Dieu procession must be recognized as a distinct entity that did much more to enflame sectarian tensions than other popular celebrations. It brought the ritual of the Catholic mass onto the street by parading the communion host at the head of the procession. This audacious use of public space was opposed by the Evangelical Protestant community, who saw the procession as an effort to cast Montreal as a Catholic city.[68]

Catholic commentators weighed in on the decision made by several Protestant Montrealers who lived along the route to decorate their homes for the occasion, saying that this was evidence that their church, through its rich popular spectacles, was the sole institution capable of bridging the city's combustible sectarian divide.[69] What else would prompt a Protestant to engage in a Catholic celebration in this way? Catholic and Protestant neighbours, of course, struck up friendships on street corners and over backyard fences. In addition, a Protestant might well have decorated their home for the procession not because they were toying with religious conversion but because they embraced a public celebration as an opportunity for revelry.

On the pages of the city's French-language newspapers, which offered the most vivid and detailed descriptions of the procession, Montrealers stood in awe of the spectacle unfolding on the streets each June. It was assumed that people, whether English or French, Protestant or Catholic, intrinsically understood both the political and spiritual implications of the event. What is particularly telling is that descriptions of Fête-Dieu, like those of other popular celebrations during this period, imagined the city as a stage from which the tensions and conflicts that marked daily life had been wiped clean. This was surely a falsely constructed narrative. The men, women, and children who participated in the Fête-Dieu procession in the hopes of summoning a profound spiritual experience would have done so alongside the hucksters, mischievous boys, prostitutes, drunkards, and petty thieves who plied their trades on the streets every day. When thousands of people lined the narrow and dusty streets of Montreal to observe the procession, it is impossible to imagine they did so without occasionally feeling crowded, hot, and jostled. Toes were no doubt trodden upon along the narrow footpaths, tempers and long-simmering interpersonal conflicts surely would have flared up. These sorts of details are entirely absent from published descriptions of Fête-Dieu and other manifestations of popular Catholicism during this period, thereby leaving it up to historians to keep such realities in mind when considering how the partisan intellectual and political frameworks of the nineteenth-century shaped journalistic depictions of crowd events.

This is not to say that all coverage of Catholic crowd events was charged with sectarian rancour. Despite the Protestant and Tory bent of the city's English elite, papers like the *Montreal Gazette* tended to publish brief and respectful descriptions of the procession in which they would note its route and order, while routinely complimenting organizers on the beautiful job they had done decorating the city for the event. There were, however, important exceptions to this conciliatory approach that remind us how contentious and politicized such events could be. In 1844, a group of Protestant clergymen and lay activists drafted a petition that was published in the *Montreal Gazette* and subsequently translated and reprinted – alongside indignant commentary – in the city's French-language newspapers. The petitioners prefaced their remarks by stating – rather disingenuously – that they had no intention of stirring up a sectarian conflict, before launching into a diatribe against the Fête-Dieu procession. They argued that the event violated the rights of Montreal's Protestant citizens, as it hindered their ability to carry out their own religious obligations on that particular Sunday. They described how the crowds that lined the streets to watch the procession made it difficult to venture to their own houses of worship. Those fortunate enough to successfully push through the throngs of celebrant Catholics discovered upon arrival that the din created by the steady ringing of church bells and the music of regimental bands made it nearly impossible to hold a proper religious service. The city's Protestant community had suffered this hardship for several years "with patience and silence," but the petitioners felt the time had come to place restrictions on the growing scale of the celebration.[70]

The petition concluded with two particularly aggressive assertions regarding sectarian conflict in Montreal. First, a statement alluded to the colony's shifting demographic composition. The authors argued that their stand on Fête-Dieu was all the more legitimate given the distinct possibility that Protestants would soon be the majority in the city, as they already were in Canada West.[71] Secondly, they took issue with the participation of the military's brass bands in the procession, suggesting that this amounted to official support for the Catholic Church and their political allies in the Reform faction.[72] Montrealers who encountered the text of this petition on the editorial page would have caught the veiled references to the recent parliamentary debates surrounding the Party Processions Act of 1843. Protestant activists were scandalized by the fact that Fête-Dieu, an event that they saw as an intervention in the same political conflicts as the Orange Order's activities, was permitted to pass itself off to the authorities as a religious procession.[73]

The heated response to the petition published in *La Minerve* demonstrates the connection being drawn in the public sphere between rational composure and legitimate political authority. The petition, *La Minerve* thundered, revealed the degree to which its signatories were "aveuglés par le plus absurde fanatisme."[74] What else besides an irrational hostility to Catholicism, they continued, could explain any interpretation of the annual procession as being something other than a highly respectable expression of piety? Indeed, this petition and the response that followed must be interpreted against the backdrop of a strong vein of anti-Catholicism that thrived across the North Atlantic World during this period. Upon acknowledging this, however, it is important not to cast this document aside, for it contains a valuable narrative of how popular demonstrations of piety were experienced on the streets of Montreal. While the Fête-Dieu procession was described in French-language newspapers as a respectable occasion to revel in the splendours of the Catholic faith, it is worth considering the possibility that not all Montrealers experienced these events in such a positive light. This alternative description of Fête-Dieu portrayed the procession as a loud and clamorous affair that clogged the streets with revellers and caused the city to vibrate with the unrelenting chiming of church bells and thundering brass bands.

The Fête-Dieu procession would remain a lightning rod for sectarian conflict through the 1840s. Shortly after establishing the *Montreal Witness*, an English-language newspaper that delivered an Evangelical Protestant perspective on current affairs, in 1846, editor John Dougall published a series of editorials denouncing the event. Calling the procession "an idolatrous and most unseemly celebration," Dougall insisted that "The gorgeous dresses, rich canopies, mimic angels, martial music, and in fact the whole affair savors much more of theatrical representation, calculated to dazzle and deceive the people, than of the sober, serious simplicity of the Gospel, which makes men wise unto salvation. Can any who are acquainted with the New Testament countenance such displays in the name of religion?"[75] Dougall saved his most pointed attack for the symbolic display that anchored the procession – the parading of the communion wafer through the city's streets. Other descriptions of the procession, even in the English-language press, tended to gloss over this aspect of the celebration, paying closer attention to details such as its order and route. For Dougall and his readers, this was an unpalatable act of religious heresy. Dougall referred to the communion wafer as "a God manufactured by man's hands, confined in a box, and carried about by creatures of dust and ash ... which is liable to be lost, stolen, or devoured by maggots."[76] This critique of Fête-Dieu allowed Evangelical Protestants like Dougall to draw a polarizing distinction between the two faiths. The popular culture of Catholicism was decried for being preoccupied with heavily stylized rituals, while the Protestant religious service was hailed as rational and austere. This was an important part of the intellectual framework through which Evangelical Protestants attacked the legitimacy of the Catholic Church's use of popular rituals. These assertions were being made against the backdrop of larger shifts in the political culture of the North Atlantic World, where legitimate authority was increasingly linked to one's ability to demonstrate restraint and decorum.[77]

Catholic commentators were compelled to defend the Fête-Dieu procession as a demonstration of disciplined Catholic piety again in 1849. The procession was scheduled to occur during the Rebellion Losses Crisis, and commentators in the English-language press questioned the wisdom of a large-scale sectarian celebration on the streets of Montreal, given the tense atmosphere of the city.[78] According to an anonymous source cited in the *Montreal Gazette*, government officials were pleading with the clergy to call off the procession, arguing that it made them vulnerable to attacks from

Tory thugs.[79] English- and French-language commentators walked a rhetorical tightrope in the lead-up to the procession, arguing that the event risked creating yet another outbreak of violence in the city, but maintaining that members of their own community would, of course, never engage in such acts.[80] As the celebration neared, the *Montreal Gazette* published an item regarding rumours swirling about town that some Catholics were considering arming themselves in case the procession encountered violence. The Catholic press attacked the very suggestion that participants in a sublime religious ritual would even consider the partisan conflicts of the day, and railed against the Protestant press for sullying their spiritual exercise with the taint of worldly preoccupations.[81]

This is another example of how descriptions of Fête-Dieu were filtered through a sectarian lens that left little space for nuance in the public sphere. The Catholic press' insistence that the event represented spiritual reflection was complicated by reports in the English-language press that it was customary for participants to fire rifles into the air at the conclusion of the procession. The French-language press admitted that this was the case, but insisted that it had never occurred in a spirit of provocation.[82] Given their subsequent silence on the matter, Protestant commentators appear to have accepted this defence.

During popular celebrations orchestrated by the Catholic Church, piety sometimes rubbed shoulders with boisterous popular culture. Not everyone who took to the streets to participate in the Fête-Dieu procession shared the same spiritual motivations that the clergy and their allies insisted was universal, nor did everyone share the ideological rigidity of the editorialists writing in *Les Mélanges religieux* and the *Montreal Witness*. The 1849 procession went off without a hitch, with thousands taking to the streets to partake in the revelry. Its success was widely acknowledged, with numerous commentators across the sectarian divide remarking on how reassuring it was to see crowds of Montrealers behaving in such a peaceable manner after months of sporadic violence.[83]

Engaging directly with the roughest aspects of society, particularly on the city's waterfront, was part of Bourget's strategy for expanding the church's influence. They responded to concerns about the docks and the adjoining streets where itinerant labourers gathered by making

Notre-Dame-de-Bon-Secours, a chapel on the city's waterfront, a pilgrimage site. The chapel was filled with religious iconography that referenced the mobility of the sailor's life. The finishing touch was put on the chapel in 1848, when Bourget dedicated an imposing statue of the Virgin Mary on the site. The church took this opportunity to organize an elaborate procession from the docks to the chapel. Ships docked in port were festively decorated for the occasion and, following a procession of Bourget and other lay and clerical figures, a group of sailors and dockworkers carried the ornate statue to the chapel on their shoulders while singing the hymn *Veni Creator Spiritus*.[84]

Like the Fête-Dieu processions discussed earlier, the event was portrayed in the Catholic press as a demonstration of the church's unique ability to bring beauty and order to a part of the city that was associated with conflict and tumult.[85] They questioned the motivation of any commentator who would shine a negative light on their efforts to encourage virtue, piety, and temperance amongst the city's itinerant sailors and dockworkers.[86] One commentator noted the specific context of rituals like this in the lived experience of globe-trotting sailors. These were men, he argued, who had spent their lives traveling to distant shores where they would surely have encountered Muslims "se prosterner jusqu'à terre, et adresser leur prière au grand prophète."[87] The church had a responsibility to expose these men to the beauty of the Catholic faith. "Le catholique," he argued, "ne doit pas rougir de faire pour la verité ce que le musilman fait pour l'erreur."[88] While there is much to unpack in this statement with regards to racial and religious chauvinism, such events must be interpreted in the context of the larger cultural conflict occurring in mid-nineteenth-century Montreal. Coming on the heels of more than a decade of political upheaval that was notably secular in its rhetoric, Catholic Montrealers were drawn to a religious movement that bristled with much of the same political energy and community aspiration. The growing popularity of the church's public ceremonies during this period cannot be attributed to piety alone. The decisions made by Montreal's Catholics during this period to line the city's streets for a procession, to attend a temperance rally, to play the trumpet in a brass band, or to dress their children in white gowns demonstrates that these sorts of events had become widely embraced as exercises in community formation. These events also have to be interpreted in the context of a public sphere shaped by political and sectarian conflict. The Catholic clergy and their advocates in the lay community used religious processions and public celebrations to assert themselves as legitimate authority figures in the city. They did so to counter similar claims by Protestant elites, and these competing assertions were deeply contested.

While commentators often portrayed the symbolic language of the Catholic Church's popular rituals as timeless or traditional, this project was, in fact, a profoundly modern means of projecting authority and power in an urban setting defined by mobility and diversity. Piety and support for the Catholic Church's expanding social project certainly prompted some to participate in these events, but it is unlikely that this sentiment was universally shared. For some Catholic Montrealers, these celebrations were part of a larger fabric of popular culture through which they nurtured relationships with kin and community. They were opportunities for leisure and camaraderie and sites in which to establish, assert, and defend personal reputations. In other words, the popular rituals the Catholic Church held on the streets during the middle decades of the nineteenth century helped Montrealers negotiate their place in a challenging urban environment.

When it came to how these events were received, place mattered. The politics of public space were contentious, with competing factions of the city's elite using crowd events to demonstrate their ability to wield social and cultural authority. The assertions made by Catholic commentators that the growing scale upon which events like Fête-Dieu were celebrated spoke to the broad public support that the institution enjoyed, and therefore enshrined the church's legitimacy were fiercely contested by certain elements in the city's Protestant minority. Notions of legitimate authority and appropriate public decorum became deeply politicized in the city's public sphere, and the streets of Montreal became a site where competing displays of authority were mounted. That this strategy was employed by the church as debates over democratic reform increasingly tied legitimate authority to public consent was no coincidence.[89] Thinking about the complex and contradictory ways they used the streets as a political space and how these actions were interpreted in the public sphere can shed significant light on the cosmopolitan and contentious political culture that took shape in Montreal during this period. The most dramatic example of this occurred in the spring and summer of 1849, when thousands took to the streets during the Rebellion Losses Crisis, a series of crowd events that threatened to rupture public life in British North America.

6

"A PICTURE OF AWFUL AND THRILLING BEAUTY": RETHINKING POPULAR POLITICS AND AUTHORITY IN THE MIDST OF THE REBELLION LOSSES CRISIS OF 1849

It is an image that remains iconic: Ste Anne's Market, the building in Montreal's west end that housed the parliament of the United Province of Canada between 1844 and 1849, is engulfed in flames against the night sky. Men, women, and children stand before it, seemingly enthralled by the destruction. Reprinted countless times since its first unveiling, Joseph Légaré's painting has become visual shorthand for the strong current of ethnic conflict that ran through pre-Confederation Canada. This chapter examines the Rebellion Losses Crisis of 1849, the moment when the political turbulence that had shaped Montreal for over a decade reached a staggering crescendo. It considers the impact of the crisis on the city's public life, and traces how elite interpretations of these events sowed the seeds for a style of modern governance that eschewed the politics of the street.

In the months leading up to the burning of parliament, public life in Montreal had been consumed by debates over the Rebellion Losses Act, a piece of legislation tabled by the Reform faction that, after the 1848 parliamentary elections, held the balance of power in the legislative assembly. The bill cleared the way for the colonial government to compensate residents of Canada East who had suffered property damage during the rebellions of 1837 and 1838. A similar

6.1 The burning of parliament.
Note the presence of frolicking children and curious onlookers,
often absent from historical narratives of the event.
Joseph Légaré, *The Burning of the Parliament Building in Montreal*, c. 1849.

measure had been taken for Canada West at the outset of the decade without causing a stir. The Rebellion Losses Act of 1849, however, energized members of the Tory faction and their supporters. They claimed to be distraught over the possibility that supporters of the Patriote insurrection could receive compensation from the public purse. This complaint masked a rift over larger issues of governance and represented a stunning reversal of where the colony stood at the end of the 1830s, when the Tory faction reigned triumphant after years of upheaval over the principle of democratic reform. Lord Elgin had decided to uphold the principle of responsible government at a moment when the Reform faction, with its strong contingent of Canadien and Catholic backers, held a decisive majority in parliament. To distraught Tory observers, this signalled the official abandonment of the imperial vision that privileged their community – one they had taken up arms to defend during the War of 1812 and the Rebellions.

Tories bitterly contested the assertion at the heart of the movement for democratic reform, which was that the party that held the most seats in parliament ought to wield authority without intervention from officials in London. They viewed colonial politics through a sectarian lens, and maintained that the imperial authorities needed to exercise authority – through the office of the governor – to ensure that the British Protestant community was protected. Failing to do so, they argued, amounted to ceding the ability to govern to a Canadien political class, whose loyalty to the crown had wavered on a number of occasions, without any checks on their power.[1] Rather than being the flowering of a democracy in Canada, they argued, this would be a step towards tyranny.[2]

Public meetings hosted by partisans on both sides grew increasingly raucous as the debates continued.[3] The day that Lord Elgin ventured into the city and sanctioned the Rebellion Losses Act in parliament, these simmering tensions reached their boiling point. Tories pelted Lord Elgin with rotten fruit and eggs as his carriage beat a hasty retreat to his official residence at Monklands, northwest of the city centre. The *Montreal Gazette* rolled out a special edition that was essentially a call to arms. Supporters of the Tory crusade against the bill were invited to assemble at sundown on the Champ-de-Mars, the city's old parade ground. Following a series of

incendiary speeches, members of the crowd marched in a spontaneous procession to Ste Anne's Market, where parliament was still
in session. As they chanted and pelted the windows with stones, a
handful of protestors began using their torches to set fire to a wooden
portico at the side of the building. Others in the crowd – including
a contingent of mischievous boys – bent and broke the pipes that
delivered gas to the lamps around the market. Within minutes, the
entire structure was in flames. By the following morning, all that
was left of the seat of colonial government in the Province of Canada
was smouldering ash.[4]

The burning of parliament did not signal the end of the Rebellion
Losses Crisis. Outbreaks of spontaneous popular violence would
occur at regular intervals for the better part of the spring and summer of 1849. Montrealers across the partisan divide drew strategically
on a wide range of customs of collective protest to make their case.
Residents of the city experienced both the ecstasy and the terror of
living in a city engulfed in political turmoil. This pushed questions
about crowds, popular violence, and legitimate authority to the
forefront of public life for a sustained period. The role that crowd
events played in shaping the crisis brought the disdain that many
had towards this style of political engagement into sharp relief. The
heated debates surrounding these events on the streets of Montreal
during the Rebellion Losses Crisis helped fuel a rethinking of the
relationship between popular politics and emerging notions of
legitimate authority.

The ubiquity of Légaré's painting helps perpetuate the assumption that the burning of parliament was an exceptional circumstance,
but the preceding chapters demonstrate that outbursts of popular
unrest were common in mid-nineteenth-century Montreal. For the
vast majority of the city's residents, political affiliation was rarely a
private concern expressed through quiet and rational deliberation.[5]
Elections involved pageantry that knit ethnic and political communities together and drew on customs of nocturnal protest like the
charivari. Historians have long argued that the events that unfolded
in Montreal during the spring of 1849 instigated a transformation in
Canada's political culture.[6] It would hasten the decline of the Tory
faction, whose vision of legitimacy was grounded in ethnicity rather

6.2 An engraving depicting the attack on parliament.
John Henry Walker, *Fire, April 25, 1849*.

than public consent. The Rebellion Losses Crisis had an enormous impact on Montreal. The city was stripped of its status as the capital of Canada, as public officials looked to a less turbulent environment in which to carry out the work of government.[7]

Though the Rebellion Losses Crisis would have an immediate impact on Montreal, there were more complicated shifts occurring beneath the surface.[8] The link between the rational and even-tempered man who governed with the public's consent and the wielding of legitimate political and cultural authority was being negotiated.[9] Community leaders from Montreal's competing factions insisted on their own restraint during the crisis while attacking their rivals for contributing to the violence. This crisis, as it was framed in the public sphere, became an opportunity for both Reformers and Tories to make the case that only they could wield authority effectively.

The Rebellion Losses Crisis and the burning of parliament are usually situated in a narrative about the emergence of democratic and sovereign political institutions in British North America in the lead-up to Confederation.[10] This is by no means inaccurate, and it is an important part of the history of Canada. Nonetheless, this analytical framework tends to underplay the implications that the crisis had on politics at a community level – its impact on the way people experienced urban life and social relations. Moreover, it flattens the story through the assumption that it was purely an exercise in partisan politics. As with crowd events discussed in previous chapters, our understanding of the Rebellion Losses Riot is filtered through a public sphere that placed everything in a partisan framework. This sometimes results in the motivation and cohesion of crowd events being portrayed in a simplistic manner. Eyewitness accounts suggest that the number of people engaged directly in the violence was dwarfed by the size of the crowds.[11] There were certainly deeply outraged Tories who took to the streets in search of revenge, but their ranks were likely swelled by boys and young men looking for thrills, accustomed to the city's popular pageantry.[12] Others might have arrived out of curiosity and then participated briefly in the first stirrings of protest on a lark while, conversely, outraged Tories might have abandoned the crowd because of a distaste for violence. We must not perpetuate the error of earlier scholars by imagining these crowds as homogeneous and single-minded entities.[13] The streets of Montreal were a vibrant social space, and residents from across the social spectrum were pulled onto them by excitement and novelty.

While the political fallout from the events was doubtless substantial, observers of every ideological stripe were, quite simply, dumbfounded by the severity of the conflict. While newspaper coverage of the event tended to focus on the partisan implications of the violence, the fire was often described in rich sensory and emotional language. One correspondent wrote to the *Montreal Gazette* to describe what he had witnessed as parliament went up in flames: "the whole heavens were illuminated; and the clear and beautiful blue of the firmament, with the moon and stars brightly shining, contrasting with the maddened flames and white light below, made a picture of thrilling and awful beauty, such as it is rarely the lot of the artist to look upon, and such as one that his pencil would vainly try to imitate."[14] Others recorded similarly awestruck realizations that what they had thought to be snow was actually ash raining down from the smouldering parliamentary library or how, as the flames reached their peak, the night sky was illuminated as though it was noon and not nearing the stroke of midnight.[15] These events did not fit into a tidy political narrative at first – they were disorienting. Montrealers struggled to grasp how the debate over responsible government, which had dominated public life for the better part of two decades, had suddenly escalated into such destruction and violence.

Regardless of their partisan leanings, the Rebellion Losses Crisis was a sobering experience for reform-oriented elites engaged in the project of making Montreal an orderly city. It encapsulated everything that troubled them about the city's popular culture. It was rough, loud, and seemingly spontaneous. Men and women felt unsafe walking the streets for fear of encountering marauding crowds bent on confrontation. The institutions that were meant to ensure their personal safety and the security of their property – the police, the military, and the fire companies – struggled to perform their duties. Furthermore, the domestic space of the city's elites, the sanctity of which was increasingly pivotal to their identity, was not off limits during the crisis. The homes of prominent politicians, including Louis Hippolyte Lafontaine, were seriously attacked.[16]

This stoked feelings of intense vulnerability in the city's public sphere and many struggled to envision a future that was not mired in sectarian conflict. They were concerned that Montreal – a rapidly growing cosmopolitan and democratizing city – was a project doomed to failure. This was a perspective shaped not only by their experience of daily life but also by their engagement with an emerging transnational public sphere. Throughout the 1840s, the city's French and English language newspapers connected elite Montrealers to their counterparts across the western world, and the threat of popular unrest in the swelling cities of the industrial revolution was a frequent topic of discussion.[17] When outbreaks of violence occurred in cities across Britain, Europe, and the United States, Montreal's newspapers frequently printed detailed summaries.[18] While the events of April 1849 were staggering to the Montreal public, this sort of coverage provided them with the cultural and political tools to make sense of what was unfolding.

At the same time, these events were more nuanced than many partisan accounts suggest. The narrative that placed the blame for sectarian violence on the city's popular classes was complicated by the vigorous participation of numerous elite Montrealers. When Lord Elgin's carriage was attacked as he made his way back to Monklands, it was well-to-do Tories who were witnessed lobbing rotten fruit and eggs at it.[19] At the assembly on the Champ-de-Mars, the rabble-rousing speeches delivered to the crowd about to converge on parliament were made by prominent figures like *Montreal Gazette* editor James Ferres.[20] Lord Elgin himself expressed surprise that his attackers had such a respectable appearance.[21] This view was echoed in the French-language press. An editorial published in *Les Mélanges religieux* argued that the actions of the Tory crowd were all the more troubling because the agitators did not resemble a typical "rabble."[22] *La Minerve* concurred, writing that the respectable character of the Tory rioters made the calamity of 25 April especially difficult to comprehend. "Est-it possible," they asked, "que des hommes instruits et intelligents conseillent ou approuvent une conduite aussi farouche et sauvage? Nous répondrions non si nous n'avions pas sous les yeux des preuves du contraire."[23]

If elite Montrealers were reaching a bi-partisan consensus about the discreditable nature of popular violence, why did so many engage in the tumult of the Rebellion Losses Crisis? The answer lies in the desperate mood that engulfed the community at the end of the 1840s. Not only had they been stripped of their monopoly on political power,[24] but the British government's adoption of free trade had plunged the city's commerce into a sharp downturn. Many were feeling pinched both politically and economically. While it might have been surprising for supporters of the Reform faction to see prominent Tories engaging in popular violence after having spent the past decade portraying themselves as the last bastion of law and order in the city, doing so was not altogether irrational. Like the migrant labourers working on the canal, the Tory elites who rioted during the Rebellion Losses Crisis turned to popular politics because they felt excluded from formal channels of power. Both factions crafted a narrative whose purpose was to legitimize their assertions of authority during the crisis. The Tories painted the push for democratic reform as an extension of the insurrections of the previous decade. Reformers defended their faction by arguing that it was they who were the legitimate defenders of British political values – values that the Tories had abandoned because they did not command sufficient public support. The Tories, they argued, had adopted a strategy of violence and intimidation because they could no longer wield authority without democratic consent.[25]

While coverage of the Rebellion Losses Crisis in the Montreal press was shaped by the fiercely partisan framework that defined public life in the city, there are other sources that provide us a more nuanced perspective. In the days that followed the riot, Police Superintendent William Ermatinger[26] invited Montrealers to visit his office and record depositions regarding what they had witnessed. Nearly one hundred Montrealers took the magistrate up on his offer. The depositions were intended to assist the authorities in their investigation into the events of 25 April. They provide insight into how Montrealers experienced the early days of the Rebellion Losses Crisis. They also remind us that the severity of the violence that took place on the night that parliament was burned to the ground was not expected or inevitable.

The people of Montreal experienced these events as they unfolded, and there did not appear to be a predictable end to the unrest. They were charged with excitement as rumours swirled across the city of emergency torchlight processions and attacks on the governor. Some clearly found this exhilarating, while others were no doubt terrified by the prospect.

If read chronologically, these depositions provide us a glimpse at the way that Montrealers experienced the escalating tensions in their city on 25 April. John Popham, a law student, was reading at the Mercantile Library Association when he heard a small gathering of men discussing the Rebellion Losses Bill. One of the men, who he was unable to identify, exclaimed "We'll be damned if we don't go down and kick them all out," which Popham believed referred to the members of the legislative assembly who had passed the bill. Upon hearing this, Popham packed up his belongings and rushed to parliament, where he informed acquaintances employed there as clerks that this type of talk was in the air.[27]

It was not only ambitious young professionals cultivating connections to parliamentarians who caught wind of these rumours. Men and women who earned their livelihoods on the streets encountered them as well. John Cooper was a carter who spent the morning of the 25th hustling for fares in the vicinity of parliament. He watched the attack on Lord Elgin's carriage from the doorway of Munro's Tavern, an establishment frequented by Tories. In the hours that followed, he explained in his deposition, his services were hired by J.H. Isaacson, a local notary and political gadfly with strong connections to the city's Tory elite. Cooper spent hours driving Isaacson around the city, visiting the offices and residences of a number of his political allies, including brewer George Dow. It was Cooper's understanding that the purpose of these hasty meetings was to plot the emergency meeting on the Champ-de-Mars and discuss the Tory response to Elgin's decision to grant the Rebellion Losses Act royal assent.

Many appear to have taken this opportunity to record depositions that cast themselves in a chivalrous light. Bartholomew Gugy, for example, recounted his efforts to lead a pair of women who had been seated in the parliamentary gallery to safety as stones began to rain down on Ste Anne's Market. He risked his own safety when

6.3 Lord Elgin's departure from Monklands to parliament to grant royal assent to the Rebellion Losses Bill. Francis Augustus Grant, *Lord Elgin and Staff leaving Government House for Parliament, April 1849*, 1849.

"on looking behind me I noticed a couple of women and it occurred to me that it would be proper to afford them the means of safe escape from the building."[28] Firefighter Robert Irwin testified that he had been escorting female companions home from a Methodist choir practice as the attack began, and that he had refused to report for duty at the firehouse until each of the women reached home.[29] Others noted that their primary concern that night had been the safety of their wives and children. While this was no doubt accurate, it draws attention to the importance assertions of bravery and masculine restraint played during the crisis.[30] These virtues were intrinsically connected to assertions of political loyalty and legitimacy. Henry Howard, a surgeon, recounted that, upon hearing news of the attack on parliament, he rushed to the scene to check on his brother Alpheus, who worked in the parliamentary library. He noted that his fears about his brother's safety were so strong that he thought nothing of entering the burning building. Being informed that his brother had fled to safety, Howard was exiting the building when he spotted the queen's portrait and, inspired by "a determined feeling of loyalty," he and several others removed the painting from the wall. As they handed the painting through a window in a nearby office, several rioters had to be restrained from attempting to kick the image of the sovereign.[31]

Woven through much of the reporting on the events of 25 April was the notion that rational men could sense the changing mood of a crowd and identify the moment when violence became inevitable. Charles Drolet[32] was a former Patriote who had recently returned from exile in the United States to establish a legal practice in Montreal. He had been only vaguely aware of the excitement that day but as he finished his tea and prepared to extinguish his lamps, he noticed that the noise from the public meeting on the Champ-de-Mars was growing louder. The bells of the fire trucks rang more fervently than ever and, worried that a fire might have broken out nearby, he took to the street to investigate. Drolet could not identify the speakers at the makeshift podium on the Champ-de-Mars but he could hear their words, which he described as being of the most violent nature. He strolled along the periphery of the crowd when he began to sense a shift in its mood and grasped the very real possibility of violence.[33]

6.4 A twentieth-century depiction of the attack on Lord Elgin's carriage. Duncan Macpherson, *History of Canada, Lord Elgin, Montreal (1849)*, ca. 1960.

Drolet's testimony reminds us that even as the threat of violence loomed over Montreal, the meeting on the Champ-de-Mars remained a social event that drew curious onlookers out onto the streets. While pacing around the parameters of the crowd, Drolet encountered friends and colleagues who had also ventured out to assess the situation. They followed the procession as it wound its way towards parliament, curious as to how far the agitators would go in expressing their anger. After arriving at Ste Anne's Market, Drolet stood on the southwest corner of Notre Dame and McGill Streets, removed from the direct threat of violence but close enough to the action that he was able to recount the names of local merchants and shopkeepers egging the violence on.[34] He noted that a Mr Ewing, owner of a tavern on Notre Dame Street, was crying out "Fire it! Fire the building!" to the rioters from the doorway of his establishment.[35] Drolet was riveted by the action, but others claimed to have been unable to bear witness to the extraordinary events. Before he returned to rescue his brother, Henry Howard gauged the mood of the crowd and decided that he did not wish to see what was about to occur. "That is an act," Howard declared as the rioting crowd tore into the building, "I would not even look at."[36]

While newspapers were consumed by the political implications of the crisis and the burning of parliament, Montrealers had to grapple with the personal consequences of the violence. The testimonies recorded by Ermatinger recount numerous stories of people who focused on protecting their loved ones and property from the unrest. William Bird was a cooper engaged at a shop near Ste Anne's Market. He was awoken on the night of 25 April by a colleague who informed him that it would be "noble" to report to the store to protect the merchandise should the violence on the street escalate.[37] Others reported watching the attack on parliament unfold before becoming overcome with concern for their families and possessions, and rushing through the streets of Montreal to protect their homes and businesses.

The Rebellion Losses Crisis did not begin with the attack on parliament, nor did it end there. Outbreaks of popular violence continued for several nights afterwards, and sporadically for much of the spring and early summer of 1849. The entire palette of pageantry and crowd

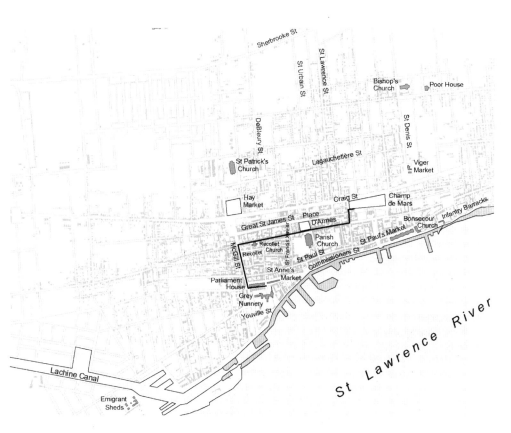

6.5 The black line depicts the route taken by the spontaneous procession
of agitated Tories and other bystanders on the night of 25 April 1849,
from their rally on the Champ-de-Mars to the parliament building.

activity was seen throughout the crisis. There were riots, spontaneous processions, and brawls. Nocturnal processions became a daily occurrence, as were raucous demonstrations in front of the offices and residences of prominent Montrealers, practices long associated with the charivari.[38] Recent migrants to the city from its hinterland as well as from rural enclaves in Ireland, however, would have been familiar with this form of extra-legal justice. Charivaris were often characterized by the donning of costumes by participants. While there are no reports of this occurring during the unrest of 1849, it was frequently noted that the nocturnal character of many of these events afforded participants a degree of anonymity sufficient to protect them from identification by the authorities.[39] This is undoubtedly why the Tories quickly adopted nocturnal processions and demonstrations as the cornerstone of their activism as the crisis began to unfold.

The severity of the attack on parliament made clear the danger posed by popular unrest and undermined confidence in the ability of the authorities to impose order on the streets. Crowds of men of both partisan stripes were organized to patrol the streets each night, a practice that many found intimidating. The Montreal residences of both Louis Hypolite Lafontaine and Francis Hincks – the former twice – were badly damaged by anti-government protestors in the weeks that followed the attack on parliament, and an attack on the home of Étienne Taché was only narrowly averted. Supporters of the Reform faction feared that a clandestine campaign was being carried out against them. Reports in the press paid attention to the strategies and the coordination of these crowds. An eyewitness account describing the first attack on Lafontaine's house, for example, described a disciplined procession of "three thousand men and two hundred boys" (almost certainly an exaggeration) marching along Saint Antoine Street to the Reform leader's house on the city's western periphery "in a very orderly manner ... obedient to one or two pairs of stentorian lungs."[40] Observers were concerned that these menacing assemblages were taking their marching orders from a leader lurking behind the scenes. There were clear links between these militant attacks and the violent rhetoric found on the pages of the city's newspapers. One editorial, for example, accused the government of being determined to drag the Canadian public "through the slime of French institutions, French ideas, and French influences."[41]

The spectre of violence loomed over Tory activism even before the attack on parliament. A letter published in the *Montreal Gazette*, for example, signed by an anonymous Tory using the pen-name "An Old Volunteer,"[42] proposed a public meeting of the city's British Protestants larger than any previous assembly, and added that the meeting ought to occur at night. This gathering of "bold and determined Saxons ... shall convince Lord Elgin, his advisors, and the French in particular, that the future has something to unfold, if the Rebellion Losses Bill be sanctioned."[43] This correspondent imitated the tone and strategy of the Tory press. They would blame the Reform government and the governor for fostering a divisive political environment where supporters of the Tory cause simply could not restrain themselves from this sort of behaviour. Despite an elite political culture that was increasingly disdainful of collective demonstrations of dissent, the *Montreal Gazette* insisted throughout the spring and summer of 1849 that there was honour in muscular protest.

The Tory press was persistent in their efforts to shift the conversation away from who had committed acts of violence on the streets of Montreal to which political faction was best equipped to restore order. This was in response to the city's Reform commentators, who argued that the actions of Tory demonstrators throughout the crisis had revealed them as unfit to wield authority.[44] All their talk of restoring calm to Montreal, Reformers argued, belied their willingness to abandon these principles when the tide turned against them.[45] Lord Elgin made similar observations regarding the Tories in his correspondence with Earl Grey in London in which he bemoaned that "reckless and unprincipled men take advantage of these circumstances to work into a fever every transient heat that affects the public mind."[46] The *Montreal Gazette*'s persistence in legitimizing and excusing the actions of the Tories who engaged in violence during the Rebellion Losses Crisis made the paper a target of the governing Reform faction. They attacked the *Montreal Gazette*'s portrayal of itself and the broader Tory community as the arbiters of respectable public behaviour while still printing editorials that were widely interpreted as calls-to-arms. In defending their actions, the editor of the *Montreal Gazette* claimed that the paper was only attempting to fulfill its journalistic responsibility to warn government officials of the profound anger coursing through the British Protestant community. If the government had simply heeded their warnings, they maintained, the legislation would have been disallowed and the crisis averted.[47] Given that their editor was amongst those detained by the authorities after delivering an incendiary address just moments before the crowd descended on parliament, it is difficult to discern just how plausible readers would have found these prevarications.

With these assertions becoming the cornerstone of public debate, Montreal crackled with political activity in the weeks and months following the destruction of parliament. Emergency public meetings were arranged under the pretence that respectable citizens needed to devise a strategy for fostering the return of a more orderly political culture. Reports of these meetings in the local press, however, suggest that few constructive proposals came out of these exchanges. Instead, they were opportunities to express community solidarity and for the leaders who organized them to cast themselves as legitimate wielders of authority.[48] Similarly, crowds continued to collect on the streets of Montreal on an almost nightly basis and political elites attempted to frame their interactions with these crowds in a way that highlighted their ability to remain composed in the face of popular unrest. The *Montreal Gazette* lavished praise on Tory luminary Bartholomew Gugy[49] when, on the evening of 28 April, he stopped a crowd of several hundred riled-up Tories from descending on the home of prominent Reform politician Étienne Taché. Gugy and a dozen unidentified acquaintances intercepted the crowd near the Haymarket and "began to expostulate with them about the impropriety of disturbing the public peace, or of destroying property and recommended them to go home quietly."[50] The crowd did just that, but not before a few hearty cheers for the queen and a triumphant march down St James Street towards Place d'Armes with Gugy held aloft on their shoulders.

As partisan newspapers attempted to piece together the events of 25 April, they remained consumed by the question of who ought to be held accountable for stirring up the passions of the Tory demonstrators. Could the events of that night have occurred without premeditation or without a central figure directing the action? Commentators from across the partisan divide were united by the notion that a small number of ringleaders should be identified and prosecuted. When the government's inquiry into the riot got under way, their attention was devoted to this undertaking. Prominent witnesses like William McDonald Dawson testified that they had seen certain demonstrators directing the crowd towards parliament. Many identified Tory rabble-rousers Alfred Perry and Alexander Courtney as having wielded authority over the crowd.[51] There were pragmatic reasons for this line of inquiry. Knowing that they would be unable to prosecute everyone, the government's strategy appears to have been to round up a few of the most notorious local agitators. There was also political utility in this strategy since by tarring their opponents as being responsible for violence, they were able to sow doubts about the Tories' ability to wield authority. It is also revealing with regard to how the public understood crowds during this period. Rather than seeing men, women, and children as a gathering of individuals with different perspectives and motivations, they were seen as a single irrational entity prone to being whipped into a frenzy by the rhetoric of a malevolent leader.

Supporters of the government do not appear to have been satisfied that so many witnesses were willing to identify Perry and Courtney as ringleaders of the attack on parliament. They had hoped to pin the blame on more prominent figures in the Tory establishment, but Perry, according to an 1849 city directory, was a frame maker and a volunteer fireman, while Courtney was the former owner of a bankrupt coffee house.[52] John Wilson, a Reform politician from Upper Canada, delivered a stirring address the day after riot demanding that investigations focus on Tories whose rhetoric about the Rebellion Losses Act had pushed men like Perry and Courtney to violence. Intelligent and educated men, Wilson argued, had a special responsibility not to arouse popular excitement.[53] Lewis Drummond crafted a stirring slogan for these suspicions in parliament a few weeks later when he thundered that "les chefs de l'émeute ne sont pas dans la rue."[54] Drummond and Wilson, and many of their allies in the Reform faction, understood that emphasizing the Tory connection to violence on the streets was the single most effective way of casting doubts on the legitimacy of the Tory cause.

Much of the give and take during the Rebellion Losses Crisis revolved around the question of transparency. These sorts of assertions were an integral component of debates about democratic reform across the globe, and discussions about popular violence were regularly viewed through this lens.[55] The violence on the streets of Montreal was construed as an attack on democratic institutions, and readers were frequently reminded that it had unfolded not only in the literal darkness of night but also in the figurative darkness of clandestine organizing. Newspapers sympathetic to the government frequently drew their readers' attention to the secretive nature of Tory strategizing,[56] which they portrayed as a betrayal of democratic politics and thus as an extension of collective violence. Judging from many of the testimonies recorded in the aftermath of the riots, it appears that government officials were actively collecting information on the nature of Tory organizing. A police officer, for example, testified that he saw unnamed "respectable" gentlemen coming and going from late night meetings at Tory haunts like Dolly's Chophouse in the Faubourg St Laurent.[57] This activity was seen as evidence that the Tories were fostering opposition to a democratically elected government that enjoyed broad public support.[58]

Montreal's Tories returned these accusations with great vigour. They argued that the social and political upheaval that gripped the city through the first half of 1849 was a direct result of the government's lack of transparency. The government's investigation into the events of 25 April, headed by William McCord, became their primary target. When McCord was appointed, the government had failed to disclose both the scope of his mandate and the budgetary resources allocated to the operation. The Tories were particularly incensed because they suspected that the government was planning to use the inquiry to destroy the careers of critics of the Reform faction.[59] McCord, the *Montreal Gazette* suggested, had been brought from his hometown of Quebec to do the government's "nasty" work.[60] The Tory press also defended the anti-government crowds who gathered nightly on the streets of Montreal for weeks after the first outbreak of violence. While the Reform faction treated these demonstrations as a menace to the fragile colonial democracy, Tories noted that they had not caused any considerable property damage since the destruction of parliament. They also argued that while the Reform press was determined to tar these young men as a threat to public order, they were in reality small groups of concerned citizens bearing witness to the government's continued bungling of the crisis.[61]

Despite their mutual animosity, the Tory and Reform press shared a similar rhetorical approach to the relationship between popular violence and political legitimacy. Tories argued that the Reform faction posed a threat to public order by organizing demonstrations of their political supremacy. Two weeks after the attack on parliament, the Reform faction had hosted a banquet at the Hôtel Tétû on Great Saint James Street. The *Montreal Gazette* described the event as a heinous provocation, and accurately predicted that it would attract a crowd of agitated Tories bent on disturbing the proceedings. Shortly after the banquet began, a crowd gathered outside and began to hurl stones at the windows of the hotel, shattering many of them. An unidentified man leaned out of the hotel and fired shots at the crowd, wounding two demonstrators quite seriously. The revelry at the banquet, needless to say, quickly drew to a close. Supporters of the government held this event up as yet another manifestation of the Tory reign of terror on the streets of Montreal. To commentators in the Tory press, however, this was evidence that arrogant Reformers were bent on flaunting their powers in ways that would perpetuate the city's sectarian tensions. "If the ministry are [sic] determined there shall be no peace in the city," thundered a *Montreal Gazette* editorial, "on their heads be all the consequences."[62]

The Montreal public encountered these competing assertions of political legitimacy on a daily basis. Many of them were grounded in rhetoric that demonstrated how ideas about race and gender were being used in efforts to exclude certain groups from the public sphere. At the end of June, they began to hear rumours that, while taking a restorative carriage ride around Mount Royal, Lady Elgin had become the target of hooting Tory louts.[63] The *Montreal Gazette* pounced on the story, which had first been printed in the *Pilot* and was subsequently reprinted and taken at face value in the French-language newspapers. They insisted that the story was the product of an overactive imagination, and an obvious attempt to slander the Tories. How would it even be possible, the *Montreal Gazette* asked, for two well-dressed gentlemen to have made their way up the mountain, as the rumour suggested, without being spotted by locals or toll-gate keepers? It seemed preposterous, the *Montreal Gazette* concluded, that someone "in the garb of a gentleman … would annoy a woman under any circumstances."[64] The controversy was short-lived, but demonstrates just how quickly competing factions of the Montreal elite were to evoke claims about masculine decorum in the midst of the broader conflict unfolding in the city.

Nobody's reputation was as fiercely contested during the crisis as Lord Elgin's. Tory attacks on the governor's decision to uphold the practice of responsible government were deeply gendered. In their continued efforts to brand the governor as a traitor to both the queen and the Anglo-Saxon race, the *Montreal Gazette* portrayed him as insufficiently masculine to stand up to the government's whims and demands. Lord Elgin, one editorial chided, had proven himself better suited to a career as "an English *schoolmistress*" than that of a British statesman.[65] Racial language was also used to attack the governor. The *Montreal Gazette* reprinted an editorial that first appeared in the Glasgow *Enquirer* arguing that Elgin's decisions proved he was unfit to govern a white settler society. In calling for his immediate removal from his post, the editorial stated that "his talents might suit to govern a nigger island, but certainly not to rule a fine and enlightened race of Anglo Canadians".[66] The Tory attack on Lord Elgin connected the dots between their critiques of the governor's character and their staunch opposition to responsible government.[67] An effectively governed colony, they argued, required a powerful Legislative Council stacked with men selected for their "good education and moral worth" and granted the power to serve as an effective check on the whims and biases of elected officials.[68] While they were not inherently opposed to an expanded colonial democracy, Tories insisted that there were decisions about governance that officials had to make without giving thought to popular consent.

Commentators sympathetic to the Reform faction, of course, saw things quite differently. Lord Elgin was hailed for maintaining his composure in the face of vitriolic and violent Tory attacks. When the carriage carrying the governor was attacked by a Tory crowd outside Munro's Tavern shortly after he sanctioned the Rebellion Losses Bill, the Reform press credited him for maintaining his *sang-froid*. They noted that he had maintained eye-contact with his attackers but had remained calm, showing only pity.[69] The governor's ability to stay above the fray had crucial implications, his supporters in the press suggested. Had he failed to do so, far more blood could have been spilled in the crisis:

> During the whole of this most painful and disgraceful scene, His Excellency, though very pale, appeared quite self-possessed, and gave no orders to the military, nor was any thing done by them to resent this usage. He bore it patiently, and, in so doing, we are satisfied did more to disarm violence than a thousand soldiers or constables could have done. Indeed, had blood been shed on that occasion, such was, we are convinced, the temper of the people, that probably several hundred lives would … have been sacrificed, and we would have been now in the very midst of a civil war of races, with partisans rushing in from all parts of the country to deluge our streets with blood.[70]

These traits continued to draw praise from Elgin's biographers in the decades that followed, with one noting that "by taking on himself the whole responsibility of sanctioning the obnoxious Bill, he had drawn down upon his own head the chief violence of a storm which might otherwise have exploded in a manner very dangerous to the Empire."[71]

Standing up to the violent actions and rhetoric of a desperate Tory faction was held up as a credit to the governor's courage, resolve, and composure, traits that were widely understood as masculine virtues. When Lord Elgin returned to the city mere days after he was first attacked and parliament was set aflame, it was held up in the Reform press as proof of his courageous dedication to democratic reform.[72] In the words of an editorial published in *Les Mélanges religieux*, the governor had proven himself to be a well-trained practitioner in the science of responsible government.[73] Navigating flare-ups of partisan and sectarian fury, they maintained, was an integral component of this science. Elgin, in his correspondence during this period, argued that remaining composed in the face of the threats that he had experienced during the crisis was simply one of the duties that had been bestowed upon him. In a letter addressed to Montreal's City Council in which he accepted their apologies for the "indignities" he had sustained, he wrote that his attention remained focused on his duties and his "desire that the perpetrators and their abettors be brought to sentiments more befitting the members of a civilized community and the subjects of a constitutional government."[74] This was a statement that, at first glance, appears to be an expression of humility and a commitment to public service. Reading between the lines, however, it was clear that Elgin was endorsing the Reform faction's interpretation of the events and, in particular, the idea that the Tories had severely damaged their reputations. The Reform faction crafted this depiction of Lord Elgin as the perfect foil to their Tory rivals, who were portrayed as unhinged and furiously clinging to political and cultural privileges that were the antithesis of their democratic ideals.

These partisan conflicts over which public figures had "kept cool" during the crisis became such a ubiquitous feature of the political landscape that they became the topic of parody in the popular culture. William Lyman and Co., a dry goods store on St Paul Street, referenced this brand of rhetoric in an advertisement that they had placed on the back page of the *Montreal Gazette*. "In times of excitement like the present," the text read, "it is especially requisite to keep cool ... we would recommend our friends to subscribe at once for ice at Lyman's, for we see by *Punch* that it is 'warranted to keep remarkably cool.'"[75] In a time and place where the public sphere rarely afforded itself an opportunity to examine the lighter side of politics, this ad demonstrates that Montrealers would have been accustomed to these assertions about composure playing a prominent role in public debates.

The most sustained and scathing parody of the public discourse around decorum came one month later, when the *Montreal Gazette* began publishing an exchange of ribald and far-fetched sendups of the Reform press' vilification of the Tories. This began after the *Pilot* reported that a gang of Tory thugs had briefly kidnapped one of their delivery boys. The *Montreal Gazette* went on the offensive by mocking the story, reporting that after gagging the boy and dragging him to an undisclosed hideaway in an east-end suburb, the thugs "stripped the flesh off his bones and, making beef steaks of it, ate him up."[76] The *Montreal Gazette* clearly found publishing light-hearted editorials to be great fun, and upped the ante a few weeks later by publishing a report that a gang of "villainous bankrupt rascals" descended upon Monklands and carried off all of the eggs laid by Lord Elgin's hens. Upon their return to the city, they kidnapped one of the new cavalry officers appointed by the government in the aftermath of the attack on parliament and hoisted him to the top of the "French Church ... where they procured a number of crows to pick his bones bare."[77]

The final instalment of the *Montreal Gazette*'s parodies was a fantastical account of William McCord and Lady Elgin being kidnapped while exiting the Donegana Hotel "by a band of political desperados ... bankrupts in fortune and standing, vocal, loyal, and commercial." The "desperados" tore off McCord's coat, slit one of his ears open, and shaved his head. They then turned their attention to Lady Elgin, playing mischievously with the strings on her bonnet, before tearing it off her head and throwing it out of the carriage.[78] This final story was the most extreme and bawdy of the three, and likely signalled how weary the city's Tories were of being denigrated by supporters of the Reform government. Farce can often be as illuminating as conventional commentary. To bring a smile to the faces of their Tory readers, the *Montreal Gazette* allowed itself to break with the conventions of the public sphere. It did so, however, in a way that emphasizes how fundamental assertions about decorum and restraint were in the renegotiation of legitimacy occurring during the crisis.

While Tory papers like the *Montreal Gazette* relished engaging in these partisan exchanges, others questioned the respectability of such pursuits. The *Montreal Witness*, the evangelical newspaper that was usually sympathetic to the Tory cause because of its strong anti-Catholic bent, published an editorial arguing that it was unmanly to invest so much energy in these squabbles. One's time was better spent tending to the spiritual affairs of the family, they insisted. The conflict between the Tories and the Reformers was a distraction that was proving damaging to otherwise happy families, friendships, churches, and social organizations. "We think it is the duty," the *Montreal Witness* chastened its readers, "of all good men to aim at allaying the present bitterness of party feeling by mutual forbearance, and avoiding as much as possible exciting topics on either side."[79] Their words might have appeared out of step with the heated politics of the Rebellion Losses Crisis but would prove influential in its aftermath, when many commentators alluded to the steady moral guidance that men needed to practice as the heads of families.[80]

The events also raised concerns about the effectiveness of the institutions charged with safeguarding the public. That a relatively small crowd was able to storm the locus of British authority in North America and burn it to the ground was taken as a dramatic indicator that the police were unable to maintain order in the city. Not surprisingly, assertions about the failure of these institutions were deeply partisan. Montrealers pouring over the details of the riot returned frequently to the question of whether it could have been prevented. This was a moment where many institutions, like the police, the civic government, and the garrison were either relatively new or else in the process of re-negotiating the contours of their jurisdiction. Should troops have been summoned sooner? Would a larger and more robust police force have been able to turn agitated protestors back from Ste Anne's Market? As outbursts of sectarian violence continued on an almost nightly basis in the city, many concluded that the events of 25 April were not exceptional but evidence of a systemic breakdown of authority.

Critiques of the police, the fire companies, and the troops circled around the issue of partisanship. These institutions were not neutral observers. The failures that occurred the night that parliament was destroyed, like those of the preceding decade, were widely understood as a product of their partisan inclinations.[81] Many of the fire companies, for instance, were made up entirely of either Canadiens or British Protestants. They included in their ranks men who were deeply engaged in the city's popular politics.[82] Eyewitness accounts of the hours leading up to the rally on the Champ-de-Mars noted that companies sympathetic to the Tory cause careened through the streets ringing their bells to alert English-speaking Montrealers about the gathering.[83] Others reported a less than vigorous response to the unfolding emergency. At a meeting held the following day, Henry Boulton, a politician from Upper Canada, recalled seeing hundreds of the city's volunteer firefighters standing with arms folded as the fire swept through Ste Anne's Market. He reminded his audience that these were men who regularly put themselves at risk to save the lives and property of fellow citizens.[84] Others chimed in with even more damning accusations, insisting that English-speaking fire companies had actively prevented Canadien fire companies from reaching the scene until it was too late to salvage the building. Auguste Desnoyers, a carter who served in a Canadien company, testified that after becoming aware of the fire he had rushed down St Paul Street towards parliament. As he approached McGill Street and Ste Anne's Market, his passage was blocked by a group of men armed with sticks and guns whose sole purpose appeared to be preventing firemen from reaching the blaze. Desnoyers, driven by a sense of duty, persisted in his efforts, and thereby found himself on the receiving end of an assault that also saw his hose and other tools destroyed.[85] That supporters of the Tories behaved in such a way during a crisis that threatened the colony's democratically elected institutions was, according to supporters of Reform, evidence of the degree to which they were willing to renounce the public good for the sake of partisanship.[86]

The most prominent target of these complaints was Alfred Perry, the captain of the Hose, Hook, and Ladder Fire Company. With connections to the Orange Order and an apparent knack for community organizing, Perry had long been amongst the most bellicose Tory activists in the city. On the night of 25 April, he delivered a fiery address to the crowd gathered on the Champ-de-Mars, and numerous eyewitness accounts placed him at the head of the procession from the rally to Ste Anne's Market.[87] Perry was one of the few arrested in the aftermath of the attack, though the charges against him did not stand up in court. He owed his escape from the law's clutches to a handful of defenders who were able to sow doubt about his involvement in the fire. Thomas Robinson, a confectioner and fellow volunteer fireman, testified that Perry had been by his side for much of the evening, working doggedly with a group of firefighters to make sure that the flames did not leap onto the roofs of adjoining buildings.[88]

The *Montreal Gazette*, in its deeply partisan coverage of the events, defended Perry and others like him being criticized in newspapers sympathetic to the government. The primary task of firefighters was to make certain that the flames did not spread to private residences in the area and, the *Montreal Gazette* editorial stated, they deserved credit for working with their "usual zeal" to contain the fire.[89]

The Tories also made much of the government's decision not to summon the troops. Allan MacNab, a Tory member of parliament from Upper Canada, noted that he rode a cab through the streets shortly before the crowd on the Champ-de-Mars began their march towards parliament, and that it was clear to him that serious trouble was brewing. The steady peeling of fire bells and the knots of onlookers milling about were clear indicators of the "the probability of a row." The Reform faction, he and other Tories insisted, should have ascertained this and immediately ordered the troops to protect important sites.[90] Other prominent officials indicated that they had felt similar concerns. Francis Hincks, the editor of the *Pilot*, recalled walking down Beaver Hall hill with Benjamin Holmes and immediately sensing that the mood had turned violent. The two prominent Reformers darted towards the Tétû Hotel, where police superintendent William Ermatinger lived, to warn him of the "excited state of feeling" in the streets.[91] Other eyewitness accounts published in the *Montreal Gazette* noted that bystanders were surprised that troops had not been called to the scene, given the tensions that had been escalating in the city for months and how they had reached a boiling point with Lord Elgin's decision to uphold the principle of responsible government.[92]

Government officials, of course, contested this take on events. In his deposition, John Taylor, the chief office clerk to the Legislative Council, reported that as the Tory procession towards parliament began, he was ordered to call the regiment to duty. Upon exiting the east door of Ste Anne's Market, however, he was surrounded by a group of menacing men who called him a spy and threatened him with bodily harm if he took another step in the direction of the barracks. This exchange delayed Taylor, and by the time his cab wound its way through the gathering crowd and across town, the attack on parliament was already underway.[93] Meanwhile, Lord Elgin, in a dispatch to Earl Grey at the colonial office in London, speculated that the absence of troops on the streets during the initial outbreak of violence likely prevented a great deal of bloodshed.[94] The tendency of the troops to react severely to agitated crowds over the preceding two decades had led to fatalities.[95] It is fair to speculate that, had troops been stationed at Ste Anne's Market before the Tories descended upon it, they might have been ordered to fire on the crowd.

As unrest continued to plague Montreal, it became clear that the institutions established to promote public order were struggling. When a crowd of Tories descended on Lafontaine's residence at the end of April, eyewitness accounts portrayed the police force as largely ineffective. When two officers arrested a man suspected of stealing silverware during the demonstration at Lafontaine's home, a crowd of six or seven English-speakers armed only with sticks attacked them, warning the officers to mind their own business.[96] The suspect escaped during the mêlée. Not every act of resistance towards the authorities was violent. When troops were stationed in front of a building housing government offices, they were mocked and harassed. A correspondent writing for the *Witness* reported that a crowd spent the better part of the day "marching when they marched, countermarching when they countermarched, and facing about. [All of this was] accompanied with laughter and often repeated cheers."[97] The Tory press suggested that the troops were failing at the principle task assigned to them – protecting the government officials attempting to carry out their duties in the midst of the crisis. When officials attempted to exit the building, the troops were unable to prevent them from being kicked and pelted with rotten vegetables.[98] These actions were consistent with reports in the Reform press that supporters of the government were being roughed up by these same crowds of men and boys as they attempted to make their way along Notre Dame Street.[99]

While the Tories critiqued the colonial government for hesitating to call out the military on the night of 25 April, they also heaped scorn on the municipal government for swearing in 200 special constables in the aftermath of the attack on parliament. Again, these actions were interpreted through a partisan lens. The Reform press presented this decision as proof that the authorities were taking decisive action to protect the city from Tory crowds. The Tories, meanwhile, were outraged that the municipal government was bankrolling a supplementary force that was, for all intents and purposes, a hastily assembled Canadien militia. They warned their supporters that these men were "armed to the teeth."[100] The swearing-in of these special constables confirmed one of their most frequently articulated concerns about responsible government: that the moment its advocates took hold of the reins of government, they would harness their power to suppress their political rivals.

Reports after the swearing-in of these special constables suggest that rather than restraining the Tory crowds on the streets of Montreal, their presence acted as a provocation. Reports were published in both the French- and English-language press of crowds of axe-wielding Tories confronting the constables, who returned gunfire in the ensuing mêlées.[101] Depositions recorded by some of these special constables suggest that their lack of training when confronting the fury of the crowds filled them with an overwhelming sense of vulnerability. Fleury St Jean, a law student who briefly served in the force, described how, within hours of being sworn in, he was ordered to join a contingent of thirty guarding the armoury at Dalhousie Square from a crowd of approximately 600 Tory men and boys. The special constables were able to hold their line with minimal gunfire, but the threat of being overwhelmed coloured their every move.[102]

After a handful of confrontations between the special constables and Tory crowds, the municipal government voted to disband the force under the pretence that the crisis was dissipating.[103] This would not be the last attempt, however, to augment the presence of law enforcement on the streets of Montreal during the crisis. The colonial government was the next to take up the challenge. Within a month of the attack on parliament, they established a new police force of roughly one hundred men, overseen by William McCord. Word of the new force spread when witnesses saw them conducting training exercises in La Prairie, a secluded parish across the St Lawrence River. They made their first appearances on the streets of Montreal in early June. Not surprisingly, the Tory press attacked the legitimacy of this newly established body, holding it up as an example of government overreach. Many of these attacks were carried out in a mocking tone. They cracked jokes about the colonial force's practice of patrolling the city streets at night in pairs. "They must," the *Montreal Gazette*'s editorial chuckled, "be afraid of goblins." In the sharp critique that followed this humorous hook, the editorialist's chief complaint was that the force appeared to devote most of its energy to protecting the homes and offices of government officials while the rest of the town was left to fend for itself.[104] The Tories saw the entire process around this new force – their hasty establishment, the secretive training in the countryside, and their nocturnal patrols – as evidence of the government's clandestine and heavy-handed efforts to quash dissent. Upon word that the colonial and municipal police forces had quickly become entangled in feuds over jurisdiction, the Tory press surmised that the reestablishment of order on the streets of Montreal would only occur when the government ceased its meddling.[105]

While the Tory press spun this unrest as evidence that the government was incapable of wielding authority, the Reform press suggested that the Tories were attacking the legitimate institutions of an elected government. Reform parliamentarian John Cameron declared that these Tory crowds contradicted the laws and customs of civilized society.[106] A correspondent reporting in *Le Canadien* concurred, accusing the crowds of keeping the city on the edge of a complete breakdown of public order. "Il faut voir et entendre ces hordes d'incendaires," he wrote, "pour se faire une idée de l'état dans lequel est maintenant la capitale."[107] *La Minerve* published an editorial unpacking the psyche of the Tory rioter, warning their readers that the men currently holding the city in a state of siege were blind to everything but their own prejudices and bigotries, and had become "machines" capable of inflicting untold destruction.[108]

There is no doubt that the Reform faction was pushing this line of argument because it was effective as partisan boilerplate. Assertions about who was best equipped to wield authority had become the focal point of public life in the city. With that being said, these assertions should not be dismissed as mere rhetoric. Like the striking canal workers discussed in chapter 3 and the partisan crowds that took to the streets during elections discussed in chapter 4, Montreal's Tories were drawing on longstanding customs of popular politics to make their voices heard. Engaging in crowd events was a strategic attempt to assert their power in the community and to communicate that they remained a viable political force. Their actions would surely have been intimidating to their political rivals. They were menacing and boisterous, and where institutions like the military, fire companies, and the police had been unable to effectively contain outbreaks of popular violence in recent memory, it is hardly surprising that their actions raised concerns.[109]

Montreal's public sphere consistently viewed decisions about policing through a partisan lens. This obscures the degree to which both Tories and Reformers disliked the burden that increasing spending on policing placed on the public purse. Given the economic downturn that had formed the backdrop for the crisis, the augmented force approved by City Council became a contentious issue.[110] The Police Commission wrote to City Council at the end of May to express their thanks for allocating funds to place extra constables on patrol. They noted, however, that it was becoming clearer by the day that additional money would be needed to uniform the new recruits. "The new force," they wrote "cannot be of much efficiency so long as they continue to be differently clothed from the old police force."[111] By mid-June, as concerns about popular violence slowly abated and financial realities set in, the Police Commission abandoned their hopes that this augmentation of their ranks would be made permanent.[112] When Alderman Bell and one of his constituents, a Mr Jones, tabled an unrelated petition calling for some officers to be hired to patrol the land adjacent the Lachine Canal, the response was distinctly that of an institution attempting to shed financial responsibilities. They were told that rather than relying on the municipal police force to address their concerns, they ought to ask the Harbour Commission to step up its patrols. The Police Commission also criticized the public for developing unrealistic expectations.[113]

The systematic failure of the police, the military, and the fire companies to restore order both on 25 April and in the weeks and months that followed prompted a great deal of handwringing. For supporters of the Reform faction it seemed that, after a decades-long struggle for democratic reform, the rule of law was now under outright attack from Tory sympathizers unwilling to cede the reins of power. On 11 May, *Le Canadien* ran an editorial with a headline that captured the mood of government supporters during the crisis: "L'émeute régne et gouverne toujours à Montréal."[114] Tories, meanwhile, argued that the actions taken by the Reform faction since taking power in 1848 proved that it was determined to govern tyrannically by removing imperial oversight. Both sides insisted that they were uniquely equipped to serve as stewards of democracy.

These competing claims about who was fit to govern in the aftermath of the attack on parliament were frequently wrapped in assertions about loyalty. For supporters of the government, all the partisan back-and-forth over the Rebellion Losses Crisis boiled down to one question: Could the actions of an outraged crowd be simultaneously violent and loyal? From their perspective, the Tory crowd who pelted the governor's carriage with eggs, dead rats, and rotten fruit were attacking British institutions and the rule of law. Reformers even drew comparisons between the Tories and the *sans-culottes* of the French Revolution.[115] The crisis thereby presented those associated with the Reform faction an opportunity to cast themselves as the upholders of public order.[116] This came after decades during which advocates for democratic reform had been portrayed as a threat to colonial stability. In the public discourse occurring during the Rebellion Losses Crisis, loyalty was measured in large part through the way that people conducted themselves on the city's streets. In the decades since the Conquest, Montreal's Tories had portrayed themselves as the staunch defenders of the colony's British connections. Tory commentators and politicians frequently linked the legitimacy of their authority to their record of taking up arms to defend the crown, most notably during the War of 1812 and the rebellions of the 1830s. The attack on parliament, supporters of the government argued, threw this legacy into doubt. Louis Joseph Papineau, himself no friend of the Reform establishment, argued that Tory loyalty was but a thin veil draped over a penchant for ethnic and political domination.[117]

The Tories took issue with this interpretation. The persistent outbreaks of violence on the streets of Montreal throughout the spring and summer of 1849 were, they argued, blinding many to the real threat to public order. Canada, they argued, was being overseen by a governor too weak to serve as an effective check on an elected government that included men who had, in living memory, taken up arms against the crown.[118] The opponents of the Rebellion Losses Bill, a *Montreal Gazette* editorial argued, were the same men

> who at the outset of the Rebellion, when called upon by [Lord Elgin's] predecessors ... rallied around the Union Jack without pausing to consider the force to which [they] would be opposed ... impelled only by the impulse which animated the loyal population of Canada, during that unhappy period, to crush all attempts made against our glorious constitution, to frustrate the endeavours of bad men, who would subvert the Government, and sever our connexion with Great Britain, impelled, your Excellency, by the stern resolve of Britons, to uphold the honour and dignity of the Crown in these Colonies.[119]

Tory commentators doubled down on their insistence that only they possessed the perspective necessary to govern the colony effectively. The policing of popular violence was of paramount importance here. When faced with the possibility that Lord Elgin would summon the troops onto the streets of Montreal to crack down on Tory crowds, a *Montreal Gazette* editorial thundered that such an order would mark the end of a longstanding and once fruitful partnership between the crown and Montreal's British Protestant community. "The Empire will weep," they stated, "when it sees the day that the British bayonet is used against the loyal subjects of the Queen, to support a French domination in a British colony."[120] Anti-French sentiment was never far beneath the surface of these assertions. Anglo-Saxons, they argued, possessed the commercial outlook, training, and other personality traits that made them well-suited to the challenges of colonial governance.[121] The Canadiens, meanwhile, were portrayed as lacking these traits. "They hate knowledge, they dread enterprise; and they live accordingly in indolence and poverty," read one particularly visceral outburst on the pages of the *Montreal Gazette*.[122] Rather than granting royal assent to the Rebellion Losses Act, another editorial insisted that Lord Elgin, having observed the Reformers in action, ought to declare Canada an "English Province" where "French laws, French tenures, and French ideas must go to the wall."[123] While Reformers were portraying the actions of the Tories as an attack on public order, Tories framed their actions as employing violence in defence of the crown. There was honour, Tories insisted, in taking up arms against the abuse of power – be it imperial officials in London abandoning longstanding alliances in the colonies or supporters of a government bent on overstepping its authority.[124]

As the spring of 1849 turned to summer, Benjamin D'Urban, the military commander whose celebrated half-century career included a stint as the governor of the Cape Colony, where the port city of Durban bears his name, was found dead in the bathroom of his suite at Montreal's Donegana Hotel.[125] The following day, the *Montreal Gazette* printed a notice asking the city's "British inhabitants [to] turn out *en masse*" at eleven o'clock for the funeral procession, which would wind its way from the hotel to the military burial ground.[126] Businesses in the city were expected to close their doors for two and a half hours in order to pay tribute to D'Urban. The *Montreal Gazette* used this occasion to make a political point when it highlighted the difference between D'Urban's career as a "gallant old soldier" and "a tried servant of our Gracious Queen" and the actions of Lord Elgin and the government.[127]

Given the partisan rancour that gripped the city, this procession could have led to another confrontation. In the end, however, it was a muted and solemn occasion. Crowds lined the streets along the one-mile route and filled the burial ground.[128] Flags were hung at half-mast and a solemn silence hung over the city. The procession knit together representatives of D'Urban's public and private life. Four military regiments accompanied the coffin down Notre Dame Street, followed by politicians, public officials, students and professors from McGill College, the deceased's servants, and, bringing up the rear, a throng of mourning citizens.[129] The only quibble mentioned in the *Montreal Gazette* was that Lord Elgin did not lower the flag at Monklands to half-mast, which they claimed broke with official protocol. The Reform press deemed the event charming and remarked that it was a delightful contrast to the scenes of disorder all spring.[130] An editorial in *La Minerve* noted that the orderly nature of the event was a testament to the work of the police, given that sinister gangs of Tory roughs continued to prowl the streets in search of trouble.[131]

6.6 Benjamin d'Urban's funeral procession.
The image can be read as a celebration of order
and authority in the midst of the Rebellion Losses Crisis.
James Duncan, *The Funeral of General d'Urban*, 1849.

That D'Urban's funeral procession was carried out without any public reports of violence suggests that the crisis was drawing to a close. One week later, the city's Catholics marched in the annual Fête-Dieu procession, discussed in the previous chapter. While nerves were on edge in the lead-up to the event, and there was sparring in the press as to whether this was an appropriate use of the city's streets given the continued threat of violence, it too went off without a hitch. Violent outbursts continued to occur sporadically through the summer. Two short yet severe tumults broke out in August, the first when nine men were arrested and charged for their role in the attack on parliament.[132] The second occurred when Louis Hypolite Lafontaine arrived at the Cyrus Hotel to testify at a coroner's inquest into the death of William Mason, the son of a local veterinary surgeon shot by a military guard protecting Lafontaine's home from attack. Just as he was giving his deposition, the hotel was attacked and set on fire by Tory demonstrators.[133] Lafontaine managed to escape thanks to the help of some soldiers on the scene.[134] The attack on the Cyrus Hotel was the last major outbreak of violence on the streets of Montreal connected to the Rebellion Losses Crisis.

This by no means suggests that Montreal's Tories now calmly acquiesced to the vision of colonial governance shared by the Reform faction and Lord Elgin. The second half of 1849 saw the emergence of the annexation movement, which advocated severing Canada's ties with Britain. Many in the British Protestant community, especially those whose livelihoods depended on the vitality of transatlantic commerce, argued that the imperial government's adoption of free trade had made the survival of Montreal's economy dependent on forging stronger ties with American markets. Unlike the conflict over responsible government, the annexation movement was not sectarian. Canadien and Irish Montrealers engaged in the politics of republicanism were also drawn to the movement and Papineau's Institut Canadien was a hotbed of annexationist organizing.[135] Despite attracting an initial burst of public attention, however, the movement was short-lived. By the first months of 1850 it was apparent that support was softening. The majority in the Canadien community were pleased with the survival of responsible government, and were persuaded by conservative commentators and the Catholic clergy that annexation posed a threat to their survival.[136] Meanwhile the British Protestant merchants who had been behind the Tories during the Rebellion Losses Crisis were placated by the reciprocity agreement between the colonial government and the United States, which allowed them greater access to American markets while remaining subjects of the crown.[137] French and English-speaking annexationists held a number of public meetings in the autumn of 1849, but this movement was essentially removed from the culture of the streets. As passionate as annexationists might have been, they saw the issue as fit for rational deliberation, not for popular demonstrations. Tory elites might have been rehabilitating their reputations through assertions of composure and restraint during these debates.

A number of historians have argued that the unrest of 1849, and the attack on parliament in particular, spurred a turn away from rough popular politics.[138] It is important to note, however, that attitudes towards the place of popular politics in public life did not change as quickly as the flames that consumed Ste Anne's Market. They were rooted in a more drawn-out and contentious cultural shift that linked legitimate authority to a vision of rational masculine citizenship. The same cultural changes that were prompting community leaders to assert their authority through parades and processions were also reinforcing the marginalization of a sizeable majority of Montrealers – including women, the poor, the Indigenous, and racial and ethnic minorities – from public life.[139] Changing cultural attitudes towards power and legitimacy were reflected in the rethinking of institutions at the colonial and civic level. The adoption of responsible government and the re-establishment of municipal authority allowed male elites to wield a previously unheard-of degree of social and political influence.[140]

The Rebellion Losses Crisis forced the city into a reckoning with the question of what constituted legitimate political engagement. It had become evident by the end of 1849 that spontaneous manifestations of popular politics no longer fell within these contours. The Tories had attempted to carve out a limited space where such acts could be construed as respectable, but their political demise suggests that these efforts did not gain traction. There would be sporadic outbreaks of collective violence on the streets of Montreal for decades to come – it was engrained in the city's popular culture.[141] What changed however, was the relationship between violence and public life. The culture of the popular classes was increasingly conceptualized in elite circles as a social problem that could be policed through the criminal justice system. This transformation was not natural or inevitable but the product of determined political action on the part of liberal elites working to create a new social order. Public figures from across the partisan and sectarian divides were united in their efforts to distance themselves from the rough popular culture that surrounded them. The messages communicated in parades and public celebrations, and in reactions to outbreaks of popular violence, gave weight to the deeply gendered, classed, and racialized notion that in a democratic society, a man who behaved in a specific way was best equipped to hold the reins of authority. While politics might have become far less combustible in Montreal as a result, many found themselves pushed to the margins of public life by this idea.

Conclusion

ON THE STREETS
AND LOOKING FORWARD
AS A TURBULENT DECADE
DRAWS TO CLOSE

In the middle of the nineteenth century, the streets of Montreal became a contentious political space. On these narrow, dusty, and muddy roads, a conflict took shape between an aspirational cohort of elite liberal reformers and a dynamic and racially diverse popular class. *Taking to the Streets* continues a long historiographical tradition of treating the middle of the nineteenth century in Montreal and what came to be the province of Quebec as a crucial moment of social change. Historians Brian Young,[1] Jean-Marie Fecteau,[2] Bettina Bradbury,[3] Donald Fyson,[4] Robert Sweeny,[5] Mary Ann Poutanen,[6] and Allan Greer[7] have studied this time and place to examine the conflicts surrounding the transition to liberal capitalism. These works pursue questions around power, privilege, property, and politics. They trace the impact that industrialization, urbanization, gender, citizenship, property, law, and democracy have had on people who lived in Montreal and its environs, and the institutions created to foster prosperity, religiosity, and public order.

Taking to the Streets builds on their work by looking at a specific space – the street – as a means of reflecting on this period of intense social change. It was the material and rhetorical experience of the street that prompted reformers to target a range of longstanding practices at the heart of how the men, women, and children of the popular classes made ends meet and forged connections to a community. We glimpse the complexity of the era's social changes and the resistance that reformers encountered from those with street-based strategies of community formation and survival. How the streets were used as a political space posed a challenge to an emerging liberal elite that eyed collective action warily and sought to do away with cultural practices they viewed as impediments to progress and prosperity. This study explores ways that the street was envisioned both as a space drawing attention to emerging notions of modernity and order, and also one where longstanding popular customs and strategies could persist. In the midst of social change, the streets of Montreal communicated assertions about legitimate social, political, and cultural authority to a cosmopolitan community. Crowd events like parades, celebrations, religious processions, and riots were not sporadic outbursts but rooted in the rhythms of daily life. The street was a site where the conflict between the social vision of liberal reformers and the moral economy of the popular classes often came into stark relief.[8] This was a highly complex process that draws our attention to the unpredictable nature of social change. The lines between rough and restrained were not always drawn clearly. Members of the city's migrant popular classes clearly embraced the parades and processions orchestrated by different segments of the city's elite, while many of these elites were themselves no strangers to the rough and tumble aspects of the city's popular culture. The streets were a place where the emerging powers of the city's bourgeois elite were most evident but, conversely, they were also a space of resistance towards the multifaceted project of reform.

Following the Rebellion Losses Crisis, a turbulent decade drew to a close in Montreal. To walk its streets during these months was to engage viscerally with the social and political transformation unfolding in the city.[9] The streets were more than the city's built environment; they were a space where social power was displayed and contested. They were sites of memory, where remnants of the city's past butted up against the promise of its future. Walking a short distance, it would have been possible to see both the vestiges of the small colonial outpost that Montreal had been at the beginning of the nineteenth century and evidence of the industrial metropolis it would become in the second half of the nineteenth century. Monuments to the city's commercial prosperity, in the form of the stately head offices of banking and insurance companies along Great St James Street and posh stores lining McGill Street, would have been juxtaposed with boarded-up windows that signalled its recent economic malaise. Strolling the streets would unleash a flood of memories for those who had lived in the city for any period of time: a tavern on Commissioners Street where the bonds of friendship were fostered over drinks; a street corner where a romantic connection was ignited during a parade; a public square where one intervened to help a friend being pummelled by supporters of a rival candidate. In a city where the vast majority of residents spent a considerable portion of their days and nights outdoors, the streets mattered on both a political and personal level.

The centrality of nineteenth-century streets as a social, cultural, and political space comes into sharper focus when considering the attention paid to them by those who wielded civic authority. Municipal officials had been granted significant new powers by the Special Council at the outset of the decade, and they used this authority to work towards making a more orderly city.[10] Softening the edges of a raucous popular culture was a daunting challenge to civic leaders, and they tapped into transatlantic discussions on the subject in search of innovative ideas. Strolling through the streets of Montreal during this period, one would have been struck by the increased presence of police officers on patrol.[11] Wielding these new tools of civic authority was not an easy task. With boisterous celebrations spilling out of taverns and brothels, carters coming to blows over fares, soldiers passed out on footpaths after nights of boozy celebration, and shoplifting lads scurrying away from merchants, exercising authority on the streets of Montreal was always difficult. Reports of police officers being assaulted and prisoners being rescued by their supporters also remind us that popular resistance was an intrinsic component of daily life.[12]

Hiring billy-club-wielding police officers to walk the beat, however, was not the only means that civic elites had at their disposal to communicate their vision of public order to the broader community. As I have shown, the 1840s brought about an uptick in the number and scale of parades that wound their way through the city's streets. Although mid-nineteenth-century Montreal lacked the grand boulevards being carved through European capitals like Paris in order to stage symbol-laden parades,[13] thoroughfares like Great St James and McGill Streets were regularly transformed into procession routes through the use of garlands and ceremonial archways. Parades can be read by the historian in a number of overlapping ways. First, they were an opportunity for segments of the city's elite to celebrate their cultural, political, and economic progress. Politically speaking, they were a means of fostering public support or the appearance thereof to further a political agenda. This was an important task in an era of democratic reform. What is more, parades provided licence for revelry. They were festive occasions where Montrealers from all walks of life could mingle with friends, neighbours, and family.[14] Those marching in the parade would be cheered on. In all likelihood, though it was never reported in the local press, these crowd events could also provide an opportunity to bellow a crude remark or two at one's social betters. Finally, what made parades an effective political tool was that in a city where circulating through the streets could be the most onerous challenge of daily life, elites could use these occasions to assert that their respective national or religious community was best equipped to wield authority. A well-orchestrated parade was leveraged as evidence that its organizers could turn the streets into a disciplined space, even if only for a matter of hours. This delivered an important message about legitimacy and power in the midst of the political and sectarian conflicts of this turbulent decade.

The resonance of the parade in this cultural landscape is made evident by the way that it was adopted by groups from across the city's social fault-lines. Both Canadien and Irish advocates of democratic reform hosted elaborate parades to mark their respective national days of celebration. These events provided an opportunity for community leaders to make public demonstrations of their masculine restraint. It was not only economic elites who found these sorts of events a useful means of defending their interests. Migrant labourers working on the Lachine Canal leaned on customs rooted in agrarian protest, like boisterous nocturnal processions, to make their voices heard. For the urban industrial working-class that was just beginning to take shape, the streets were a place that they could make their presence known, lodge appeals for public sympathy and support, and intimidate those seen to be standing in their path. Finally, the Catholic Church – an institution whose vision of social order occasionally clashed with that of the economic and cultural leaders who organized the St Jean Baptiste and St Patrick's Day celebrations – also leaned heavily on popular customs. At the outset of the 1840s, the church harnessed the cultural and political vacuum opened by the collapse of the Patriotes in the rebellions of 1837 and 1838 to create a larger social space for itself in the city and colony.[15] The church began to wield more clout politically and institutionally.[16] They used interventions in street culture to draw more Montrealers into the fold. By the end of the decade, Catholic Montrealers were attending mass more frequently, lining the streets to watch processions like the annual Fête-Dieu, and participating in other rituals like the stations of the cross, pilgrimages, and religious retreats. These events articulated an idea that was also being delivered from the pulpit during mass: that the Church could serve as an anchor for people struggling with the challenges imposed by the urban experience. It would be a comfort for the labourer toiling on the docks, the migrant overcome with the strain of displacement, and the mother struggling with the unrelenting demands of providing for a family. For both the Irish and the Canadiens, the Church's calendar of cultural events could serve as a rallying point. An institution looking to expand the contours of its authority had to engage with the city's street culture. The Church's ability to do this effectively played a pivotal role in the development of a vivid and experiential brand of Catholicism that shaped public life in Montreal deep into the twentieth century.[17]

Despite the best efforts of different factions of the elite to communicate their vision of an orderly city, Montreal remained an unruly place. On the precipice of industrialization, it was a commercial city. The waterfront was its economic heart, and it was a place where migrants took up gruelling labour. Cacophonous taverns lined Commissioners Street, which looked out onto the waterfront.[18] But while it might have appeared discordant and disorderly to the uninitiated, this popular culture was rooted in strategies employed by economic migrants to navigate a landscape defined by mobility and precarity. Many of the men working at the docks were looking to earn money to continue their migratory journeys. They were joined on the streets of Montreal by, amongst others, British soldiers stationed at the garrison and women who relied on prostitution to make ends meet. Businesses in the city, from boarding houses to brothels and taverns, catered to this transient population. Daily life for these Montrealers was rarely sequestered into cramped private spaces. It was lived exuberantly on footpaths, in parks, courtyards, and alleyways. This was the context in which the streets of Montreal worked as a political space, the site of elaborate parades, violent outbreaks of collective violence, and other sorts of crowd events.

At the end of the 1840s, the vast majority of residents lived in the city centre. Change, however, was afoot. The scale of migration into and through the city had increased rapidly during this decade.[19] Montreal experienced economic and social transformations that were occurring on a global scale, as industrialization and the transition to a capitalist economy touched off a period of sustained urbanization. Migrants stepped off steamships pulling into Montreal's harbour in a wide array of conditions. Many, however, most notably those fleeing the famine and social crisis unfolding in Ireland, were destitute. Diseases like cholera and typhus touched off periodic epidemics in port cities around the globe, and as a hub of migration, Montreal was not spared. These events strained social relations.[20] The emigrant sheds hastily erected in the city's southwest corner, on land owned by the Grey Nuns adjoining what had once been the town's verdant commons, demonstrated an effort to exert governmental control. The city these migrants encountered was being reshaped by processes of social and geographic segregation that altered its physical form and public life.[21] Economic elites began to flee the city centre for garden suburbs creeping up the base of Mount Royal. The process of suburbanization would continue in the second half of the nineteenth century, as improvements to transportation made the promise of an idyllic semi-rural existence accessible to a growing segment of the community.[22] Meanwhile, ramshackle working-class suburbs took shape on the city's urban fringes, allowing labourers proximity to the factories and warehouses being built at a distance from the city centre.[23] These changes would impact the tone of street-based popular culture significantly in the years that followed, as residents became increasingly ensconced in neighbourhoods where class, ethnic, and racial differences were less palpable than they had been in a more compact walking city.

The Rebellion Losses Crisis proved to be a transformative moment for Montreal. In its aftermath, imperial officials had hastily elected to move the capital to Toronto in Canada's western hinterland where, they hoped, marauding crowds would be less likely to interrupt government proceedings. In Montreal, sectarian conflicts continued to engulf politics in a millenarian haze. To those engaged in public life, the violence of the previous decade, which reached its climax with the attack on Ste Anne's Market, was legible, even rational. The restoration of order did not appear inevitable. As straightforward as it might be for historians to grasp the way these issues were resolved in the decades that followed, to many Montrealers at the time it seemed as though society was coming unhinged, to be tossed on to the scrapheap of history's failed projects. How did the city avoid this fate?

Answering that question requires an examination of both politics and demographics. Just as many commentators sympathetic to the Reform faction had suggested during the Rebellion Losses Crisis, the Tory faction would not survive the transition to responsible government. The ethnic hostility that coursed through their platform and their language meant that they would have little chance of cobbling together a parliamentary majority in the Province of Canada. Fragments of the old Tory faction joined the Reform faction to establish a Liberal-Conservative party that would wield enormous political power in the lead-up to Confederation in 1867. Their opposition consisted of the Clear Grits, a collection of reformers bound together by the assertion that the Liberal-Conservative majority had not done enough to bring to fruition a truly democratic Province of Canada, and the Rouge faction, whose critiques of the ruling party and the Catholic Church earned it the sustained support of Canadien liberals.[24] This retooling of the party system made a significant impact on the streets of Montreal. It softened the relationship between ethnic and sectarian divisions and political affiliation and electoral politics became less mired in these tensions. The move to a secret ballot furthered the process.[25] A shifting political agenda also made an impact on the influence that popular politics had on public life. Due to their continuous reference to assertions of difference, the debates over democratic reform that had been the centrepiece of political life in the 1840s spilled into violent confrontations on the streets. In the decade that followed, however, the debates over economic development that became the cornerstone of politics did not have the same polarizing effect. Instead, they laid the groundwork for a century of economic dominance of the territory in the midst of becoming Canada. The Victoria Bridge, opened in 1860, connected Montreal to a year-round harbour in Portland, Maine, and gave it a continuous connection to global trade. Meanwhile, railways helped Montreal became the hub of a transcontinental and transnational trade in grain from the west, allowing financial elites in the city to prosper from the colonial dispossession of the Indigenous population of what was being reconstituted into western Canada.

The transformation of the city's demographic composition continued in the subsequent decade. The famine migration from Ireland began to subside in the first few years of the 1850s. Irish migrants in search of a better life became more likely to land in America after court rulings overturned laws that had made entry there more economically burdensome.[26] The Reciprocity Treaty of 1854, which increased trade between British North America and the United States, brought renewed prosperity to Montreal. The city's capitalists invested heavily in industrial enterprises and required reliable access to migrant labour to staff their factories. As Irish migration into the city declined, rural Canadiens filled this role. The brief period when the majority of Montrealers spoke English drew to a close and, during the second half of the nineteenth century, the city's working-class became predominately Canadien. This demographic shift also contributed to the changing tenor of public life. Montreal remained a migrant city but the men, women, and children arriving from the rural hinterland often had stronger connections to the community than the transient labourers of the 1840s did. The city's popular culture did not suddenly dissipate, but engaging in its rougher elements was no longer an essential component of the migrant's survival strategy.

Popular unrest would continue to loom over Montreal through the next two centuries. Antipathy between the city's Catholics and an activist Evangelical Protestant community sparked a riot at the Haymarket during the summer of 1853 when Alessandro Gavazzi, an excommunicated Italian priest turned anti-papal activist, was invited by the Congregationalist community to give an address at Zion Church. A confrontation ensued between Gavazzi's supporters and a protesting crowd of Irish Catholics. The troops intervened, firing muskets into the crowd and killing twelve people. Many commentators in the press warned of an unwelcome resumption of the sectarian violence of the 1840s, but these hostilities became less frequent as the years passed.[27] Serious violence broke out during the St Patrick's Day festivities in 1876, when the shooting of an Orange Order activist led to a mass Protestant demonstration that turned ugly.[28] Opposition to the city's public smallpox vaccination program in 1885 ignited rioting that had an ethnic tinge,[29] as did raucous demonstrations against the federal government's decision to impose conscription during the world wars. When the National Hockey League suspended Montreal Canadiens star Maurice Richard during the 1955 playoffs, fans in the city reacted with a nocturnal riot that spoke to deeper tensions between the English- and French-speaking communities.[30] Hockey fans continued to celebrate the victories and defeats of their beloved Canadiens with outbursts of exuberant vandalism well into the twenty-first century. It was labour agitation, however, that did the most to fuel concerns about popular unrest and violence.[31] Through the middle decades of the twentieth century, laws were passed and enforced that were explicitly designed to compel striking workers to practice restraint in their protest by imposing restrictions on their use of public space. This harkened back to legislation passed by the Special Council in the aftermath of the Rebellions of 1837 and 1838 against popular assembly.[32]

Urban growth and technological change have altered the way that people use the streets, yet they remain a site of contention. Maintaining control of this space continues to be a core objective of those who wield authority. The project of creating the sort of orderly city envisioned by its bourgeois elite is complex. At its core, though, it is built around a conflict over how people ought to use the streets that often pits elites against the popular classes. As was the case in the 1840s, twenty-first-century Montrealers do not share equal access to the streets. While different factions of the city's economic and cultural elite might be lauded for organizing elaborate parades and processions, the city's poor and marginalized communities come under persistent scrutiny for how they use public space. The continued relevance of these issues is illustrated by the police shooting of Fredy Villanueva, an eighteen-year-old Honduran immigrant lingering in a park in the city's north end with friends on a summer night in 2008. Whose actions come under scrutiny, and whose do not, remains an effective measure of privilege. One's freedom to access public space continues to be mediated by questions of race, class, gender, and sexuality, demonstrating how social status shapes the urban experience in a myriad of ways.

The street-based popular culture of 1840s Montreal left an imprint on the city. Two decades into the twenty-first century, Montreal's boosters continue to brand it as a place where people take to the streets. To a degree that distinguishes it from most other North American centres, Montreal presents itself as a city of festivals where communal experiences like attending outdoor concerts are central to a unique urban identity.[33] Recent decades have seen investments in public spaces and street architecture that would have been appreciated by the reform-oriented elites of the mid nineteenth century, who dreamed of an urban experience anchored by peaceful strolls along genteel boulevards. As was the case in the mid nineteenth century, however, this culture of collective experience on the street also opened up a window of opportunity for those looking to engage in and disrupt public life. Crowd events that are frequently conceptualized as innocuous festivities take on a heightened meaning in certain political circumstances. Take, for example, the annual Canada Day and St Jean Baptiste Day festivities during the constitutional crises of the early 1990s, when parades once again took on a sharply contested political significance. Meanwhile, marginalized communities have continued to use the streets as a place to make their case for greater inclusion into the public sphere. The custom of parading, for example, has been harnessed by both the LGBTQ community and the Caribbean community, just as Irish migrants and the Canadien community did in the 1840s. It has been employed by feminist activists determined to "take back the night" from the threat of male violence. The 2012 protests against tuition hikes mentioned in the introduction did not emerge in a vacuum. The movement took hold because popular customs of protest had been fostered in an intergenerational chain, largely through the intertwined actions of the student, LGBTQ, and labour movements.

Taking to the streets is a persistent component of the urban experience in Montreal. There is a material culture to draw upon that includes everything from the design of banners to a repertoire of chants and songs, from the mapping of routes to the practice of banging on pots and pans. In order to fully make sense of these customs, historians must reflect on elements that seem to lie just beyond our grasp. We must take into consideration the exhilaration that can come with engaging in crowd activities, and the unacknowledged ways in which the bonds of community formation are formed and fostered. We must also take into account that gathering in crowds can be a powerful means of intimidating political and cultural foes. This was a crucial factor in the development of political institutions across British North America, but especially in raucous port cities like Montreal. Finally, we must reflect on the relationship between the threat of unruly popular action, democracy, and the project of liberal governance. The spectre of the riotous crowd, for example, did much to legitimize innovative practices in urban policing, a trend that has been altered but not abated in the nearly two centuries since the events described in *Taking to the Streets* unfolded.

In some crucial ways, we have been bequeathed the urban streets that the reformers of the mid nineteenth century conjured in their most audacious dreams. Social hierarchies are firmly embedded in the landscape. Access to collective experiences, in the form of protest and celebration, are fleeting and tightly constrained. A stroll through the streets of twenty-first-century Montreal reveals the value placed on consumption and commerce over human interaction. It reminds us of the overwhelming priority given to the fluid circulation of privately owned automobiles by the urban planners of the twentieth century. While mid-nineteenth-century Montrealers would have experienced modest surveillance in the form of patrolling police officers, their twenty-first-century counterparts find themselves under the gaze of a web of closed circuit cameras recording nearly every step of their journeys through the city. This has produced the sort of restrained urban culture that the reform-oriented elites of the nineteenth century were advocating for. It is not without its advantages. Twenty-first-century Montrealers make their way through a city where acts of interpersonal violence are rarer than they were in the mid nineteenth century. If given a choice, many would likely choose the comfort and security of the present day over the tumultuous experiences that punctuated urban life in centuries past. Still, we must pause to reflect on the sacrifices that were made to fulfill this liberal project. It has significantly weakened the ability of those bereft of power to challenge the vision of those who cling to it. Furthermore, this achievement of order is often only illusory. Beneath the surface of the streets lies a persistent tension, a reminder that that the discipline being exerted by those who wield power is in perpetual need of reinforcement.

The triumph of a reformed urban landscape is never complete. Its defenders have to practice eternal vigilance in its defence. Sizeable public expenditures are devoted to maintaining and expanding the ability of the state to place limits on people's access to public space, confirming that this remains an issue of the upmost importance to those who wield authority. The liberal order that became hegemonic over the course of the twentieth century finds itself under attack by the entangled forces of inequality, populism, and environmental catastrophe, and the urban street will likely be a vital forum for the social and cultural conflicts instigated by these tensions. The repertoire of cultural practices that people use to make their voices heard will once again be flexed and renewed. There are Montrealers yet to be born, and future Montrealers scattered around the globe who have yet to set their sights on the city, who will one day take to its streets in jubilation, exaltation, frustration, and anger. Many will do so to put forth the argument that they belong there and that their voices and the demands of their community need to be heard and given weight in the city. Their actions will continue to shape the contours of the public sphere, and prod and provoke those who hold the reins of power. Most will only be dimly aware that their actions have a genealogy that binds them to Montreal's raucous nineteenth-century past; that their actions have been part of a much longer conversation about who ought to be able to wield authority and how they ought to be able to do so in a modern society. The passage of time changes cities, but there are patterns that somehow manage to persist. The powerful few who view the cultural practices of those ostracized on the basis of their race, economic status, gender, or sexuality as impediments to their cultural and political projects will continue to encounter the challenge of sustained resistance. While this book draws to a close, the story of Montreal's streets as a political space still has countless pages yet to be written.

Notes

Introduction

1 A vibrant scholarly literature has already emerged around the student strike of 2012. An interesting introduction to it can be found in Ancelovici et Dupuis-Déri, eds, *Un printemps rouge et noir*. See also Weinstock, "Occupy, *Indignados*, et le printemps érable."

2 Some notable examples include Rudé, *The Crowd in the French Revolution* and Hobsbawm, *Primitive Rebels*.

3 Zemon Davis, "The Reasons of Misrule," 74.

4 Thompson, "The Moral Economy of the English Crowd in the Eighteenth Century."

5 For a synthesis of this literature, see Rogers, *Crowds, Culture, and Politics*, 1-17; Holton, "The Crowd in History." For how this work has been interpreted recently by historians of Quebec, see Fahrni, "Who Now Reads E.P. Thompson?"

6 Desan, "Crowds, Community, and Ritual," 57.

7 The classic text to note here is Thompson's *The Making of the English Working Class*.

8 For a selection of his extensive work, see Tilly, *Popular Contention in Great Britain, 1758–1834*; *From Mobilization to Revolution*; *The Politics of Collective Violence*.

9 For an overview of his work, see Hanagan, "Charles Tilly and Violent France."

10 Rogers and Shubert, "Spectacle, Monument, and Memory," 266–7. This literature was heavily influenced by Hobsbawm and Ranger, eds, *The Invention of Tradition*.

11 See, for example, Anderson, *Imagined Communities*; Colley, *Britons*; Truesdell, *Spectacular Politics*; Waldstreicher, *In the Midst of Perpetual Fêtes*.

12 There is no greater example of this line of questioning than that found in Hall's seminal "The Tale of Samuel and Jemima."

13 For an overview of Marx's and Foucault's analyses of power, which informed my take on these themes, see Smart, *Foucault, Marxism and Critique*.

14 Habermas, *The Structural Transformation of the Public Sphere*, trans. by Burger; Holendahl, "Jürgen Habermas: 'The Public Sphere' (1962)," trans. by Russian.

15 Eley, "Nations, Public and Political Cultures"; Calhoun, *The Roots of Radicalism*, chapter 4.

16 See, for example, works such as Wilentz, *Chants Democratic*; Ryan, *Women in Public*; Ryan, *Civic Wars*; Davis, *Parades and Power*; Vernon, *Politics and the People*.

17 This process is the central problématique of Mary Ryan's influential and provocative *Civic Wars*.

18 In this respect, it addresses the landmark work of historian Jean-Marie Fecteau, *La liberté du pauvre*.

Chapter One

1 *Montreal Gazette*, 10 February 1841.

2 Ibid.

3 For more on earlier calls for a union between Upper and Lower Canada, see Curtis, "Le redécoupage du Bas-Canada dans les années 1830"; Lamonde, *Histoire sociale des idées au Québec, 1760–1896*, 91.

4 The outrage amongst Canadien elites at the Act of Union is dealt with at length in Lamonde, *Histoire sociale des idées au Québec*, Chapter IX, and Monet, *The Last Cannon Shot*, chapters 1–2.

5 For more on English-speaking mobilization during the Rebellions, see Young, "The Volunteer Militia in Lower Canada, 1837–1850."

6 For more on the treatment of Patriotes by the authorities in the aftermath of the Rebellions, see Henderson, "Banishment to Bermuda"; Boissery, *A Deep Sense of Wrong*; Greenwood,

"The Montreal Court Martial 1838–9: Legal and Constitutional Reflections."

7 The idea that the Canadien political elite were in a state of resigned disarray in the aftermath of the Act of Union is found throughout the historical literature on the period. Stephen Kenny, however, has nudged us towards a more nuanced perspective on this period, arguing that Canadiens continued to find ways to protest administrative misrule in Canada. See "'Cahots' and Catcalls."

8 See, for more on this, Poutanen, "Bonds of Friendship, Kinship, and Community."

9 An extensive literature on the process of middle-class identity formation during this period emphasizes a tight distinction between the public sphere of work and civic engagement and the private sphere of domestic life. See, for some examples, Hall and Davidoff, *Family Fortunes*; Tosh, *A Man's Place*; Blumin, *The Emergence of the Middle Class*, chapter 5. For some Canadian examples, see the essays in Guildford and Morton, eds, *Separate Spheres*.

10 Works that have shaped my perspective on the process of modernity and its relationship to urban space include Harvey, *Paris: Capital of Modernity*; Berman, *All That Is Sold Melts into Air*; Vernon, *Distant Strangers*.

11 See Davis, *Parades and Power*, chapter 1; Ryan, "The American Parade"; Gunn, *The Public Culture of the Victorian Middle Class*, chapter 7.

12 For more insight into Montreal's role in the commercial and cultural networks of the Aboriginal nations of northeastern North America, and the impact that colonization had on this world, see Havard, *The Great Peace of Montreal of 1701*.

13 On the French fur trade on the North American continent and diplomacy with aboriginal peoples, see Havard, *The Great Peace of Montreal of 1701*; Podruchny, *Making the Voyageur World*.

14 For more on Montreal society during this period, see Dechêne, *Habitants et marchands de Montréal au XVII siècle*.

15 For a collection of essays that draws attention to the global and continental implications of the Seven Years' War and pays particular attention to the Indigenous experience, see Hofstra, ed., *Cultures in Conflict*.

16 See Calloway, *The Scratch of a Pen*, chapter 5.

17 The reaction of Canadien society to the British conquest has been a point of contention amongst historians for the better part of a century. See Fyson, "The Conquered and the Conqueror; Brunet, "Les Canadiens après la conquête"; Igartua, "A Change in Climate."

18 Lawson, *The Imperial Challenge*; Welland, "Commercial Interest and Political Allegiance."

19 On the loyalist migration into what became Canada, see Moore, *The Loyalists*. Recent literature emphasizes the global nature of this migration. See the essays in Bannister and Riordan, eds., *The Loyal Atlantic*.

20 This is the subject of Ducharme's *Le concept de liberté au Canada à l'époque des révolutions atlantiques, 1776–1838*.

21 This sphere of cultural and political activism is documented extensively in Lamonde, *Histoire sociale des idées au Québec*.

22 For more on this see Curtis, "Le redécoupage du Bas-Canada dans les années 1830." In *The Politics of Codification*, Brian Young points out that a vocal group of Canadien liberals were also supportive of efforts to reform some of the less coherent aspects of French civil law.

23 Linda Colley's *Britons* provides an extensive overview of the role of anti-French sentiment in shaping British identity in the eighteenth and nineteenth centuries.

24 For more on nativism during this period, see Oxx's recent survey of the topic, *The Nativist Movement in America*. The literature on Irish identity formation during this period is also helpful here. See Roediger, *The Wages of Whiteness*; Ignatiev, *How the Irish Became White*.

25 For discussions of political violence in pre-Rebellion Montreal, see Bradbury, "Widows at the Hustings" and Jackson, *The Riot that Never Was*.

26 On the 92 Resolutions and the response to them in Lower Canada and London, see Lamonde, *Histoire sociale des idées au Québec*, chapter IV.

27 For an overview of the rebellions of 1837 and 1838 and a survey of the scholarly literature on the topic, see Bernard, *The Rebellions of 1837 and 1838 in Lower Canada*.

28 On the Doric Club, see Kyte Senior, *British Regulars in Montreal,* 26, 108; Ryerson, *Unequal Union,* 52.

29 Bernard, *The Rebellions of 1837 and 1838 in Lower Canada.*

30 Greer's *The Patriots and the People* interprets the rebellion as a rural insurgency by demonstrating how the peasants in Montreal's hinterland drew on longstanding customs of agrarian protest.

31 Ibid., chapter 5.

32 For an overview of the Special Council period and their policy agenda, see Watt, "Authoritarianism, Constitutionalism, and the Special Council of Lower Canada, 1838–1841."

33 There is an extensive literature on Durham's time in Canada. Alongside Lambton, Buller, and Gibbon Wakefield, *The Report and Despatches of the Earl of Durham, Her Majesty's High Commissioner and Governor-General of British North America,* see Curtis, "The Most Splendid Pageant Ever Seen"; Ajzenstat, *The Political Thought of Lord Durham*; Henderson, "Uncivil Subjects."

34 The evolution of the movement for democratic reform in the Province of Canada in the aftermath of the Rebellions is dealt with at length in Bédard, *Les Réformistes* and Monet, *The Last Cannon Shot.*

35 Both Jeffrey McNairn and Carol Wilton demonstrate in great detail how political ideas spread across the frontier towns of Upper Canada in the first half of the nineteenth century. See McNairn, *The Capacity to Judge* and Wilton, *Popular Politics and Political Culture in Upper Canada.*

36 For both a quantitative and qualitative analysis of Montreal's growth over the course of the nineteenth century, see Olson and Thornton, *Peopling the North American City.*

37 Olson and Thornton, "The Challenge of the Irish Catholic Community in Nineteenth-Century Montreal."

38 For an overview of the public health situation in early nineteenth-century Montreal, see Robert, "The City of Wealth and Death."

39 On the typhus outbreak of 1847, see Charest-Auger, "Les réactions montréalaises à l'épidémie de typhus de 1847" and Horner, "The Public Has The Right to be Protected From A Deadly Scourge."

40 Recent work on Irish migration to North America during this period points out that migrants from rural areas of Ireland

may well have grown familiar with some aspects of the urban economy, as its influence stretched deep into the rural hinterland. Correspondence with kin who had migrated earlier might also have provided them with some sense of what to expect upon arrival in cities like Montreal. See, for example, Jenkins, *Between Raid and Rebellion*, chapter 3.

41 In the context of Montreal, see Bradbury, *Working Families*. Mary Anne Poutanen points out that, in a garrison town like Montreal, prostitution provided a means for women to contribute to the survival of their families; see *Beyond Brutal Passions*.

42 For more on the agrarian origins of popular resistance, see Thompson, "The Moral Economy of the English Crowd in the Eighteenth Century; Palmer, *Cultures of Darkness*, chapter 2.

43 The threat of crowds was heightened by their tendency to take to the streets at night which, amongst other things, provided participants with a degree of anonymity. See Palmer, *Cultures of Darkness*, chapter 2.

44 The literature on the development of working-class or popular culture in pre-Confederation Canada is not extensive, and most of what there is focuses on the emergence of organized labour – a social movement that often explicitly excluded marginalized groups like non-whites, women, and others who occupied the most precarious positions that the labour market had to offer. There are a few exceptions. See, for example, Way's study of the Irish migrants employed on the construction of canals in North America during this period, *Common Labour*. For more on the process of community formation in mid-nineteenth-century Montreal, see Olson and Thornton, *Peopling the North American City*, chapter 11.

45 This was part of a growing emphasis on character and independence in the way that legitimate authority was defined, asserted, and understood in the age of democratic reform. See, for other examples, Morgan, *Public Men and Virtuous Women*; McKay, "The Liberal Order Framework," 625; Vernon, *Politics and the People*.

46 See McKay, "The Liberal Order Framework," 629; For an overview of Gramsci's writing on authority and the concept of a passive revolution, albeit from a more contemporary perspective, see Morton, *Unravelling Gramsci*.

47 For extensive discussions of how this process of marginalization and exclusion worked, see Ryan, *Civic Wars* and Calhoun, *The Roots of Radicalism.*

48 Several landmark works pushed me in this direction as a graduate student, including Ryan's *Civic Wars* and *Women in Public,* Stansell's *City of Women,* Clark's *The Struggle for the Breeches,* and Morgan's *Public Men and Virtuous Women.*

49 The connections between crowds and madness were most famously drawn by Le Bon in *The Crowd.* For more on Le Bon's influence, see Rogers, *Crowds, Culture and Politics in Georgian Britain,* Introduction.

50 On the role of the Catholic Church in the emergence of the state and the concept of the social in nineteenth-century Quebec, see Fecteau, "La dynamique sociale du catholicisme québécois au XIXe siècle."

51 In his reflections on his years spent in Montreal, British military commander James Alexander wrote of the "gaieties usual in a garrison town" in reference to the calendar of events and celebrations around which elite Montrealers organized their social lives. See Alexander, *Passages in the Life of a Soldier, or Military Service in the East and West, in Two Volumes,* 37.

52 A handful of these secret societies were mentioned in an editorial in *La Minerve,* 8 February 1847. Although such activity was rarely mentioned in the press, the tone of the article suggests that politically engaged Montrealers would have been aware of their existence.

53 Jeffrey McNairn argues in *The Capacity to Judge* that the first half of the nineteenth century in Upper Canada was marked by a re-conceptualization of political life around the pursuit of independent and informed debate.

54 See Ducharme, *Le concept de liberté au Canada.*

55 See Young, *The Politics of Codification.*

56 This topic is dealt with at length in Curtis' *The Politics of Population.*

57 Historians Jean-Marie Fecteau and Donald Fyson have debated the timeline of state formation and regulation in urban Quebec, with Fecteau pointing to the middle of the nineteenth century as a turning point and Fyson making the case for a more gradual

evolution dating back to the French regime. See Fecteau, "Primauté analytique de l'expérience et gradualisme historique"; Fyson, "Réplique de Donald Fyson"; and Fecteau, "En guise de (provisoire) conclusion."

58 On the impact that the famine migration had on urban governance, see Gallman, *Receiving Erin's Children*; Horner, "'If the evil now growing around us be not staid.'"

59 Joyce, *The Rule of Freedom*, Introduction.

60 For insight on questions around public space and politics, see Bradbury and Myers, "Negotiating Identities in Nineteenth- and Twentieth-Century Montreal."

61 For more on nineteenth-century regulation, see Fecteau, *La liberté du pauvre*; Poutanen, "Regulating Public Space in Early-Nineteenth-Century Montreal"; Noel, *Canada Dry*; Heron, *Booze*, chapter 3.

62 Michèle Dagenais places the creation of municipal governments in British North America in the context of the transition to liberal governance. See "The Municipal Territory."

63 On the gradual evolution of policing in Lower Canada, see Fyson, *Magistrates, Police, and People*, chapter 4.

64 See Poutanen, "Regulating Public Space in Early-Nineteenth-Century Montreal"; Fyson, *Magistrates, Police, and People*, chapter 6.

65 Again, debates about the emergence of a liberal order in nineteenth-century British North America have shaped my perspective on this. See McKay, "The Liberal Order Framework"; Sandwell, "The Limits of Liberalism."

Chapter Two

1 Eaton explained in his letter to the Police Commission that he had previously been the proprietor of a commercial building on St Paul Street that was destroyed in a fire in 1841, but was, by the following year, "recovering from his misfortunes by supplying the public with rolls in the mornings." Archives de la Ville de Montréal (henceforth AVM), VM43 S3, *Fonds de la Commission de la Police*, 3 April 1844.

2 Ibid., 17 March 1843.

3 Ibid., 3 April 1844.

4 Ibid.

5 Ibid.

6 Ibid.

7 The concept of class identity as a product of social interaction is most associated with the work of E.P. Thompson. See *The Making of the English Working Class*. The influence of this conception of class can be seen in the literature on urban life in nineteenth-century America. See, for example, Blumin, *The Emergence of the Middle-Class*, 12; Ryan, *Civic Wars*, 14; Scobey, *Empire City*, 30–4.

8 The need to place crowd events within the context of daily life has been central to the more recent literature, which has been critical of the groundbreaking work published in the 1960s and 1970s which tended to treat occurrences like riots as sporadic and exceptional. For further discussions, see Davis, *Parades and Power*, 14; Harrison, "The Ordering of the Urban Environment," 145; Rogers, *Crowds, Culture, and Politics in Georgian Britain*, 13; Ryan, *Civic Wars*, 14; Mungar, "Contentious Gatherings in Lancashire, England, 1750–1893," 75. Understanding rituals in the context of daily life is one of the most crucial questions anthropologists explore. See, for example, Turner, *The Ritual Process*.

9 Alderman Benjamin Holmes was a fervent supporter of urban tree-planting, arguing that trees, more than anything else, would transform the appearance and the culture of Montreal's streets. *La Minerve*, 20 February 1843.

10 An 1843 editorial in *La Minerve* was particularly explicit on the topic of the politics of promenading, contrasting the respectability of those who took leisurely strolls through the city, winding their way up the slope of Mount Royal to enjoy the fresh air, to the city's popular classes, who preferred to spend their evenings "dans les cabarets … dans un état d'ivresse abrutissant!" 20 February 1843.

11 Street widenings were also associated with the sort of creative destruction necessary for the ascendancy of a capitalist economy during this period. These wide boulevards were not only aesthetically pleasing to urban reformers, but they were singularly capable of awakening streams of inert capital by pushing up real estate prices and creating new opportunities for development.

For a study of this process in Montreal, see Gilliland, "The Creative Destruction of Montreal." For more on the class and gender politics of the stroll, see Scobey, "Anatomy of the Promenade."

12 For more on the relationship between street lighting and authority, see Poutanen, "Regulating Public Space," 43; Bouman, "Luxury and Control."

13 *La Minerve*, 20 February 1843. Paris was a frequent reference point for members of Montreal's Canadien elite. For example, in the fall of 1843, notices appeared in *La Minerve* about an exhibition of a detailed panorama of Paris. For an admission price of fifteen cents, curious Montrealers were invited to spend an afternoon or evening studying this minutely detailed relief of "la grande cité européenne." *La Minerve*, 21 September 1843.

14 Joyce, *The Rule of Freedom*; McKay, "The Liberal Order Framework."

15 Fecteau's *La liberté du pauvre* provides a vivid overview of these debates.

16 For a detailed description of the duties of Montreal's police force, see *Regulations for the Governance of the Police Force, Rural and City, Province of Canada with Instructions as to the Legal Authorities and Duties of Police Constables* (Montreal: J. Starke and Company, 1841). In the secondary literature, see Greer, "The Birth of the Police in Canada"; Rogers, "Serving Toronto the Good"; Fyson, *Magistrates, Police, and People*, chapter 4. One particularly influential look at the evolution of policing is Cobb's *The Police and the People*.

17 The Police Commission dealt frequently with demands for sanitary improvements, especially during outbreaks of epidemic disease. See, for examples, VM43 S2, *Fonds de la Commission de la Police*, 31 May 1849; AVM VM43 S3, *Fonds de la Commission de la Police*, 7 May 1847; AVM VM43 S2, *Fonds de la Commission de la Police*, 28 October 1847; AVM VM43 S2, *Fonds de la Commission de la Police*, 14 May 1847. The 1840s witnessed the first stirrings of the sanitary reform movement in Montreal, which lobbied civic authorities for better drainage and garbage collection. See Gagnon, *Questions d'égouts*. In her study of sanitary reformers in nineteenth-century British Columbia, Megan Davies argues that these activists were determined to impose their vision of order on the rough urban

landscapes they encountered. A similar inclination is evident amongst the reformers of mid-nineteenth-century Montreal. Davies, "Night Soil, Cesspools, and Smelly Hogs on the Streets," 17. See also Bradbury, "Pigs, Cows, and Boarders," 9.

18 For a discussion of how this sphere of activity helped foster a liberal society in Canadian cities in the second half of the nineteenth century, see Ferry, *Uniting in Measures of Common Good*.

19 Both Patrick Joyce and Penelope Edmonds provide insights into the important role that urban grids, which were often more a statement of ambition for civic elites than an expression of reality, were crucial to visions of an orderly city during this period. See Joyce, *The Rule of Freedom*, 11; Edmonds, *Urbanizing Frontiers*, chapter 3.

20 Glackmeyer, *The Charter and By-Laws of the City of Montreal* (Lovell, 1865), 372. Efforts to improve the urban landscape focused on public squares like Place d'Armes, where trees were planted and stone gates constructed during this period. See Choko, *The Major Squares of Montreal*, trans. Kathe Roth, 37.

21 Glackmeyer, 371.

22 See Curtis, *The Politics of Population*; Greer and Radforth, eds, *Colonial Leviathan*.

23 For some examples, see Bibliothèque et Archives nationales du Québec, centre d'archives de Montréal (hereafter BANQ-M), TL32 S1, SS1 (Quarter Sessions Documents, henceforth QSD), Deposition of James McCormack, 2 December 1843; QSD, Deposition of David Malhiot, 4 October 1844; QSD, Deposition of Daniel Thauvette, 2 August 1844. The danger that police officers faced in the line of duty was well documented in the persistent demands for pay hikes throughout this period. See, for example, AVM VM43 S3, *Fonds de la Commission de la Police*, 28 October 1847.

24 Fyson, "The Trials and Tribulations of Riot Prosecutions." It is hardly surprising, then, that crowds were central to the way that a number of petty criminal offenses were constructed. See, for example, the section on Disorderly Persons in the *Revised Acts and Ordinances of Lower Canada*, 159–68. For example, in order to legitimize an indictment against someone arrested for public drunkenness, constables often emphasized the way that the suspect had caused a crowd of spectators to gather around them.

25 *Ordinances Made and Passed by His Excellency the Governor General and Special Council for the Affairs of the Province of Lower Canada: Volume Fifth*, 70. See Greer, "The Birth of the Police," 24.

26 *Montreal Witness*, 26 March 1849.

27 Ibid.

28 Ibid.

29 Horner, "'If the evil now growing around us be not staid.'"

30 Classic studies of gendered aspects of the emerging middle-class culture during this period include Tosh, *A Man's Place*, and Davidoff and Hall, *Family Fortunes*.

31 *Montreal Witness*, 26 March 1849.

32 For a more in-depth discussion of the relationship between class and gender in shaping women's experience of the nineteenth-century city, see Stansell, *City of Women* and Perrot, *Femmes publiques*.

33 Dagenais, "The Municipal Territory."

34 AVM, VM43 S2, *Fonds de la Commission de la Police*, 27 April 1847.

35 For more on the attitudes of Canadian merchants to their urban surroundings, see Bliss, *A Living Profit*.

36 AVM, VM43 S2, *Fonds de la Commission de la Police*, 16 July 1847.

37 Ibid., 28 October 1847.

38 Ibid.

39 Ibid., 9 February 1844. In their study of the Orange Order in nineteenth- and twentieth-century Canada, Cecil Houston and William Smyth note that Orangemen were heavily involved with sabbattarian campaigns during this period. This suggests the possibility that, while couched in the language of gentility, there were more connections between these campaigns and the city's rough sectarian politics than we might assume. See *The Sash Canada Wore*, 156.

40 Glackmeyer, *The Charter and Bylaws of the City of Montreal*, 97; 106; 396; 399.

41 AVM, VM43 S2, *Fonds de la Commission de la Police*, 26 January 1844.

42 Ibid.

43 Warburton, *Hochelaga or England in the New World*, 210. For a discussion of the harbour area as a space where Montrealers encountered the messiest aspects of social and economic change, see Gilliland, "Muddy Shore to Modern Port."

44 *La Minerve*, 6 July 1843.

45 AVM, VM43 S2, *Fonds de la Commission de la Police*, 9 February 1844.

46 Ibid.

47 For examples, see BAnQM, E17 TL32 S1, SS1, Deposition of Sub-Constable McGuire, 7 November 1843; BAnQM, E17 TL32 S1, SS1, Deposition of Henry Hebert, 19 March 1840; BAnQM, E17 TL32 S1, SS1, Deposition of Charles St Germain, 6 February 1841.

48 For example, a group of residents and business owners along McGill Street, one of the city's major north-south thoroughfares, emphasized the intimidating presence of crowds of carters in an 1844 petition to the municipal government. AVM, VM43 S2, *Fonds de la Commission de la Police*, 5 January 1844.

49 Ibid., May 1847.

50 *La Minerve*, 3 August 1843.

51 The literature on middle-class identity formation during the long nineteenth century is informative here. See Gunn, *The Public Culture of the Victorian Middle-Class*; Morgan, *Public Men and Virtuous Women*, chapter 4; Blumin, *The Emergence of the Middle Class*; Davidoff and Hall, *Family Fortunes*; Tosh, *A Man's Place*.

52 QSD, Deposition of Constable Joseph Vaillancourt, 17 June 1845.

53 This specificity with regards to gender persists through judicial documents and the records of the Police Commission. If taken at face value, it suggests that girls did not engage in this sort of disorderly public behaviour. While this seems unlikely, there is no evidence to suggest otherwise.

54 AVM, VM43 S2, *Fonds de la Commission de la Police*, 22 November 1849.

55 See Baldwin, *Domesticating the Street*, 147–8; Bradbury and Myers, "Introduction," 1.

56 AVM, VM43 S2, *Fonds de la Commission de la Police*, 24 August 1848.

57 Ibid.

58 Ibid., 22 November 1849.

59 QSD, Deposition of Henry Driscoll, 30 October 1846.

60 This was not unique to Montreal, but part of a broader set of concerns about the place of boys in an age of rapid urbanization.

Egerton Ryerson was raising concerns about idle boys on the streets of Toronto in *A System of Public Elementary Instruction for Upper Canada,* 1–8. For more on the problem, see Winter, *London's Teeming Streets,* 67; Baldwin, *Domesticating the Street,* chapter 6.

61 *Montreal Witness,* 5 March 1849.

62 Jean-Marie Fecteau argues that juvenile delinquents held a special place in the imagination of nineteenth-century social reformers because they were believed to be susceptible to their methods, in contrast to adult criminals, seen as being too hardened in their ways. See *La liberté du pauvre,* 181.

63 For more on the expansion of schooling in nineteenth-century Lower Canada and Quebec, see Curtis, *Ruling by Schooling.*

64 AVM, VM43 S2, *Fonds de la Commission de la Police,* 27 December 1849.

65 QSD, Grand Jury Presentment, 18 January 1844.

66 Ibid.

67 Historians have written about public schooling during this period as representative of the expanding reach of the state in the 1840s. Education also became an important site of resistance as communities lashed out at their loss of local control on the issue. An important case study is Nelson's "Rage against the Dying of the Light." For a more general history of the rise of public schooling in nineteenth-century Quebec, see Charland, *L'entreprise éducative au Québec, 1840–1900.*

68 This arrangement was mentioned in criminal depositions recorded in a case where children were being bullied on their daily procession to school. QSD, Depositon of Eusèbe Archambault, 27 January 1841; QSD, Deposition of Pierre Pivin, 27 January 1841; QSD, Deposition of Théophile Cousineau, 27 January 1841; QSD, Deposition of Adelaide Butler, 27 January 1841; QSD, Deposition of Adelaide Bebille, 27 January 1841; QSD, Deposition of William Power, 27 January 1841.

69 AVM, VM43 S2, *Fonds de la Commission de la Police,* 17 November 1846.

70 QSD, Depositon of Eusèbe Archambault, 27 January 1841; QSD, Deposition of Pierre Pivin, 27 January 1841; QSD, Deposition of Théophile Cousineau, 27 January 1841; QSD, Deposition of Adelaide

Butler, 27 January 1841; QSD, Deposition of Adelaide Bebille, 27 January 1841; QSD, Deposition of William Power, 27 January 1841.

71 QSD, Deposition of Adelaide Butler, 27 January 1841; QSD, Deposition of Adelaide Bebille, 27 January 1841. The adults involved in the altercation were John Gallagher, William Gallagher, William Steel, and Stephen Samuels. The four were listed as labourers. It was also noted that William Steel was an "idiot."

72 *Les Mélanges religieux*, 3 October 1845.

73 A similar case continued to be made a century later. It is interesting to compare later approaches to these problems, given the considerably expanded reach of the state by the middle decades of the twentieth century. See Sutherland, "'We always had things to do.'"

74 For a more detailed discussion of the role of the tavern in nineteenth-century working-class life, see Palmer, *Cultures of Darkness*, chapter 10; and DeLottinville, "Joe Beef of Montreal."

75 For discussions on the connections between temperance, respectability, and the politics of identity, see Heron, *Booze*, 55–8; Holman, *A Sense of Their Duty*, 131–3; Fingard, "Race and Respectability in Victorian Halifax," 171.

76 Alexander, *Passages in the Life of a Soldier*, 37.

77 *Montreal Gazette*, 20 January 1844.

78 Ibid.

79 See Noel, *Canada Dry*.

80 A typical deposition for these types of arrests resembled the one recorded by a police constable in June 1845: "Paul Leclaire was arrested by the deponent last night, in a state of drunkenness and unable to walk and to take care of himself, on the footpath of Commissioners Street of the said city, thereby impeding and incommoding the peaceable passengers passing and repassing in the said street." QSD, Deposition of Thomas Donaghue, 20 June 1845. Dozens of such cases were heard during of the quarterly sessions of the lower criminal courts. Most resulted in petty fines or short sentences in the House of Correction. For more on how the judicial systems dealt with these sorts of crimes, see Fyson, *Magistrates, Police and People*, chapter 7.

81 *Souvenir of the Golden Jubilee of St Patrick's Total Abstinence and Benefit Society, 1840–1890*, 24.

82 AVM, VM43 S2, *Fonds de la Commission de la Police*, 26 August 1843.

83 Ibid.

84 AVM, VM43 S2, *Fonds de la Commission de la Police*, 7 September 1843.

85 AVM, VM43 S2, *Fonds de la Commission de la Police*, 19 February 1844.

86 AVM, VM43 S2, *Fonds de la Commission de la Police*, 26 March 1847.

87 AVM, VM43 S2, *Fonds de la Commission de la Police*, 6 July 1848.

88 *Montreal Gazette*, 20 February 1844.

89 Craig Heron argues that temperance activists likely exaggerated some of their accounts to draw attention to their cause. Heron, *Booze*, 43.

90 Relying on judicial records is hardly an ideal means of crafting a reliable portrait of ordinary people in the nineteenth-century city. Depositions were tweaked to resemble a common script of criminality, and were mediated by the voices of the powerful and well-connected men appointed to serve as magistrates. No other source, however, provides such a rich description of the social interactions of the popular classes during this period. This is especially important when it comes to broadening our understanding of the daily experiences of those who did not sit down to write the sorts of letters and memoirs that elites did. While many of these depositions offer only meager descriptions of instances when men and women were arrested for drunkenness, a small portion provide a more textured set of details. For more on the problems these documents pose to historians, see Shoemaker, "Using Quarter Sessions Records as Evidence for the Study of Crime and Criminal Justice."

91 QSD, Deposition of Michael Lynch, 10 October 1847.

92 QSD, Deposition of Joseph Cherry, 11 January 1841; QSD, Deposition of Hugh McLaughlin, 11 January 1841.

93 QSD, Deposition of Joseph St Aubin, 12 January 1841; QSD, Deposition of Charles St German, 12 January 1841.

94 QSD, Deposition of Louis Lacroix, 3 August 1844.

95 QSD, Deposition of Henry Donaghue, 9 February 1844.

96 Taverns were a vital source of community solidarity during this period. See Olson and Thornton, "The Challenge of the Irish

Catholic Community," 343. For other examples, see Heron, *Booze*, 26–9; Palmer, *Cultures of Darkness*, 219–20.

97 The Police Commission had to regularly discipline officers caught drinking on the job. For example, see AVM, VM43 S2, *Fonds de la Commission de la Police*, 29 November 1849.

98 QSD, Deposition of James Willard, 23 February 1840.

99 QSD, Presentment of Grand Jury, 18 January 1844. In his groundbreaking study of prostitution in nineteenth- and twentieth-century Paris, Alain Corbin argues that the discourse surrounding prostitution only became medicalized in the 1860s. It was then that measures such as Britain's Contagious Diseases Act were adopted. Prior to the 1860s, as the evidence from Montreal illustrates, discussions about prostitution were focused almost entirely on public order. Corbin, *Les filles de noce*.

100 QSD, Presentment of Grand Jury, 18 January 1844.

101 Joachim Schlör makes a similar argument about nineteenth-century Paris, Berlin, and London. *Nights in the Big City*, trans. Pierre Gottfried Imhof and Dafydd Rees Roberts, 178.

102 Poutanen, *Beyond Brutal Passions*.

103 QSD, Deposition of John Dredge, 27 February 1840; QSD, Deposition of Toussaint Gareau, 27 February 1840.

104 QSD, Deposition of Robert Laid, 29 November 1843; QSD, Deposition of François Dupuis, 29 November 1843.

105 QSD, Deposition of Joseph Bourdon, 17 August 1844; QSD, Deposition of Desange Tapin, 17 August 1844.

106 Mary Anne Poutanen makes a similar argument in "To Indulge Their Carnal Appetites," 308.

107 QSD, Deposition of William Moore, 11 January 1847; QSD, Deposition of Louis Bourbon, 11 January 1847.

108 QSD, Deposition of William Moore, 11 January 1847; QSD, Deposition of Louis Bourbon, 11 January 1847.

109 Senior, *British Regulars in Montreal*, 9.

110 QSD, Deposition of Louis Lacroix, 3 November 1843.

111 QSD, Deposition of Rosannah Lewis, 29 December 1844.

112 Ibid.

113 QSD, Deposition of John McGillivery, 2 December 1840; QSD, Deposition of Charles Coulomb, 2 December 1840.

114 QSD, Deposition of James Jackson, 2 December 1840.

Chapter Three

1 The note is included with the depositions recorded in front of the Queen's Bench in Montreal relating to the rioting that occurred during and following the strike. BA-NQ-M, TL19 S1 SS1 (henceforth QBD), *Depositions to the Court of Queen's Bench*, Deposition of Joseph Frobisher McDonald, 5 February 1843.

2 When violence broke out again in the spring of 1843, *La Minerve* ran an editorial asking plaintively "si cet état de chose aura une fin?" *La Minerve*, 3 April 1843.

3 For more on striking canal workers in the United States, see Way, *Common Labour*. A number of notable strikes occurred on the canals upriver from Montreal following the events at Lachine. For a summary of the events at Beauharnois, located just up the St Lawrence River from Montreal, see Boily, *Les Irlandais et le canal de Lachine*. These were followed by serious strikes and riots during the construction of the Welland Canal near St Catharines, Ontario. See Bleasdale, "Class Conflict on the Canals of Upper Canada in the 1840s."

4 See Desloges and Gelly, *The Lachine Canal*, 20–4.

5 This is in keeping with the way that these events have been analyzed by Canadian labour historians and political economists. Clare Pentland, in his detailed study of the strike published in 1948, argues that it was a decisive turning point in Canadian labour relations. Because the labourers worked in close quarters and under intense surveillance, Pentland argued that the expansion of the Lachine Canal by the Board of Works foreshadowed the kind of factory work that would become familiar to a growing segment of the working class as the nineteenth century progressed. "The Lachine Strike of 1843," 256. Pentland also argues that the events of 1843 marked a turning point in Canadian labour relations because the Board of Works accepted bids from contractors in a way that encouraged men like Henry Mason to slash wages to beat out competing bids. Ibid., 261. Pentland's notion of the Lachine Canal Strike as a precursor to the labour struggles in the second half of the nineteenth century was echoed in the subsequent works of Marxist historians Stanley Ryerson and Bryan Palmer.

See Ryerson, *Unequal Union*, 182–4; Palmer, *Working Class Experience*, 2nd ed., 50. Raymond Boily provides a narrative account of the events of 1843 in *Les Irlandais et le canal de Lachine*, a volume that also includes a generous collection of primary documents concerning the strikes at Beauharnois and Lachine. It is the only major French-language account of the Lachine Canal strike. Ruth Bleasdale's study of popular violence on canal projects in Upper Canada during this period adds nuance to the analyses of earlier Marxist interpretations by arguing that the action of the strikers was an entirely rational response to the conditions they faced, and that their efforts to attain higher wages and better working conditions were successful. Bleasdale, "Class Conflict on the Canals of Upper Canada in the 1840s."

6 For more on this, see McCalla, *Planting the Province*; Marjorie Cohen, *Women's Work, Markets, and Economic Development in Nineteenth-Century Ontario*.

7 See Olson and Thornton, *Peopling the North American City*, especially chapter 11.

8 There could well have been a linguistic divide here as well although, as Sherry Olson and Patricia Thornton have argued, it is difficult to ascertain how much Gaelic was ever spoken in Montreal. It is possible that because most of this workforce had spent the better part of the last decade in the United States, English was the dominant language for both the Cork and Connaught factions. See Olson and Thornton, "The Challenge of the Irish Catholic Community," 355. On the other hand, Peter Toner has uncovered evidence that Gaelic remained widely used amongst the Irish migrant community in New Brunswick during this period. See "The Origins of the New Brunswick Irish, 1851."

9 Ignatiev, *How the Irish Became White*, 95. For more on the violent confrontations between Corkonians and Connaughtmen in the 1830s, see Way, *Common Labour*, 200.

10 Historians of Irish popular resistance have debunked the notion that these forms of popular agitation were ancient in their origin. They date this kind of activism to the 1760s, when itinerant bands of informally organized labourers engaged in the same sorts of clashes and confrontations that were occurring along the banks

of the Lachine Canal during the winter of 1843. Kenny, *Making Sense of the Molly Maguires*, 13. The forms of retributive and extra-legal practices carried out by these Irish peasants targeted those who were thought to have committed social and economic injustices. While exploitative landlords were often targeted in late-eighteenth- and early-nineteenth-century Ireland, it was public works contractors and mine owners who found themselves on the receiving end in North America. Kenny, *Making Sense of the Molly Maguires*, 8-9; Huggins, *Social Conflict in Pre-Famine Ireland*, 16-17; Jones, *Rebecca's Children*; Ignatiev, *How the Irish Became White*, 92. The influence of E.P. Thompson's concept of the moral economy is evident in this historiography. See in particular Thompson, "The Moral Economy of the English Crowd," 79. These actions, historians have argued, were prompted by the transition to capitalist landholding practices in rural Ireland occurring at this time. As with the violence on the outskirts of Montreal, the popular resistance that emerged in rural Ireland was characterized by its rich material culture, with disguises, decorations, and carefully choreographed processions being central to its strategies. Roberts, "Caravats and Shanavests," 66.

11 Tulchinksy, "The Construction of the First Lachine Canal, 1815–1826."

12 Careless, *The Union of the Canadas*, 16.

13 Way, *Common Labour*, 207–10; 233–4.

14 For a case study of how this transformation unfolded in Ireland, see Gearóid Ó Tuathaigh, *Ireland before the Famine.*

15 For more on this, see Radforth, "Sydenham and Utilitarian Reform," 77; Boily, *Les Irlandais et le canal de Lachine*, 18–19.

16 Way, *Common Labour*, 231.

17 Hamilton Killaly to Charles Bagot, 17 August 1842, volume 117, reels 6125-6, Letterbooks of the Chairman of the Board of Works and Commissioners of Public Works, R182-224-X-E, Library and Archives Canada (hereafter LAC).

18 Martin Paquet's survey of shifting attitudes towards immigration and inclusion in Quebec history points to a need to study these issues on a micro level. His analysis begins with the observation that immigrants have, since the earliest colonization of New

France, been marginalized. Under shifting ideological pretences, cultural and political elites have constructed these conditions as the embodiment of a natural social order. Paquet, *Tracer les marges de la cité*, 18. On a similar note, Sherry Olson argues in her study of ethnic partition in Montreal during the 1840s that the arrival of large numbers of immigrants led to a series of interlocking social and ethnic hierarchies casting the Irish as the "undeserving" or the "other." Olson, "Ethnic Partition of the Work Force in 1840s Montreal," 167.

19 See Tilly, "Citizenship, Identity and Social History," S7.

20 In their exploration of collective violence in the nineteenth and early twentieth centuries, the Tillys note the way that political elites repeatedly constructed outbreaks of rioting as dangerous and irrational expressions "of the times being out-of-joint." C. Tilly, L. Tilly, and R. Tilly, *The Rebellious Century*, 2. The propensity of Montreal elites to frame their concerns about large-scale immigration around the danger of collective violence reinforces this argument.

21 *Montreal Gazette*, 7 February 1843.

22 Ibid.

23 *Montreal Transcript*, 7 February 1843.

24 *Les Mélanges religieux*, 10 February 1843.

25 *Le Canadien*, 3 April 1843.

26 *Montreal Gazette*, 7 February 1843.

27 Ibid.

28 Thomas Begly to Charles Atherton, 10 February 1843, volume 117, reels 6125-6, Letterbooks of the Chairman of the Board of Works and Commissioners of Public Works, R182-224-X-E, LAC.

29 QBD, Deposition of Donald Duff, 3 February 1843.

30 Ibid.

31 QBD, Deposition of Edward McGreevy, 5 February 1843. It was John Rogers, the chief foreman, who noted the flags and banners in his testimony. QBD, Deposition of John Rogers, 5 February 1843.

32 QBD, Deposition of Jeremiah Higgins, 5 February 1843.

33 Ibid.

34 For revealing eye-witness accounts of the nocturnal parades of the Cork faction, see QBD, Deposition of Bryan Owens, 3 February

1843; QBD, Deposition of Francis Getting, 4 February 1843; QBD, Deposition of Joseph Frobisher McDonald, 5 February 1843.

35 Even their foes recognized their discipline. The *Montreal Gazette* reported that members of the Cork faction had refused liquor offered to them as a sign of good faith during the dispute, and noted that the men participating in the nightly parades had an appearance of sobriety. *Montreal Gazette*, 23 June 1843.

36 Bryan Palmer's work is particularly revealing with regard to these customs of nocturnal protest. See, *Cultures of Darkness*, 23–47. Palmer's argument that the night belonged to the sorts of ruffians who offended even the bourgeois sensibilities of those who sympathized with them is certainly reflected in the experiences of the striking canal workers.

37 QBD, Deposition of Étienne Courville, 4 February 1843.

38 Ibid.

39 Craig Calhoun's re-thinking of the relationship between radicalism and tradition offers rich insights on this subject. See *The Roots of Radicalism*.

40 For some examples of this narrative, see QBD, Deposition of Joseph Frobisher McDonald, 5 February 1843; QBD, Deposition of Donald Duff, 3 February 1843; QBD, Deposition of Charles Turner, 5 February 1843.

41 Immigration was a hotly contested political issue in the years surrounding the rebellions and through the 1840s. At the centre of this debate by 1843 was Edward Wakefield, a well-connected politician who had proposed and supported systematic immigration schemes as a progressive measure to deal with poverty in the British Isles. Canadien politicians opposed these measures, seeing them as an attempt to flood Lower Canada with English-speaking immigrants. See Fitzpatrick, *Irish Emigration, 1801–1921*, 14. A much smaller wave of Irish immigrants had raised concerns in 1832 during a major cholera outbreak in Montreal. See Bilson, *A Darkened House*.

42 QBD, Deposition of Joseph Frobisher McDonald, 5 February 1843.

43 Ibid.

44 Ibid.

45 QBD, Deposition of Henry Mason, 5 February 1843. In fact, from

the moment that these sorts of disruptions had begun to occur across the colony, the Board of Works and the private contractors building the canals had forcefully lobbied the government for a strong military presence in the vicinity of these projects, setting a hugely important precedent for military policing of labour strife in Canada. An early example can be seen in a letter from Board of Works President Hamilton Killaly to Governor Bagot, which called not only for soldiers to be sent to the Welland Canal following rioting amongst the Irish labourers there, but also recommended that William Beverly Robinson, the superintendent of the canal, be immediately appointed Justice of the Peace for the Niagara district. Hamilton Killaly to Charles Bagot, 17 August 1842, volume 117, reels 6125-6, Letterbooks of the Chairman of the Board of Works and Commissioners of Public Works, R182-224-X-E, LAC.

46 *Montreal Transcript*, 11 March 1843; *Montreal Gazette*, 7 March 1843.

47 Olson and Thornton, *Peopling the North American City*, chapter 3.

48 QBD, Deposition of Thomas Fallen, 3 February 1843; QBD, Deposition of Bryan Owens, 3 February 1843.

49 QBD, Deposition of Thomas Fallen, 3 February 1843; QBD, Deposition of Bryan Owens, 3 February 1843.

50 QBD, Deposition of Michael Murray, 5 February 1843.

51 See, for example, QBD, Deposition of Hugh Logan, 5 February 1843.

52 See, for example, QBD, Deposition of Andrew Caughey and Michael Kelly, 4 February 1843; *Le Canadien*, 6 March 1843.

53 See, for example, *Montreal Gazette*, 7 February 1843; *Le Canadien*, 10 February 1843.

54 For an overview of the parliamentary crisis unfolding during this period, see McNairn, *The Capacity to Judge*, chapter 5.

55 *Le Canadien*, 6 March 1843.

56 *Montreal Transcript*, 7 March 1843.

57 Ibid. Only *Le Canadien* made any mention of involvement by non-canal workers in this particular riot. Tellingly, their coverage suggested that the brawl had been part of an effort to intimidate Montreal residents who intended to testify against the strike's ringleaders when the men charged in earlier riots were brought before the courts. *Le Canadien*, 8 March 1843.

58 *La Minerve*, 23 March 1843; *Les Mélanges religieux*, 24 March 1843.

59 Benjamin Holmes had emigrated from Ireland to Canada as a child with his family in the first decade of the nineteenth century. As an adult he had embarked on successful careers as a clerk, a banker, and a politician. A longtime Tory, Holmes switched his allegiance to the Reform faction in 1842. See the entry on Holmes by Lorne Ste Croix in the *Dictionary of Canadian Biography*.

60 *Mélanges religieux*, 24 March 1843.

61 *La Minerve*, 23 March 1843. *La Minerve* referred to the striking canal workers on numerous occasions as "les mutins." Their sympathy was directed towards the contractors, whose agreement with the Board of Works involved strict deadlines to complete the work before the upcoming shipping season. Like the English-language newspapers, *La Minerve* consistently published editorials targeting the lawlessness of the labourers. See, for example, *La Minerve*, 2 February 1843.

62 *Montreal Gazette*, 25 March 1843.

63 *Montreal Transcript*, 28 March 1843.

64 Calhoun's assertion that the public sphere was shaped by active exclusion is important to consider here. Calhoun, *The Roots of Radicalism*, 5.

65 *Montreal Gazette*, 25 March 1843.

66 Ibid.

67 *Montreal Transcript*, 7 March 1843; *Le Canadien*, 12 April 1843.

68 Senior's analysis of how the troops handled civil disturbances like the Lachine Canal Strike in *British Regulars in Montreal* is enlightening with regard to the attitudes of the garrison's authorities about civil unrest. She argues that the strike occurred in the context of changing attitudes towards the role of the military in civil affairs, and that the troops demonstrated unprecedented restraint by not turning their rifles on the canal workers. Her assertion, however, that the Cork / Connaught rivalry was a sectarian divide appears to be inaccurate, given the fact that both were from heavily Catholic regions of Ireland and both sides were eager to seek conciliation with the assistance of a Roman Catholic priest.

69 *Montreal Transcript*, 11 March 1843; *Les Mélanges religieux*, 10 March 1843. Holmes' visit was not without controversy. A correspondent for the *Montreal Herald* saw any attempt to

negotiate with the Irish workers as foolhardy, suggesting instead that they ought to be forced out of the area and replaced with Canadiens, who had proved themselves in the past to be less combative and willing to work for lower wages. This was met with a stern rebuke in *La Minerve* and from Benjamin Holmes and the St Patrick's Benevolent Society, which reaffirmed its commitment to providing charitable assistance to Irish immigrants. *La Minerve*, 23 March 1843.

70 *Montreal Gazette*, 28 March 1843.

71 For more on the importance of public demonstrations in shaping the respectable identities of Irish elites in nineteenth-century Canada, see Cottrell, "St. Patrick's Day Parades in Nineteenth-Century Toronto"; Trigger, "Irish Politics on Parade."

72 *Montreal Gazette*, 20 June 1843; *Les Mélanges religieux*, 24 March 1843.

73 *Montreal Gazette*, 25 March 1843; *Les Mélanges religieux*, 20 June 1843.

74 This would be the conclusion that the Board of Works made by the end of March, as their report placed much of the blame for the unrest on the unscrupulous practices of the contractors, who were removed from the project. Thomas Begly to W. Evans, 29 March 1843, volume 117, reels 6125-6, Letterbooks of the Chairman of the Board of Works and Commissioners of Public Works, R182-224-X-E, LAC.

75 Boily, *Les Irlandais et le canal de Lachine*, 58.

76 Bleasdale, "Class Conflict on the Canals of Upper Canada in the 1840s."

77 Pentland, "The Lachine Strike of 1843," 278.

78 See volume 117, reels 6125-6, Letterbooks of the Chairman of the Board of Works and Commissioners of Public Works, R182-224-X-E, LAC; Pentland, "The Lachine Strike of 1843," 273-8.

79 *Montreal Transcript*, 11 March 1843. The failure to convict the strikers was the end result of a trial that prompted a controversy of its own. Benjamin Hart, who had been a prominent advocate for the rule of law in the aftermath of the rebellions, argued that by detaining the strikers the authorities were violating their habeas corpus rights. This, Hart argued, was an assault on British values.

Montreal Gazette, 7 March 1843. For more on the difficulties faced by the state in prosecuting rioters, see Fyson, "The Trials and Tribulations of Riot Prosecutions."

80 Paquet, *Tracer les marges de la cité*, 116–22; Greer and Radforth, *Colonial Leviathan*, 10.

81 The only opposition to the bill came from Louis Hippolyte Lafontaine, and he did so only on the grounds that the right to bear arms was an important right under British law, and the legislation in question might inadvertently compromise this right for citizens who lived in the vicinity of the public works. Lafontaine appears to have been working under the assumption that the men employed on the public works were not entitled to those rights. Bleasdale, "Class Conflict on the Canals," 34.

82 Thomas Begly to Mills, 30 March 1843, volume 117, reels 6125-6, Letterbooks of the Chairman of the Board of Works and Commissioners of Public Works, R182-224-X-E, LAC.

83 *La Minerve*, 22 January 1844. Benjamin Holmes once again intervened in the debate, reminding council members of the squalor the canal workers lived in, noting that many slept in cabins that would make the stables of most council members seem luxurious.

84 For an overview of the epidemic in Montreal, see Charest-Auger, "Les réactions montréalaises à l'épidémie de typus de 1847"; Horner, "'The Public Has the Right to be Protected from a Deadly Scourge.'"

85 See, for example, AVM VM 43, Fonds de la Commission de Police, 28 June 1849.

86 Historical geographer Jason Gilliland argues that the importance placed on improving the infrastructure along the waterways of Upper and Lower Canada is illustrative of the way that Montreal's harbour and the Lachine Canal ought to be conceptualized as spaces intrinsically linked to capitalist development and the expansion of global trade. See "Muddy Shore to Modern Port," 461. Gilliland's argument echoes Way's that canal workers experienced the harshest exposure to the most negative aspects of capitalism.

Chapter Four

1 *Montreal Gazette*, 14 May 1844.
2 The links between authority, social change, and how people carry themselves in public are the subject of Richard Sennett's landmark *The Fall of Public Man*, a text which influences much of my analysis here.
3 Calhoun, *The Roots of Radicalism*.
4 This argument is shaped by the contributions to the historiography that suggest that the decade following the rebellions was pivotal in the emergence of the project of liberal governance in Canada. See McKay, "The Liberal Order Framework"; Ducharme and Constant, "A Project of Rule Called Canada - The Liberal Order Framework and Historical Practice"; McKay, "Canada as a Long Liberal Revolution." British historian Matthew McCormack examines the links between these ideals of masculine restraint and political power in *The Independent Man*.
5 See, for examples of this, McNairn, *The Capacity to Judge*; Watt, "Duty bound and ever praying"; Wilton, *Popular Politics and Public Culture*.
6 This approach speaks to the work of Jürgen Habermas and his critics. See Habermas, "The Structural Transformation of the Public Sphere." For a concise and engaging survey of Habermas' writing on the public sphere and subsequent critiques with regards to gender and class, see Eley, "Nations, Public and Political Cultures."
7 *La Minerve*, 21 August 1843.
8 *La Minerve*, 11 July 1844.
9 For the wording of the act, see An Act to Restrain Party Processions 1843 Cap.VI, in *The Provincial Statutes of Canada*, 17. For analysis and debate in the Montreal press, see *La Minerve*, 20 November 1843.
10 This is known in the historiography as "The Metcalfe Crisis." See Monet, *The Last Cannon Shot*, 137–50; *Montreal Gazette*, 30 April 1844.

11 Similar efforts were made to curtail the rougher manifestations of
Orangeism in Ireland, which created the same degree of partisan
rancour and were eventually abandoned. An important survey of
measures taken to curtail Orange marching in Ireland is found in
Bryan, *Orange Parades*, especially 36–8. The Act was repealed in
Canada in 1851.

12 Gregory Kealey makes this argument with regards to the
Orange Order in Toronto after the Rebellion Losses Crisis. See
"Orangemen and the Corporation."

13 For more on controversies relating to the Orange Order, collective
violence, and public spaces, see Radforth, "Collective Rights, Liberal
Discourse and Public Order." It is difficult to gauge the degree to
which the Orange Order was active in Montreal. In their survey of
the organization, Cecil Houston and William Smyth note that there
were roughly six lodges in Montreal in 1850, a much smaller number
proportionally than there were in the cities of Upper Canada. With
that being said, they suggest that members of the order in Montreal
were more radicalized than their Upper Canada brethren because
of the strong Catholic presence in the city. Houston and Smyth, *The
Sash Canada Wore*, 51–5.

There were also rumours of connections between the troops
stationed at the garrison in Montreal and the Orange Order. Senior,
British Regulars in Montreal, 16. The presence of the Orange Order
on the streets of Montreal cannot be traced consistently through
the press, despite the strong anti-Catholic sentiment in Protestant
and Tory newspapers like the *Montreal Witness* and the *Montreal
Gazette*. If the Orangemen of Montreal marched on 12 July, it
was not reported in the local press. The rioting during the 1844
by-election produced a rare exception to this rule. The man who
was wrestling with Julien Champeau when the troops intervened,
William Dyer, was identified as an Orangeman who told a number
of bystanders during the riot that he would have papist blood on his
hands before he slept that night. The *Montreal Gazette* virulently
denied these allegations. *Montreal Gazette*, 30 April 1844.

14 *Les Mélanges religieux*, 28 June 1849.

15 Ryan, *Civic Wars*; Jones, *Republicanism and Responsible
Government*.

16 Monet, *The Last Cannon Shot*, 150; Careless, *The Union of the Canadas*, 61–9.

17 *Montreal Gazette*, 29 March 1844.

18 Bernard, *Les rouges*; Lamonde, *Histoire sociale des idées*, 297.

19 Lamonde, *Histoire sociale des idées*, 309.

20 See, for example, Careless, *The Union of the Canadas*.

21 McNairn, *The Capacity to Judge*.

22 Benjamin Jones traces these ideas across the British world in the middle decades of the nineteenth century. See *Republicanism and Responsible Government*.

23 Morgan, *Public Men and Virtuous Women*, 219; Bruce Curtis, "Class, Culture and Administration," 126; Greer and Radforth, "Introduction." For how this process occurred in other contexts, see Calhoun, *The Roots of Radicalism*, chapter 4; Eley, "Culture, Nation and Gender"; Hall, McClelland, and Rendall, *Defining the Victorian Nation*.

24 See, for examples, Greer and Radforth, *Colonial Leviathan*.

25 Paquet, *Tracer les marges de la cité*, 112.

26 For more on voting in Lower Canada, see Séguin, "Pour une nouvelle synthèse sur les processus électoraux du XIXe siècle québécois."

27 For some examples that relate specifically to Montreal, see Careless, *The Union of the Canadas*, 44; Jackson, *The Riot that Never Was*. More recent work has begun to unpack the impact that this violence had on the negotiation of access to the public sphere during this period. See, for example, Bradbury, "Widows at the Hustings."

28 Séguin, "Pour une nouvelle synthèse," 76.

29 *Montreal Gazette*, 13 April 1844.

30 *Montreal Gazette*, 11 April 1844.

31 *Montreal Gazette*, 16 April 1844.

32 *Montreal Gazette*, 11 April 1844.

33 *Montreal Gazette*, 23 March 1844.

34 *Montreal Gazette*, 2 March 1844.

35 *Montreal Gazette*, 21 March 1844.

36 *La Minerve*, 1 April 1844.

37 *La Minerve*, 29 February 1844.

38 *La Minerve*, 15 April 1844.

39 *La Minerve*, 4 March 1844.

40 Jackson, *The Riot that Never Was*; Bradbury, "Widows at the Hustings."

41 For more on the medical inquest into Champeau's death, see Duffin, "The Great Canadian Peritonitis Debate – 1844–1847."

42 See, for example, Séguin, "Pour une nouvelle synthèse," 93–7.

43 Ryan, *Women in Public*, 32. Even sites that tend to be conceptualized as masculine during this period were not as homogeneous as we might suspect: A letter addressed to the Police Commission two months prior to the by-election decried the lack of accommodation made available to women who attended the weekly meetings of Montreal's City Council, noting that space could easily be set aside for approximately fifteen to twenty seats for this purpose. AVM, VM43 S3, *Fonds de la Commission de la Police*, 5 February 1844.

44 *Montreal Gazette*, 21 March 1844.

45 *Montreal Gazette*, 2 May 1844.

46 *Montreal Gazette*, 23 April 1844. Attempts on the part of the city's Reform faction to have the soldier whose bayonet killed Champeau held criminally responsible for the act resulted in a jury that split evenly along ethnic lines. Senior, *British Regulars in Montreal*, 67.

47 *Montreal Gazette*, 27 April 1844.

48 *Montreal Gazette*, 2 May 1844.

49 *Montreal Gazette*, 16 March 1844.

50 *Montreal Gazette*, 23 May 1844.

51 *La Minerve*, 2 May 1844.

52 *La Minerve*, 18 April 1844.

53 Senior, *British Regulars in Montreal*, 67.

54 *La Minerve*, 11 April 1844.

55 Ibid.

56 *Montreal Gazette*, 16 April 1844; *La Minerve*, 15 April 1844.

57 *La Minerve*, 22 April 1844.

58 *Les Mélanges religieux*, 7 April 1846.

59 For more on how Montreal's courthouse communicated power through architecture, see Fyson, *Magistrates, Police, and People*, 321–3.

60 It is necessary here to comment on the relationship between the franchise and popular politics in Montreal. As was the case in the United States, the franchise in Canada was quite broad, with only the poorest residents restricted from voting. While the Lachine Canal workers did not have the right to vote, most artisans did. This made Montreal very different from Britain, where popular politics was linked to struggles by artisans to gain the right to vote, most notably through the Chartist movement. See, for example, Hall, "The Rule of Difference"; Clark, *The Struggle for the Breeches*. The main issue with voting and election in Canada, therefore, was not who could vote, but whether voters were being intimidated or prevented from voting at the polling station.

61 For more on the rowdy popular politics of the Orange Order, see Kealey, "Orangemen and the Corporation."

62 The petition was discussed at length in *La Minerve*, 2 April 1846.

63 *Les Mélanges religieux*, 3 April 1846; *Les Mélanges religieux*, 7 April 1846. Unfortunately, neither editorial provides the actual number of signatures.

64 *Les Mélanges religieux*, 3 April 1846.

65 *Montreal Gazette*, 19 March 1846.

66 Lafontaine was especially vocal on the issue. Reacting to an election riot in Belleville in 1842, he bemoaned that people's rights were violated when they were prevented from voting by intimidating crowds. *Louis Hippolyte Lafontaine – Correspondance général. Tome I: Les ficelles du pouvoir*, 50–1.

67 Fecteau, "Mesures d'exception et règle de droit," 486-8; Watt, "Authoritarianism, Constitutionalism, and the Special Council."

68 *Montreal Gazette*, 25 April 1844.

69 Ibid. For more on the activities of English-speaking national societies in early nineteenth-century Montreal, see Leitch, "The Importance of Being English?"

70 Lamonde, *Histoire sociale des idées*, 176.

71 *La Minerve*, 8 June 1843.

72 Shortly after the society's re-establishment, a report in *La Minerve* celebrated its successful membership drive, noting that not only elites but also members of the city's "classe ouvrière" were signing on. *La Minerve* was particularly pleased that a youth group had

become the society's vanguard, and that some young members had established a youth group that took principled stands against luxury and foreign goods. *La Minerve*, 24 April 1843.

73 Archdiocese - Archives de la chancellerie de Montréal (hereafter ACDM) 780.019 Fonds Société St Jean Baptiste, *Souvenir du 24 juin 1874*, 8. For more on the growth of mutual aid societies in nineteenth-century Quebec, see Petitclerc, *Nous protégeons l'infortune*, particularly chapter 1.

74 *Les Mélanges religieux* ran an editorial in which it contrasted the sober parade with the boozy banquet. They praised the Quebec City branch of the Société St Jean Baptiste's decision to postpone the banquet to the day after the parade in order to ensure the sobriety of the parade. They called on the Montreal branch to adopt this practice, and it appears as though they did. *Les Mélanges religieux*, 16 mai 1843. This move towards a performative sobriety occurred across the sectarian divide. Orange Order lodges across Canada went dry during this period to foster a more respectable image for the group and their parades, which were under attack from the Reform faction in parliament. Houston and Smyth, *The Sash Canada Wore*, 114.

75 *La Minerve*, 17 January 1843.

76 For a particularly detailed description of the annual St Patrick's Day parade, see *La Minerve*, 18 March 1847.

77 Interestingly, throughout the 1840s it appears as though the celebration of St Patrick's Day was able to unite Irish Montrealers from across the Protestant / Catholic divide. This truce would end in the early 1850s, when the event became more explicitly nationalist and Protestants withdrew their participation. Trigger, "Irish Politics on Parade," 183.

78 Goheen, "Symbols in the Streets," 238.

79 For more on this topic, see Goheen, "Symbols in the Streets;" Goheen, "Parading: A Lively Tradition in Early Victorian Toronto"; Ryan, "The American Parade"; Ryan, *Civic Wars*, 64; Davis, *Parades and Power*, 2.

80 Davis, *Parades and Power*, 159; Ryan, "The American Parade," 137.

81 Some work in Canadian History has highlighted the links between reputation and spectacle. See Nelles, *The Art of Nation-Building*,

240–1; Curtis, "The Most Splendid Pageant Ever Seen."

82 The Canadien community and the temperance movement shared St Jean Baptiste as a patron saint, a connection frequently pointed out by Canadien community leaders.

83 Members of temperance societies were obligated to pay a small deposit on their instruments and were thus likely composed of relatively well-to-do artisans and members of the middling classes. Band members were reminded that they were serving as ambassadors for the temperance movement, and could be fined if seen drinking or on the premises of a tavern or gambling den. Records suggest that these rules might have resulted in a rapid turnover in personnel in these bands. ACDM, 790.21 Fonds Chiniquy, Règlement de la société musicale de la témperance Canadienne de Montréal.

84 Ryan, *Civic Wars*, 72; Ryan, "The American Parade," 143.

85 *Montreal Gazette*, 8 February 1844.

86 Ryan, "The American Parade," 133; Davis, *Parades and Power*.

87 For an example of this sort of coverage, see *Les Mélanges religeux*, 25 June 1844.

88 Curtis, *Ruling by Schooling Quebec*.

89 *La Minerve*, 25 March 1844. For more coverage of St Patrick's Day parades, see *Montreal Gazette*, 18 March 1845; *Montreal Gazette*, 18 March 1846; *Les Mélanges religieux*, 20 March 1849; *Montreal Gazette*, 19 March 1849.

90 While the temperance societies were involved in the celebration of St Patrick's Day throughout the decade, the 1843 parade was specifically meant to celebrate the career of Reverend Phelan, the priest who had founded the St Patrick's Temperance Society at the outset of the decade and had inspired thousands of Irish Montrealers to take the pledge each year. *Montreal Transcript*, 16 March 1843.

91 *Montreal Gazette*, 16 March 1843.

92 *Les Mélanges religieux*, 21 March 1843.

93 *La Minerve*, 27 June 1844.

94 *Les Mélanges religieux*, 23 June 1848.

95 For more on Garneau and the writing of Quebec history, see Bergeron, *Lire François-Xavier Garneau, 1809-1866*.

96 *Les Mélanges religieux*, 30 June 1846.

97 For more on this, see Ismer, "Embodying the Nation."

98 See, for example, *La Minerve*, 26 June 1848; *L'Avenir*, 27 June 1848.

99 See, for example, *Montreal Gazette*, 25 June 1845; *Montreal Gazette*, 25 June 1846.

100 For interesting discussions of this process of marginalization in the context of nineteenth-century British North America, see Bradbury, *Wife to Widow*; Harring, *White Man's Law*.

Chapter Five

1 For insight into this historical moment, see Lambton's *Lord Durham's Report on the Affairs of British North America*. For a recent assessment of Durham's time in Canada and the attitudes of him and his entourage towards French Canada and its institutions, see Curtis, *Ruling by Schooling Quebec*, chapter 8.

2 *La Minerve*, 31 August 1843.

3 Two of the leading historians of nineteenth-century Quebec have argued convincingly that the liberalism that shaped public life during this period made the state hesitant about intervening too heavily in social matters like health and education. This left a gap for the Catholic Church and other religious institutions to fill. See Fecteau, "La dynamique sociale du Catholicisme," 503; Bradbury, *Wife to Widow*, 398.

4 See Dagenais, "The Municipal Territory."

5 For an overview of Montreal's public sphere during this period, see Lamonde, *Histoire sociale des idées au Québec, 1760–1896*, chapter 4.

6 The academic literature on the public sphere is informative here. See Habermas, *The Structural Transformation of the Public Sphere* as well as more recent critiques of his analysis, including Eley, "Nations, Publics, and Political Cultures."

7 See Ryan, *Civic Wars*.

8 For more on this process, see Ferry, *Uniting in Measures of Common Good*; McKay, "The Liberal Order Framework."

9 Tosh, *A Man's Place*.

10 For an overview of the Ultramontane ideology with regards to state

and society, see Eid, *Le clergé et le pouvoir politique au Québec*, chapter 2.

11 The relationship between liberalism and Ultramontane Catholicism is explored by Fecteau in *La liberté du pauvre*, chapter VII.

12 Perin, *Ignace de Montréal*, chapter II; Voisine, "L'ultramontanisme Canadien-français au XIXe siècle," 77.

13 This apparent shift in French Canada's religious culture has fueled a decades-long academic debate around the question of whether it constituted a religious revival and, if it did, whether it marked a sudden transformation in the aftermath of the rebellions or a more drawn-out shift that had been percolating since the 1820s. The two leading figures in this exchange, Louis Rousseau and René Hardy, base their competing assertions on extensive quantitative evaluations of how many Catholics in Lower Canada were taking communion during major masses or entering religious orders during this period. See Hardy, "À propos du réveil religieux dans le Québec du XIXe siècle"; Rousseau, "À l'origine d'une société maintenant perdue"; Rousseau et Remiggi, "Le renouveau religieux à Montréal au XIXe siècle"; Rousseau, "À propos du 'réveil religieux' dans le Québec du XIXe siècle"; Hudon, "Le renouveau religieux québécois au XIXe siècle"; Hardy, *Contrôle social et mutation de la culture religieuse au Québec, 1830–1930*, chapter 2; Rousseau et Remiggi, *Atlas historique des pratiques religieuses: Le Sud-Ouest du Québec au XIXe siècle*, Introduction.

14 *Les Mélanges religieux*, 28 May 1847. Charles Chiniquy received a similar welcome at the docks when he arrived in Montreal to deliver one of his celebrated temperance lectures in July 1849. See Trudel in *Chiniquy*, 2nd ed., 99.

15 For a discussion of how colonial authorities used these sorts of public rituals to assert their power, see Curtis, "The Most Splendid Pageant Ever Seen"; Perin, *Ignace de Montréal*, 42.

16 The politicization of these rituals also occurred in English Canada several decades later. See Radforth, "Collective Rights, Liberal Discourse, and Public Order."

17 Galarneau, "Monseigneur de Forbin-Janson au Québec en 1840–1841," 128–9.

18 *Les Mélanges religieux*, 26 December 1840.

19 Ibid.

20 Voisine, "Ultramontanisme canadien-français au XIXe siècle", 74.

21 *Les Mélanges religieux*, 13 January 1841.

22 *Les Mélanges religieux*, 26 December 1840.

23 See Galarneau, "Monseigneur de Forbin-Janson au Québec en 1840–1841," 130; Voisine, "Ultramontanisme canadien-français au XIXe siècle," 73. This was despite the fact that Forbin-Janson advocated for the rights of the exiled Patriotes. Galarneau, "Monseigneur de Forbin-Janson au Québec en 1840–1841," 138.

24 *Les Mélanges religieux*, 13 January 1841.

25 *Les Mélanges religieux*, 29 January 1841.

26 *Les Mélanges religieux*, 8 January 1841.

27 Bradbury, *Working Families*, chapter 5; Poutanen, "Bonds of Friendship, Kinship, and Community."

28 Bradbury, *Wife to Widow*.

29 The literature on how women negotiated their marginalized status during this period is enlightening here. See Danylewicz, *Taking the Veil*; Ryan, *Civic Wars*, particularly chapter 6; Stansell, *City of Women*.

30 Rousseau et Remiggi, *Atlas historique des pratiques religieuses*.

31 For a larger discussion of Catholic temperance activism in Lower Canada / Canada East during this period, see Ares, "Les campagnes de tempérance de Charles Chiniquy."

32 *Les Mélanges religieux*, 19 January 1841.

33 Ibid; Ares, 270.

34 Bourget also made this argument. See *Mandements, lettres pastorales, circulaires et autres documents publiés dans le diocèse de Montréal depuis son érection jusqu'à l'année 1869*, vol.1, 104.

35 *Souvenir of the Golden Jubilee of St Patrick's Total Abstinence and Benefit Society, 1840–1890*, 22–5.

36 This interpretation has been made by Trudel in *Chiniquy*; Noel, "Dry Patriotism."

37 See, for example, Rorabaugh, *The Alcoholic Republic*, 188.

38 For more on these tensions, see Blocker, *American Temperance Movements*, 191.

39 Harrison, *Drink and the Victorians*, 19.

40 See Olson and Thornton, *Peopling the North American City*,

particularly chapter 11. In his study of Chiniquy and the
temperance movement in Quebec, Jean-Patrice Ares argues that
self-regulation and the creation of rituals and routines of sobriety
were central to the movement. See "Les campagnes de tempérance
de Charles Chiniquy."

41 Eid, *Le clergé et le pouvoir au Québec*, 33; Noel, "Dry Patriotism,"
192; Bernard, *Les rouges*.

42 The city's Anglophone Protestant temperance movement drew on
ideas and practices that were sweeping the Anglo-American World
during this period, on which there is a vast historical literature.
See, for examples, Harrison, *Drink and the Victorians*; Shiman,
The Crusade against Drink in Victorian England; Cook, "Through
sunshine and shadow"; Martin, *Devil of the Domestic Sphere*;
Heron, *Booze*, chapters 3–5.

43 Noel, "Dry Patriotism," 201.

44 For an example of Charles Chiniquy making these connections
in his writing, see *Manuel des sociétés de tempérance dédié à la
jeunesse du Canada*, 3rd ed., 30.

45 Ibid., 64.

46 Ibid., 42.

47 Trudel, *Chiniquy*, 101; 126–7.

48 Lachance, *La saga des Papineau*, chapter 21.

49 Trudel, *Chiniquy*, 127. Incidentally, women did eventually become
an essential component of Chiniquy's parting with the Catholic
Church. Following accusations that he seduced a young woman
following a temperance rally, Bourget had him shuffled off to a
parish in the American Midwest, where he would eventually shift
his spiritual allegiance to an evangelical brand of Protestantism.

50 Ian McKay argues that these gendered ideals were crucial
components of the liberal political that emerged during this period.
See "The Liberal Order Framework," 625.

51 Caulier, "Bâtir l'Amérique des dévots; Danylewicz, *Taking the Veil*;
Hudon, "La sociabilité religieuse à l'ère du vapeur et du rail," 142.

52 A French language guidebook to performing the Stations of the
Cross referred to the practice as "la pieuse coutûme des âmes
fervantes." The women reading the guidebook, which was sold in
Montreal, would certainly have been empowered by the notion

expressed within, that devout women were the vanguard of
Catholicism. *Instruction sur le chemin de la croix, avec les pratiques
de cette devotion dediée à la très-sainte-vierge*, 24.

53 *Le Canadien*, 26 May 1843.

54 For an overview of conflicts over Fête-Dieu in Montreal over the
course of the nineteenth century, see Sheito, "Une fête contestée."

55 *Les Mélanges religieux*, 27 June 1848.

56 Looking at Catholic processions as a means of understanding how
the popular classes engaged with their religion is an approach best
exemplified by Robert Orsi in his study of Italian Harlem in the
late nineteenth and early twentieth century. *The Madonna of 115ᵗʰ
Street: Faith and Community in Italian Harlem, 1880–1950*.

57 Ollivier Hubert argues that this focus on order and precision was
a defining trait of Catholic rites during this period. Disorderly
movements and behaviour, clerical figures surmised, would
weaken the emotional impact of these rituals. See *Sur la terre
comme au ciel*, 271–4.

58 *Les Mélanges religieux*, 26 June 1848. Bishop Bourget, Roberto
Perin argues, was a keen student of the city's spatial politics. See
"Elaborating a Public Culture in Nineteenth-Century Quebec,"
95–7.

59 Mary Ryan suggests that we interpret parades as a representation of
an idealized social order. This is a fruitful exercise in this case. See
"The American Parade," 132.

60 *Les Mélanges religieux*, 16 June 1846.

61 See, for example, Hubert, *Sur la terre comme au ciel*, 222–4; and
Bryan, *Orange Parades*, 172.

62 *La Minerve*, 9 February 1843.

63 *Les Mélanges religieux*, 16 June 1846.

64 This interpretation is in keeping with the analysis popularized by
Turner in *The Ritual Process*. Turner argued that rituals created a
liminal space where the structures of everyday life could be both
elaborated and challenged. In his work on sectarian parading
in twentieth-century Northern Ireland, Dominic Bryan builds
on Turner's work, noting that these sorts of rituals provided an
opportunity for people to see the community ordered in a way that
empowered them. Bryan, *Orange Parades*.

65 *Les Mélanges religieux*, 16 June 1846.

66 *Les Mélanges religieux*, 18 June 1841.

67 *Les Mélanges religieux*, 20 June 1843.

68 Christine Sheito makes a similar argument with regards of the collective rights of Catholics. "Une fête contestée," 74.

69 *Les Mélanges religieux*, 20 juin 1843. The most stunning example of this was observed during the 1849 procession, when George Moffatt, a Protestant merchant who was accused of egging on Tory thugs during the Rebellion Losses Riot, decorated his store with flowers and saplings for Fête-Dieu. Henri Comte, *La Fête-Dieu à Montréal de 1658 à 1933*, 18.

70 *Montreal Gazette*, 5 June 1844; *La Minerve*, 7 June 1844.

71 For more on the politically charged debates over demographic change, see Curtis, *The Politics of Population*, 7–9; "Le redécoupage du Bas-Canada dans les années 1830," 63.

72 Sheito, "Une fête contestée," 36.

73 An Act to Restrain Party Processions 1843 Cap. VI, in *The Provincial Statutes of Canada*, 17. This sense that the Catholic Church and its adherents were gradually gaining official sanction from the colonial authorities played a significant role in fostering the hostility that would explode during the Rebellion Losses Crisis of 1849.

74 *La Minerve*, 7 June 1844.

75 *Montreal Witness*, 8 June 1846.

76 Ibid.

77 For more on this, see Morgan, *Public Men and Virtuous Women*. An important context here is the role that anti-Catholicism played in the formation of a British identity in the second half of the eighteenth and first half of the nineteenth centuries. English-speaking Protestant Montrealers were engaged in this process. See Colley, *Britons*, 5.

78 *Montreal Gazette*, 13 June 1849.

79 Ibid.

80 *Les Mélanges religieux*, 12 June 1849.

81 Ibid.

82 *Montreal Gazette*, 12 June 1849. An editorial printed in *Les Mélanges religieux* mocking these allegations took the *Montreal*

Gazette's reporting as evidence that violent anarchists at the Tory newspaper were bent on destroying the Catholic religion. *Les Mélanges religieux*, 15 June 1849.

83 *Les Mélanges religieux*, 12 June 1849.

84 *Les Mélanges religieux*, 6 October 1848.

85 For more on the lives of dock labourers and sailors in the city, see DeLottinville, "Joe Beef of Montreal"; Ingram, "Saving the Union's Jack."

86 *Les Mélanges religieux*, 6 October 1848.

87 Ibid.

88 Ibid.

89 For more on the impact of democratic discourse on the political culture of Quebec and the North Atlantic World during this period, see Ducharme, *Le concept de liberté au Canada à l'époque des Révolutions atlantiques*, and Vernon, *Politics and the People*.

Chapter Six

1 This vision is vigorously defended by Donald Creighton in *The Commercial Empire of the St. Lawrence, 1760–1850*, 354. In their commentary on the parliamentary debates on the Rebellion Losses Act, the *Montreal Gazette* lamented that public opinion had not been gauged on the issue, and that Lord Elgin risked setting a precedent whereby the governor could be manipulated by whatever faction held a majority in parliament. *Montreal Gazette*, 28 March 1849.

2 Buckner, *The Transition to Responsible Government*, 300.

3 Many recognized that political debate had taken a rough turn when women stopped filling the benches of the visitor's gallery in parliament. *La Minerve*, 26 April 1849.

4 For eyewitness accounts of the riot, see the *Montreal Gazette*, 27 April 1849; *Witness*, 30 April 1849; *La Minerve*, 26 April 1849; *Le Canadien*, 27 April 1849; *Les Mélanges religieux*, 27 April 1849; *Pilot*, 27 April 1849.

5 Jeffrey McNairn argues persuasively that analyses of responsible government need to take into account the growing emphasis placed on the ability of men to engage in rational debate in a public

setting. The events of 1849 provide vivid examples of this rhetoric, as political leaders were attacked for their real or perceived connections to the unrestrained politics of the crowd. McNairn, *The Capacity to Judge*, 12.

6 Three works of political and economic history highlight the Rebellion Losses Crisis as a turning point. Jacques Monet argues that the crisis was a crucial test of responsible government. *The Last Cannon Shot*, 334–42. This perspective is shared by J.M.S. Careless' study of the political maneuverings of the Act of Union period, *The Union of the Canadas*, 121–7. Donald Creighton portrays the firing of parliament as the last furious gasp of Montreal's English-speaking merchant elite, whose world was being turned upside down by political and economic policies being carried out in Britain and Canada in *The Empire of the St. Lawrence*, 349–85.

7 They eventually settled on rotating the seat of government between Quebec and Toronto, two cities that were no strangers to popular violence. *Le Canadien*, which was published out of Quebec, launched a campaign to have the capital moved there on a permanent basis. A letter to the editor signed by a M. Laterrière encapsulated their argument succinctly. He warned that violence was likely to remain at least a periodic feature of Montreal society, and that Quebec was a more appropriate seat of government as it was English in sentiment. *Le Canadien*, 18 May 1849. The *Montreal Gazette* defended Montreal, noting that similar violence had occurred in places like Quebec and Toronto, and that Montreal's Tory crowds deserved commendation for there having been no deaths attributable to them during the rioting. *Montreal Gazette*, 24 May 1849.

8 Similar observations about the long-term consequences of the popular unrest of the 1840s are made by McKay in "The Liberal Order Framework" and Kealey in "Orangemen and the Corporation."

9 Geoff Eley makes a strong case for engaging in a gendered historical analysis of this process. Elite men, he argued, harnessed shifting ideologies around gender to parlay their economic might into cultural authority. This observation rings true in the way that

Montreal's reform-oriented elites spoke about remaining rational and composed in the face of popular unrest. Eley, "Nations, Public and Political Cultures," 312.

10 For an example of this, see Careless, *The Union of the Canadas*, 121–7.

11 This observation was made, for example, in the report on the destruction of parliament published in *Les Mélanges religieux*, 27 April 1849.

12 Debates about the coherency of crowds have long been an important part of scholarly work on popular protest. Desan, for example, has critiqued E.P. Thompson for exaggerating the coherency and discipline of crowds in "Crowds, Community and Ritual," 61.

13 This point was emphasized by Nicholas Rogers in his survey of the historiography on crowds in British History, *Crowds, Culture and Politics*, 3–17. Holton has also written about the dangers of ignoring the ambivalence of crowds or resorting to reductionism in considering their motivations. "The Crowd in History," 227.

14 *Montreal Gazette*, 27 April 1849.

15 Ibid.

16 For the importance of domestic space with regards to elite identity, see Davidoff and Hall, *Family Fortunes*, chapter 3; Tosh, *A Man's Place*; Fecteau, *La liberté du pauvre*, 74.

17 For more on how elites in other urban centres reacted to a rough popular culture where spontaneous crowd events figured heavily, see Davis, *Parades and Power*.

18 For a survey of nineteenth-century popular violence, see C. Tilly, L. Tilly, and R. Tilly, *The Rebellious Century*.

19 This would have been surprising because of the rhetoric of the day that connected popular unrest and the urban poor but, in fact, it was not out of the ordinary. As Mary Ryan demonstrates in her study of public life in three nineteenth-century American cities, merchants often figured prominently in vigilante crowds that portrayed themselves as the defenders of democratic values. Ryan, *Civic Wars*, 162.

20 Other speakers included Augustus Heward, a broker at the Bank of Montreal, whose head offices were occupied by Peter McGill, the scion of an elite Montreal family with deep connections to Tory

circles, and Henry Montgomerie, who resided on Devonshire Place on the genteel slopes of Mount Royal. Only the fourth speaker could claim any connection to the popular classes: Alfred Perry was an engine maker and firefighter from a humble immigrant background. Biographical information collected from *The Montreal Directory 1849*.

21 *Further Papers Relative to the Affairs of Canada*, 5.

22 *Les Mélanges religieux*, 4 May 1849.

23 *La Minerve*, 26 April 1849.

24 At the local level, the municipal government created at the beginning of the 1840s wielded important new authorities, and featured a strong Canadien and Irish contingent with deep connections to the Reform faction.

25 Jones, *Republicanism and Responsible Government*.

26 Ermatinger, the son of a Swiss merchant in the fur trade and the daughter of an Ojibwa Chief, was the descendent of a storied family. For more, see Stewart, *The Ermatingers*.

27 QBD, Deposition of John Popham, 28 June 1849.

28 QBD, Deposition of Bartholomew Augustus Conrad Gugy, 23 June 1849.

29 QBD, Deposition of Robert Irwin, 4 May 1849.

30 Historians have noted the emphasis placed on masculine restraint and respectability in shaping the political worldview of the nineteenth-century middle class. See, for example, Holman, *A Sense of Their Duty*, and Morgan, *Public Men and Virtuous Women*, 142. Peter Bailey's work, in which he explores the fluid, performative aspects of respectability with regards to Victorian popular culture is important here. See *Popular Culture and Performance in the Victorian City*, 45.

31 QBD, Deposition of Henry Howard, 23 June 1849.

32 For more on Drolet's life, see Carman Miller's entry in the *Dictionary of Canadian Biography*.

33 Although the words of the speakers may have been disturbing, the scene was later described in less threatening terms by a *Montreal Gazette* reporter. In an effort to defend the respectability of the gathering, he noted that the crowd was sparse and consisted of both men and women. *Montreal Gazette*, 27 April 1849.

34 QBD, Deposition of Charles Drolet, 28 April 1849.

35 Ibid.

36 QBD, Deposition of Henry Howard, 23 June 1849.

37 QBD, Deposition of William Bird, 20 July 1849.

38 For more on charivaris in nineteenth-century Canada, see Hardy, "Le charivari dans l'espace québécois"; Greer, *The Patriots and the People*; Palmer, "Discordant Music."

39 There was a long tradition of nocturnal protest in the western world. Men and women had long taken advantage of the anonymity provided by darkness to transgress social and cultural conventions, and this was clearly the case with prominent Montrealers during the Rebellion Losses Crisis. David Harvey has argued that elite anxiety about crowds was rooted in the way they usurped authority by creating anonymous spaces. Harvey, *Paris*, 223. For a longer discussion of nocturnal protest, see Palmer, *Cultures of Darkness*, chapter 2.

40 *Montreal Gazette*, 7 May 1849.

41 *Montreal Gazette*, 7 March 1849.

42 The pen-name suggests that the writer had served in militias defending the crown in 1837 and 1838, or as far back as 1812.

43 *Montreal Gazette*, 7 March 1849.

44 Lewis Drummond made these allegations in parliament shortly after the house reconvened, causing the Tory side to erupt in cries of indignation. *Montreal Gazette*, 3 May 1849.

45 *Les Mélanges religieux*, 8 June 1849. The Catholic press alluded to the Gordon Riots of 1780, when anti-Catholic crowds were stirred up by the violent rhetoric of Lord George Gordon. See Rogers, *Crowds, Culture and Politics*, 152–98. William Weir, a keen observer of Montreal's political scene, argued in his memoirs that the Rebellion Losses Bill was simply an excuse to justify a Tory revolt that had been brewing since their losses in the election of the previous year. See Weir, *Sixty Years in Canada*, 27.

46 Walrond, *Letters and Journals of James, Eighth Earl of Elgin*, 70.

47 *Montreal Gazette*, 14 May 1849. The newspaper defended their coverage of the debates over the Rebellion Losses Bill and their incendiary special edition that called for the gathering on the Champ-de-Mars by claiming that their inflammatory language

was an attempt to warn the government how dire the political tension in the city was. *Montreal Gazette*, 5 May 1849.

48 A meeting was called for the city's "merchants and other respectable citizens" two days after the riot. Placards and notices in the *Montreal Gazette* made it clear that this was to be a gathering of the city's English-speaking merchants. How foes of the Tories perceived this event would certainly have been coloured by the decision to hold it on the Champ-de-Mars, just like the gathering that preceded the attack on parliament. See the *Montreal Gazette*, 27 April 1849.

49 Gugy was one of the few French-speaking Tories active in the city's politics during this period. He was the son of a prominent Swiss Protestant family that had settled in Lower Canada in the eighteenth century. He had been placed in charge of the rural police force by the Special Council. For more on Gugy, see Jacques Monet's entry in the *Dictionary of Canadian Biography*; also, see Greer, "The Birth of the Police in Canada," 30–1.

50 *Montreal Gazette*, 30 April 1849.

51 Moyse Brassard, a master joiner, pointed his finger at Courtney for urging the crowd towards violence, and also noted seeing *Montreal Gazette* editor James Ferres in the thick of the action. QBD, Deposition of Moyse Brassard, 21 July 1849. William McDonald Dawson blamed Alfred Perry for the riot. He testified that Perry "appeared to exercize great control over the assemblage and to be their most active leader." He sensed that many in the crowd attended the meeting on the Champ-de-Mars with the expectation that there would be an attack on parliament. QBD, Deposition of William McDonald Dawson, 26 April 1849.

52 *The Montreal Directory*.

53 *Le Canadien*, 27 April 1849.

54 *La Minerve*, 9 May 1849.

55 Jones, *Republicanism and Responsible Government*.

56 See, for example, *Les Mélanges religieux*, 11 May 1849.

57 QBD, Deposition of Louis Lacroix, 27 June 1849. Montreal's Tories established the British American League at meetings of this nature in the midst of the Rebellion Losses Crisis. It would become the driving force behind the annexation movement. *Les Mélanges*

religieux reprinted a long essay from a conservative French periodical on secret societies during the crisis. They drew parallels between the clandestine efforts of Montreal's Tories and secretive fraternal societies in France. These organizations, the essay argued, were sinister by their very definition and existed for the sole purpose of stirring up sectarian conflict and, ultimately, usurping the power of elected governments. *Les Mélanges religieux*, 28 June 1849.

58 *Les Mélanges religieux*, 11 May 1849.

59 *Montreal Gazette*, 9 June 1849.

60 *Montreal Gazette*, 28 June 1849.

61 *Montreal Gazette*, 3 May 1849.

62 *Montreal Gazette*, 10 May 1849.

63 *Les Mélanges religieux*, 26 June 1849. Concern for the well-being of Lady Elgin was widespread throughout the crisis. Many of the petitions in support of the government and governor mentioned her specifically. For example, a petition of loyalty signed by a group of Algonquin men mentioned that their wives had expressed concern for Lady Elgin's safety and had asked that this be reflected in their text. *La Minerve*, 14 June 1849.

64 *Montreal Gazette*, 27 June 1849.

65 *Montreal Gazette*, 6 June 1849.

66 *Montreal Gazette*, 12 June 1849. This was surely an allusion to Lord Elgin's former posting in Jamaica.

67 The gender politics of democratic reform were contested throughout this period. Cecilia Morgan credits debates over responsible government in nineteenth-century Upper Canada with opening up a distinctly masculine sphere of political debate. Morgan, *Public Men and Virtuous Women*, 219.

68 *Montreal Gazette*, 15 May 1849.

69 *Les Mélanges religieux*, 27 April 1849.

70 *Montreal Witness*, 7 May 1849.

71 Walrond, *Letters and Journals of James, Eighth Earl of Elgin*, 99. Such sentiments are commonplace in Elgin's personal correspondence from this time. In a letter to Earl Grey, Lord Elgin once more shrugged off the attacks of his political foes for the sake of the public good, noting that he "thought it better to endure any amount of personal indignity, than to have recourse to measures

from which the design of pitting race against race could be inferred. *Further Papers Relative to the Affairs of Canada*, 6.

72 *Le Canadien*, 4 June 1849. Reform commentators argued that Lord Elgin's cool demeanour throughout the crisis was the embodiment of responsible government. This analysis even found its way into the historiography on the topic, and is discussed in detail in Careless, *The Union of the Canadas* and Monet, *The Last Cannon Shot*, 342.

73 *Les Mélanges religieux*, 15 June 1849.

74 AVM, VM1, *City Council Minutes*, 9 May 1849. In a response to a petition of support from the Catholic clergy of Quebec City, Lord Elgin wrote that he felt his moderate stance throughout the Rebellion Losses Crisis to be the fulfillment of a "sacred duty." *Further Papers Relative to the Affairs of Canada*, 8.

75 *Montreal Gazette*, 9 May 1849.

76 *Montreal Gazette*, 6 June 1849.

77 *Montreal Gazette*, 27 June 1849.

78 *Montreal Gazette*, 28 June 1849.

79 *Montreal Witness*, 21 May 1849.

80 See, for example, Davidoff and Hall, *Family Fortunes*, chapter 3; Tosh, *A Man's Place*. Major General Rowan, the military commander appointed in the summer of 1849, echoed this view during his inaugural address. He reminded military, civil, and religious leaders that their primary duty was to return to their families and communities to appease the tension that had developed during the previous months. *La Minerve*, 31 May 1849.

81 Scott See has argued that concerns over the ability of urban police forces to protect elites and their property from violence played a significant role in subsequent processes of state formation, as municipal governments invested more public funds into police forces, encouraging their gradual professionalization. "Nineteenth-Century Collective Violence," 35.

82 See Horner, "Like a Thread of Gold."

83 The ringing of fire bells is mentioned by the French-Canadian press as the most obnoxious means by which the Tories were holding the city under siege. *Les Mélanges religieux*, 11 May 1849; *Le Canadien*, 6 June 1849.

84 *Montreal Gazette*, 27 April 1849.

85 QBD, Deposition of Auguste Desnoyers, 5 May 1849. Desnoyers' experience does not appear to have been an isolated one. A merchant by the name of Benjamin Hutchins reported seeing a group of men carrying out similar attacks, while Michael Gannon observed another group furiously unscrewing a hose from a water pump, thus sabotaging the fire companies' efforts to extinguish the blaze. QBD, Deposition of Benjamin Hutchins, 28 April 1849; QBD, Deposition of Michael Gannon, 28 April 1849.

86 *La Minerve* had long been accusing the city's English-speaking fire companies of being little more than a rabble of Tory thugs. See, for example, *La Minerve*, 3 May 1849.

87 QBD, Deposition of Étienne Bélinge, 9 May 1849.

88 QBD, Deposition of Thomas Robinson, 4 May 1849.

89 *Montreal Gazette*, 27 April 1849.

90 Ibid.

91 Hincks, *Reminiscences of His Public Life*, 193–4.

92 *Montreal Gazette*, 27 April 1849.

93 QBD, Deposition of John Taylor, 23 June 1849.

94 *Further Papers Relative to the Affairs of Canada*, 5–6. A high-ranking military official, James Alexander, supported the government's reluctance to call out the troops or order the police to fire on crowds during the Rebellion Losses Crisis. In his memoirs he recalled warning the municipal authorities to halt their practice of drilling armed police constables in front of Bonsecours Market, as it was likely to provoke disgruntled Tories, "all ready for a fight as they were." Alexander, *Passages in the Life of a Soldier*, 21.

95 See, for example, the discussion on the role troops played on the streets of Montreal during the election riot of 1844 in chapter 4 and Senior, *British Regulars in Montreal*, 60–6. Senior argues by the end of the 1840s the troops were unwilling to engage with agitated urban crowds. Senior, *British Regulars in Montreal*, 209.

96 QBD, Deposition of Charles Touron, 3 May 1849.

97 *Montreal Witness*, 30 April 1849.

98 Ibid.

99 *Les Mélanges religieux*, 4 May 1849.

100 *Montreal Gazette*, 2 May 1849.

101 *Montreal Gazette*, 30 April 1849.

102 *QBD*, Deposition of Fleury St Jean, 9 May 1849.

103 *Les Mélanges religieux*, 1 May 1849.

104 *Montreal Gazette*, 9 June 1849.

105 Ibid.

106 *Les Mélanges religieux*, 4 May 1849.

107 *Le Canadien*, 4 May 1849.

108 *La Minerve*, 7 May 1849.

109 This sentiment can be interpreted as part of a larger struggle by the authorities to re-tool longstanding practices of policing social unrest. For more on this in the context of Montreal and Quebec, see Fecteau, "Mesures d'exception et règle de droit" and Fyson, "The Trials and Tribulations of Riot Prosecutions."

110 AVM, VM1, City Council Minutes, 18 June 1849.

111 AVM, VM1, City Council Minutes, 31 May 1849.

112 AVM, VM1, City Council Minutes, 18 June 1849.

113 AVM, VM43 S2, *Fonds de la Commission de la Police*, 28 June 1849. The final mention of an augmented police force during this period occurred in late September of that year, when the Police Commission voted to end voluntary night patrols and to thank those who had carried out these duties. AVM, VM43, S2, *Fonds de la Commission de la Police*, 29 September 1849.

114 *Le Canadien*, 11 May 1849. These discussions fueled the ultimately successful suggestions that the colonial capital of the Province of Canada needed to be removed from Montreal immediately.

115 *Le Canadien*, 27 April 1849; *Le Canadien*, 4 May 1849. An editorial published in *Les Mélanges religieux* reminded readers that they had stood alongside Tories in condemning acts of insurrectionary violence unfolding across Europe in 1848. The Tories, they noted, were now engaged in similar acts of terror on the streets of Montreal. *Les Mélanges religieux*, 12 June 1849. The Reform press rejoiced when the *Times* of London published an editorial comparing the Montreal's Tories with English Chartists and Irish rebels. The *Montreal Gazette*, of course, took issue with this comparison. *Montreal Gazette*, 6 June 1849.

116 This was not the first time that Canadien politicians had suggested that they were the true defenders of British institutions in Lower

Canada / Canada East. In the 1830s a number of politicians had suggested that the Patriotes were engaged in a struggle for institutions that would meet the lofty standards that guided British imperialism. See Greer, *The Patriotes and the People*. This is also discussed in Creighton, *The Commercial Empire of the St. Lawrence*, 159. The contested and performative nature of loyalty persisted in the decades that followed. See Radforth, *Royal Spectacle*.

117 *Le Canadien*, 14 March 1849. Papineau had been the sole Canadien politician opposed to the Rebellion Losses Act, on the grounds that it conferred legitimacy on the Act of Union. See Fernand Ouellet's entry on Papineau in the *Dictionary of Canadian Biography* and Monet, *The Last Cannon Shot*, chapter 16.

118 Throughout the union period, the position that the governor's oversight of the elected assembly was the hallmark of British governance rather than responsible government had been an important feature of Tory rhetoric in Canada. Creighton, *The Commercial Empire of the St. Lawrence*, 354. For more on how responsible government came to be the litmus test for advocates of democratic reform across the British Empire during this period, see Jones, *Republicanism and Responsible Government*.

119 *Montreal Gazette*, 4 April 1849. In a political precursor to the Rebellion Losses Crisis, British Protestant Tories had reacted in outrage when Governor Bagot reached out to Canadiens upon taking office in 1842, arguing that the politicians Bagot was bringing into government had betrayed the crown during the rebellions. Careless, *The Union of the Canadas*, 70.

120 *Montreal Gazette*, 2 May 1849. In her history of the garrison in Montreal, Elinor Kyte Senior argues that the events of 1849 did indeed rupture the formerly close relationship between Montreal's Tories and the troops stationed in the city. *British Regulars in Montreal*, 107.

121 This line of argument was part of the fabric of public life in Canada. For example, in his study of the Montreal Constitutional Association, Bruce Curtis examines the stance that British Protestant merchants took with regards to the 92 Resolutions of the Patriotes in the mid-1830s. While paying lip service to a liberal

worldview, the Montreal Constitutional Association consistently defended the practice of empowering a small English-speaking elite because they believed that the Canadiens were not sufficiently rational to govern themselves. Curtis, "Le redécoupage du Bas-Canada," 65. In *Legacies of Fear,* Frank Greenwood traces these sentiments as far back as the signing of the Quebec Act in 1774 against the backdrop of the French Revolution.

122 *Montreal Gazette,* 21 March 1849.

123 *Montreal Gazette,* 7 May 1849. Tories also insisted that Lord Elgin ought to have acknowledged that with continued immigration from the British Isles, Tories would soon enjoy the support of the majority of voters. The Governor's dogmatic commitment to responsible government had stripped a "temporary minority" of their rights. *Montreal Gazette,* 15 May 1849.

124 The Tory press occasionally drew parallels between their critique of responsible government and the American revolutionaries of the 1770s, suggesting that the Boston Tea Party was something of a precursor to the attack on parliament. This disdain for tyranny was a trait that many Tories believed to be ethnic in nature – a characteristic of Anglo-Saxon people. *Montreal Gazette,* 8 June 1849.

125 d'Urban had been called to Montreal from his residence at Sorel to assist in the efforts to restore law and order to the city. His obituary in *Le Canadien* speculated that the turmoil of the Rebellion Losses Crisis played a role in his death, though he had been burdened by ill health for months. *Le Canadien,* 30 May 1849.

126 *Montreal Gazette,* 28 May 1849. For a description of the funeral, see Alexander, *Passages in the Life of a Soldier,* 26.

127 *Montreal Gazette,* 28 May 1849.

128 James Alexander suggested that there were ten thousand people lining the length of Notre Dame Street. His military connections might have led him to exaggerate the size of the crowd, but we should not doubt that this was a significant moment. See *Passages in the Life of a Soldier,* 26.

129 *Montreal Gazette,* 29 May 1849.

130 See, for example, *Le Canadien,* 30 May 1849.

131 *La Minerve,* 31 May 1849.

132 Despite Lewis Drummond's insistence that prominent Tory leaders be held responsible for their fiery rhetoric, none were. The nine men arrested, however, did include James Orr, the owner of Orr's Hotel, a popular Tory gathering place. The others were Alexander Courtney, Joseph Ewing, Robert Cooke, James Bone, James Nelson, Robert Howard, George Jamieson, and John Dyer, famed for his participation in the rioting that marked the by-election in the west ward in April 1844. Their trials were delayed until October 1850, and were widely seen as a fiasco after numerous witnesses refused to testify. Donald Fyson argues that this was in keeping with the challenges the authorities faced when it came to prosecuting rioters, many of whom had to be released on the grounds of Habeas Corpus. See Fyson, "The Trials and Tribulations of Riot Prosecutions," 190–1.

133 Lafontaine's deposition details damages during two major attacks on his home in the western suburbs of Montreal. He was quite candid about the anxiety he experienced as a target of Tory intimidation and violence. See Aubin et Blanchet, eds, *Mon cher Amable*, 20 August 1849.

134 For an excellent description of the tumult and fire at the Cyrus Hotel, see ACDM 780.019 Fonds Société St. Jean Baptiste de Montréal – Correspondance générale, *Souvenir du 24 juin 1874* (Montréal: Société St. Jean Baptiste, 1874), 46–8. See also Monet, *The Last Cannon Shot*, 342.

135 Careless, *The Union of the Canadas*, 128; Phillipe Sylvain, "Quelques aspects de l'antagonimse libéral-ultramontain au Canada français," 134. Canadien annexationists argued that severing ties with Britain was a logical next step in the progression of their nation, and cited Louisiana as an example of a French culture surviving under American rule. Monet, *The Last Cannon Shot*, 347–9.

136 Ibid., 351.

137 Ryerson, *Unequal Union*, 237.

138 See, for example, Kealey, "Orangemen and the Corporation"; Fyson, "The Trials and Tribulations of Riot Prosecutions."

139 Mary Ryan has written eloquently on this same cultural shift in the American context. See *Civic Wars*, 131; "Gender and Public Access." Also, see Vernon, *Politics and the People*, Introduction.

140 Greer and Radforth, "Introduction," 8; Dagenais, "The Municipal Territory."

141 See Fyson, "Blows and Scratches, Swords and Guns."

Conclusion

1 See Young, *The Politics of Codification*; *Patrician Families and the Making of Quebec*; *In Its Corporate Capacity*.

2 See Fecteau, *Un nouvel ordre des choses*; *La liberté du pauvre*.

3 See Bradbury, *Working Families*; *Wife to Widow*.

4 See Fyson, *Magistrates, Police, and People*.

5 See Sweeny, *Why Did We Choose to Industrialize?*

6 See Poutanen, *Beyond Brutal Passions*.

7 See Greer, *The Patriots and the People*.

8 For more on Thompson's notion of a moral economy, see "The Moral Economy of the Crowd in the Eighteenth Century." In the context of Quebec, see Fahrni, "Who Now Reads E.P. Thompson?"

9 Berman's examination of Goethe's recounting of the legend of Faust offers a particularly rich contemplation of social and cultural change during the process of modernity. *All That Is Solid Melts into Air*, chapter 1.

10 On the Special Council, see Watt, "Authoritarianism, Constitutionalism, and the Special Council."

11 For a nuanced take on policing in Montreal, Donald Fyson's work is helpful, as it traces continuity and change on this front back to the eighteenth century. See *Magistrates, Police, and People*, chapter 4.

12 On crowds rescuing prisoners, see Fyson, "The Trials and Tribulations of Riot Prosecutions."

13 On the urban boulevard as a staging ground for parades, see Truesdell, *Spectacular Politics*.

14 For overviews of parading as a popular custom and as a means of exercising authority, see Davis, *Parades and Power* and Ryan, "The American Parade."

15 See Eid, *Le clergé et le pouvoir politique au Québec*, chapter 1.

16 See Perin, *Ignace de Montréal*, chapter 3.

17 For recent work on this topic, see Geneviève Zubrzycki, *Beheading the Saint*.

18 While dealing with a later period, DeLottinville's "Joe Beef of Montreal" remains a helpful study of the waterfront cultural landscape.

19 For an extensive study of how Montreal functioned as a hub of migration, see Olson and Thornton, *Peopling the North American City.*

20 See Horner, "The public has the right to be protected from a deadly scourge."

21 For more on segregation and the commodification of land during this period, see Sweeney, *Why Did We Choose to Industrialize,* chapter 8.

22 For more on the suburbanization of elite Montrealers during this period, see MacLeod, "Salubrious Settings and Fortunate Families"; Bérubé, *Des sociétés distinctes.*

23 For the suburbanization of the city's working-class, see Lewis, *Manufacturing Montreal.*

24 See Bernard, *Les Rouges.*

25 For more on voting by secret ballot, see Grittner, "Privilege at the Polls."

26 For a discussion of the United States' Supreme Court rulings on the Passenger Cases, see Neuman, *Strangers to the Constitution,* 28.

27 Horner, "Shame upon you as men!"

28 Cross, "The Irish in Montreal, 1867–1896."

29 Bliss, *Plague.*

30 Duperreault, "L'affaire Richard."

31 For more on labour disputes in twentieth-century Montreal, see Carel, "Mémoires de grèves, 1949 et 1972"; Petitclerc et Robert, "La loi spéciale et son contexte historique."

32 See Watt, "Authoritarianism, Constitutionalism, and the Special Council of Lower Canada, 1838–1841," chapter 3.

33 Macdonald, "Imagining the City of Festivals."

Bibliography

Archival Sources

Archives de la Ville de Montréal (AVM)
VM1   Fonds du Conseil de ville de Montréal
VM43   Fonds de la Commission de la Police

Archdiocese-Archives de la Chancellerie de Montréal (ACM)
401.130   Conférences ecclésiastiques (1839–1849)
780.019   Société St Jean Baptiste de Montréal – SSJBM –
          Correspondance générale
790.21   Sociétés de tempérance et de charité établies dans le diocèse
          de Montréal, le 25 Janvier 1842.
901.053   Mgr I Bourget, évêque de Montréal –
          Lettres envoyées pour les années 1843–1852

Bibliothèque et Archives nationales du Québec à Montréal (BANQ-M)
TL19   Fonds Cour du banc de la reine
TL32   Fonds Cour des sessions générales de la paix

Library and Archives Canada (LAC)
R182–224–X–E Letterbooks of the Chairman of the Board
             of Works and Commissioners of Public Works.

Newspapers

La Minerve
L'Avenir
Le Canadien

Les Mélanges religieux
Montreal Gazette
Montreal Transcript
Montreal Witness
Pilot

Digital Libraries and Other Digital Sources

Bibliothèque et Archives nationales du Québec-Collections,
    http://www.banq.qc.ca/collections/index.html
Dictionary of Canadian Biography Online,
    http://www.biographica.ca/index-e.html
Early Canadiana Online,
    http://www.canadiana.org
McCord Museum Collection,
    http://www.mccord-museum.qc.ca/en/keys/collection

Published Primary Sources

Alexander, James. *Passages in the Life of a Soldier, or Military Service in the East and West, in Two Volumes*. London: Hurst and Blackett, 1857.

Chiniquy, Charles. *Manuel des sociétés de tempérance dédié à la jeunesse du Canada*. 3rd ed. Montréal: Jean-Baptiste Rolland, 1849.

Exercice du Chemin de la Croix avec les pratiques de cette dévotion. Tours: R. Pornin et Cie., 1844.

Glackmeyer, Charles. *The Charter and By-Laws of the City of Montreal*. Montreal: Lovell, 1865. *Louis Hippolyte Lafontaine – Correspondance générale. Tome I: Les ficelles du pouvoir*, edited by Éric Bédard. Montréal: Les Éditions Varia, 2002.

Hincks, Francis. *Reminiscences of His Public Life*. Montreal: William Drysdale, 1884.

Lachance, Micheline. *La Saga des Papineau: D'après les mémoires inédits du dernier seigneur de Montebello*. Montréal: Québec Amerique, 2013.

Lambton, John George, Charles Buller, and Edward Gibbon Wakefield. *The Report and Despatches of the Earl of Durham, Her Majesty's High Commissioner and Governor-General of British North America*. London: Ridgeways, 1839.

Lamonde, Yves, and Claude Larin, eds. *Louis-Joseph Papineau: Un demi-siècle de combats – Interventions publiques*. Montréal: Fides, 1998.

Louis Hippolyte Lafontaine – Correpondance general. Tome 3: Mon cher Amable: Lettres de Louis Hippolyte La Fontaine à divers correspondants, 1848–1864. Montréal: Les Éditions Varia, 2005.

Mandements, lettres pastorales, circulaires et autres documents publiés dans le diocèse de Montréal depuis son érection. Montréal: J. Chapleau et fils, 1887.

Ordinances Made and Passed by His Excellency the Governor General and Special Council for the Affairs of the Province of Lower Canada Volume 5. Quebec: John Charlton Fisher and William Kemble, 1839.

Papers Relative to the Affairs of Canada. London: W. Clowes, 1849.

Regulations for the Governance of the Police Force, Rural and City, Province of Canada with Instructions as to the Legal Authorities and Duties of Police Constables. Montreal: J. Starke and Company, 1841.

Revised Acts and Ordinances of Lower Canada. Montreal: Derbishire and Desbarats, 1845.

Ryerson, Egerton. *A System of Public Elementary Instruction for Upper Canada*. Montreal: Lovell and Gibson, 1847.

Souvenir of the Golden Jubilee of St Patrick's Total Abstinence and Benefit Society, 1840–1890. Montreal: Dominion Illustrated Co., 1890.

The Montreal Directory. Montreal: Lovell and Gibson, 1849.

Walrond, Theodore, ed. *Letters and Journals of James, Eighth Earl of Elgin*. London, J. Murray, 1872.

Warburton, George. *Hochelaga or England in the New World*. London: Henry Colburn, 1846.

Weir, William. *Sixty Years in Canada*. Montreal: John Lovell and Sons, 1903.

Secondary Sources

Ajzenstat, Janet. *The Political Thought of Lord Durham*. Montreal: McGill-Queen's University Press, 1988.

Akenson, Donald. *The Irish in Ontario: A Study in Rural History*. Montreal: McGill-Queen's University Press, 1984.

Ancelovici, Marcos et Francis Dupuis-Déri. *Un printemps rouge et noir: Regards croisés sur la grève étudiante de 2012*. Montréal: Éditions Écosociété, 2014.

Anderson, Benedict. *Imagined Communities: Reflections on the Origin and Spread of Nationalism*. London: Verso, 1983.

Ares, Jean-Patrice. "Les campagnes de tempérance de Charles Chiniquy: Un des principaux moteurs du réveil religieux montréalais de 1840. Master's thesis, Université de Québec à Montréal, 1996.

Bailey, Peter. *Popular Culture and Performance in the Victorian City*. Cambridge: Cambridge University Press, 1998.

Baldwin, Peter. *Domesticating the Street: The Reform of Public Space in Hartford, 1850–1930*. Columbus: Ohio State University Press, 1999.

Bannister, Jerry, and Liam Riordan, eds. *The Loyal Atlantic: Remaking the British Atlantic in the Revolutionary Era*. Toronto: University of Toronto Press, 2012.

Bédard, Éric. *Les réformistes: Une génération canadienne-française au milieu du XIXe siècle*. Montréal: Boréale, 2009.

Bergeron, Gérard. *Lire François-Xavier Garneau, 1809–1866: Historien national*. Québec: Institut québécois sur la culture, 1994.

Berman, Marshall. *All That Is Solid Melts into Air: The Experience of Modernity*. London: Penguin Books, 1982.

Bernard, Jean-Paul. *Les rouges: Libéralisme, nationalisme et anti-cléricalisme au milieu du XIXe siècle*. Montréal: Presses de l'université du Québec, 1971.

– *The Rebellions of 1837 and 1838 in Lower Canada*. Ottawa: Canadian Historical Association, 1996.

Bernier, Gérald, and Daniel Salée. *Entre l'ordre et la liberté: Colonialisme, pouvoir et transition vers le capitalisme dans le Québec du XIXe siècle*. Montréal: Boréal, 1995.

Bérubé, Harold. *Des sociétés distinctes: Gouverner les banlieues bourgeoises de Montréal, 1880–1939*. Montreal: McGill-Queen's University Press, 2014.

Bilson, Geoffrey. *A Darkened House: Cholera in Nineteenth-Century Canada*. Toronto: University of Toronto Press, 1980.

Bleasdale, Ruth. "Class Conflict on the Canals of Upper Canada in the 1840s." *Labour / Le Travail* 7 (Spring 1981): 9–39.

Bliss, Michael. *A Living Profit: Studies in the Social History of Canadian Business, 1883–1911*. Toronto: McClelland and Stewart, 1974.

– *Plague: A Story of Smallpox in Montreal*. Toronto: Harper Collins, 1991.

Blocker, Jack. *American Temperance Movements: Cycles of Reform.* Woodbridge, CT: Twayne, 1989.

Blumin, Stuart. *The Emergence of the Middle-Class: Social Experience in the American City, 1760–1900.* Cambridge: Cambridge University Press, 1989.

Boily, Raymond. *Les Irlandais et le canal de Lachine.* Montréal: Leméac, 1980.

Boissery, Beverley. *A Deep Sense of Wrong: The Treason, Trials and Transportation to New South Wales of Lower Canadian Rebels after the 1838 Rebellion.* Toronto: University of Toronto Press, 1995.

Bouman, Mark. "Luxury and Control: The Urbanity of Street Lighting in Nineteenth-Century Cities." *Journal of Urban History* 14.1 (November 1987): 7–37.

Bradbury, Bettina. "Pigs, Cows, and Boarders: Non-Wage Forms of Survival among Montreal Families, 1861–1891." *Labour / Le Travail* 14 (Fall 1984): 9–46.

– "Widows at the Hustings: Gender, Citizenship and the Montreal By-Elections of 1832." In *Re-Thinking Canada: The Promise of Women's History*, edited by Mona Gleason and Adele Perry, 73–94. 5th ed. Toronto: Oxford University Press, 2006.

– *Wife to Widow: Lives, Laws and Politics in Nineteenth-Century Montreal.* Vancouver: University of British Columbia Press, 2011.

– *Working Families: Age, Gender and Daily Survival in Industrializing Montreal.* Don Mills: Oxford University Press, 1993.

Bradbury, Bettina, and Tamara Myers. "Introduction: Negotiating Identities in Nineteenth- and Twentieth-Century Montreal." In *Negotiating Identities in 19th and 20th Century Montreal*, edited by Bettina Bradbury and Tamara Myers, 1–21. Vancouver: University of British Columbia Press, 2005.

Brunet, Michel. "L'église catholique du Bas-Canada et le partage du pouvoir à l'heure d'une nouvelle donne, 1837–1854." CHA *Historical Papers* (1969): 137–51.

Bryan, Dominic. *Orange Parades: The Politics of Ritual, Tradition and Control.* London: Pluto Press, 2000.

Buckner, Phillip. *The Transition to Responsible Government: British Policy in British North America, 1815–1850.* Westport, CT: Greenwood Press, 1985.

Calhoun, Craig. *The Roots of Radicalism: Tradition, the Public Sphere, and Early-Nineteenth-Century Social Movements.* Chicago: University of Chicago Press, 2014.

Calloway, Colin. *The Scratch of a Pen: 1763 and the Transformation of North America.* Oxford: Oxford University Press, 2006.

Carel, Ivan. "Mémoires de grèves, 1949 et 1972." *Bulletin d'histoire politique* 21.2 (Winter 2013): 30–43.

Careless, J.M.S. *The Union of the Canadas: The Growth of Canadian Institutions, 1841–1857.* Toronto: McClelland and Stewart, 1968.

Caulier, Brigitte. "Bâtir l'Amérique des dévots: Les confréries de dévotion montréalaises depuis le régime français." *Revue d'histoire de l'Amérique française* 46.1 (Summer 1992): 45–66.

Charest-Auger, Maude. "Les réactions montréalaises à l'épidémie de typhus de 1847." Master's thesis, Université du Québec à Montréal, 2012.

Charland, Jean-Pierre. *L'entreprise éducative au Québec, 1840–1900.* Sainte-Foy: Presses de l'Université Laval, 2000.

Choko, Marc. *The Major Squares of Montreal.* Montreal: Meridian Press, 1990.

Clark, Anna. *The Struggle for the Breeches: Gender and the Making of the British Working Class.* Berkeley: University of California Press, 1997.

Coates, Colin. *The Metamorphoses of Landscape and Community in Early Quebec.* Montreal: McGill-Queen's University Press, 2000.

Cobb, Richard. *The Police and the People: French Popular Protest, 1789–1820.* Oxford: Oxford University Press, 1972.

Cohen, Marjorie. *Women's Work, Markets, and Economic Development in Nineteenth-Century Ontario.* Toronto: University of Toronto Press, 1988.

Colley, Linda. *Britons: Forging the Nation, 1707–1837.* New Haven: Yale University Press, 1992.

Comte, Henri. *La Fête-Dieu à Montréal de 1658 à 1933.* Montreal: Arbour et Dupont, 1943.

Cook, Sharon. *"Through sunshine and shadow": The Women's Christian Temperance Union, Evangelicalism, and Reform in Ontario, 1874–1930.* Montreal: McGill-Queen's University Press, 1995.

Corbin, Alain. *Les filles de noce: Misère sexuelle et prostitution aux 19e et 20e siècles.* Paris: Aubier Montaigne, 1978.

Cottrell, Michael. "St. Patrick's Day Parades in Nineteenth-Century

Toronto: A Study of Immigrant Adjustment and Elite Control."
Social History / Histoire sociale 25.49 (May 1992): 57–74.

Creighton, Donald. *The Commercial Empire of the St. Lawrence, 1760–1850*. Toronto: The Ryerson Press, 1937.

Cross, Dorothy. "The Irish in Montreal, 1867–1896." Master's thesis, McGill University, 1969, 167–72.

Curtis, Bruce. "Class, Culture and Administration: Educational Inspection in Canada West." In *Colonial Leviathan: State Formation in Nineteenth-Century Canada*, edited by Allan Greer and Ian Radforth, 103–33. Toronto: University of Toronto Press, 1992.

– "Le redécoupage du Bas-Canada dans les années 1830: Un essai sur la 'gouvernementalité' coloniale." *Revue d'histoire de l'Amérique française* 58.1 (Summer 2004): 28–65.

– "'The Most Splendid Pageant Ever Seen': Grandeur, the Domestic, and Condescension in Lord Durham's Political Theatre." *Canadian Historical Review* 89.1 (March 2008): 55–87.

– *The Politics of Population: State Formation, Statistics and the Census of Canada, 1840–1875*. Toronto: University of Toronto Press, 2002.

– *Ruling by Schooling Quebec: Conquest to Liberal Governmentality – A Historical Sociology*. Toronto: University of Toronto Press, 2012.

Dagenais, Michèle. "The Municipal Territory: A Product of the Liberal Order?" In *Liberalism and Hegemony: Debating the Canadian Liberal Revolution*, edited by Michel Ducharme and Jean-François Constant, 202–20. Toronto: University of Toronto Press, 2009.

Danylewicz, Marta. *Taking the Veil: An Alternative to Marriage, Motherhood and Spinsterhood in Quebec, 1840–1929*. Toronto: McClelland and Stewart, 1987.

Davidoff, Leonore and Catherine Hall. *Family Fortunes: Men and Women of the English Middle Class, 1780–1850*. London: Routledge, 1987.

Davies, Megan. "Night Soil, Cesspools, and Smelly Hogs on the Streets: Sanitation, Race, and Governance in Early British Columbia." *Social History / Histoire sociale* 38.75 (May 2005): 1–36.

Davis, Susan. *Parades and Power: Street Theatre in Nineteenth-Century Philadelphia*. Philadelphia: Temple University Press, 1985.

Dechêne, Louise. *Habitants et marchands de Montréal au XVII siècle*. Montréal: Plon, 1974.

DeLottinville, Peter. "Joe Beef of Montreal: Working-Class Culture and the Tavern, 1869–1889." *Labour / Le Travail* 8/9 (Fall 1981/ Spring 1982): 9–40.

Desan, Suzanne. "Crowds, Community, and Ritual in the Work of E.P. Thompson and Natalie Davis." In *The New Cultural History*, edited by Lynn Hunt, 47–71. Berkeley: University of California Press, 1989.

Desloges, Yvan, and Alain Gelly. *The Lachine Canal: Riding the Waves of Industrial and Urban Development, 1860–1950*. Québec: Septentrion, 2002.

Ducharme, Michel. *Le concept de liberté au Canada à l'époque des révolutions Atlantiques, 1776–1838*. Montreal: McGill-Queen's University Press, 2010.

Ducharme, Michel, and Jean-François Constant. "Introduction: A Project of Rule Called Canada – The Liberal Order Framework and Historical Practice." In *Liberalism and Hegemony: Debating the Canadian Liberal Revolution*, edited by Michel Ducharme and Jean-François Constant, 3–32. Toronto: University of Toronto Press, 2009.

Duperreault, Jean. "L'affaire Richard: A Situational Analysis of the Montreal Hockey Riot of 1855." *Canadian Journal of History and Sport* 12.1 (May 1981): 66–93.

Eid, Nadia. *Le clergé et le pouvoir politique au Québec: une analyse de l'idéologie ultramontaine au milieu du XIXe siècle*. Montréal: Hurtubise, 1978.

Eley, Geoff. "Nations, Public and Political Cultures: Placing Habermas in the Nineteenth Century." In *Habermas and the Public Sphere*, edited by Craig Calhoun, 289–332. Cambridge: MIT Press, 1992.

Fahrni, Magda. "Who Now Reads E.P. Thompson? Or, (Re)reading *The Making* at UQAM." *Labour / Le Travail* 72 (2013): 291–6.

Fecteau, Jean-Marie. "En guise de (provisoire) conclusion." *Revue d'histoire de l'Amérique française* 61.2 (Fall 2007): 299–301.

– "La dynamique sociale du catholicisme québécois au XIXe siècle: Éléments pour une réflexion sur les frontières et les conditions historiques de possibilité du 'social.'" *Social History / Histoire sociale* (November 2002): 507–8

– *La liberté du pauvre: Sur la régulation du crime et de la pauvreté au XIXe siècle québécoise*. Montréal: VLB, 2004.

– "Mesures d'exception et règle de droit: Les conditions d'application

de la loi martiale au Québec lors des rébellions de 1837–1838."
McGill Law Journal 32 (1986–87): 465–95.

– "Note critique: Primauté analytique de l'expérience et gradualisme historique: Sur les apories d'une certaine lecture du passé." *Revue d'histoire de l'Amérique française* 61.2 (Fall 2007): 281–94.

– *Un nouvel ordre des choses: La pauvreté, le crime, et l'État au Québec, de la fin du XVIII siècle à 1840.* Outremont: VLB, 1989.

Ferry, Darren. *Uniting in Measures of Common Good: The Construction of Liberal Identities in Central Canada.* Montreal: McGill-Queen's University Press, 2008.

Fingard, Judith. "Race and Respectability in Victorian Halifax." *The Journal of Imperial and Commonwealth History* 20.2 (May 1992): 165–95.

Fitzpatrick, D. *Irish Emigration, 1801–1921.* Dublin: Dundalgan Press, 1984.

Fyson, Donald. "Blows and Scratches, Swords and Guns: Violence between Men as Material Reality and Lived Experience in Early-Nineteenth-Century Lower Canada." Paper presented to the Annual Meeting of the Canadian Historical Association, Université de Sherbrooke, May 1999.

– "The Conquered and the Conqueror: The Mutual Adaptation of the *Canadiens* and the British in Quebec, 1759–1775." In *Revisiting 1759: The Conquest of Canada in Historical Perspective*, edited by Phillip Buckner and John Reid, 190–217. Toronto: University of Toronto Press, 2012.

– *Magistrates, Police, and People: Everyday Criminal Justice in Quebec and Lower Canada, 1764–1837.* Toronto: University of Toronto Press, 2006.

– "Réplique de Donald Fyson." *Revue d'histoire de l'Amérique française* 61.2 (Fall 2007): 294–9.

– "The Trials and Tribulations of Riot Prosecutions: Collective Violence, State Authority and Criminal Justice in Quebec, 1841–1892." In *Canadian State Trials*, vol. 3, *Political Trials and Security Measures, 1840–1914*, edited by Barry Wright and Susan Binnie, 161–203. Toronto: University of Toronto Press, 2009.

Gagnon, Robert. *Questions d'égouts: Santé publique, infrastructures et urbanisation à Montréal au XIXe siècle.* Montréal: Boréal, 2006.

Galarneau, Claude. "Monseigneur de Forbin-Janson au Québec en
1840–1841." In *Les ultramontaines Canadien-français*, edited by
Nive Voisine et Jean Hamelin, 121–42. Montréal: Boréal, 1985.

Gentilcore, Louis. *Historical Atlas of Canada*, vol.2, *The Land
Transformed, 1800–1891*. Toronto: University of Toronto Press, 1993.

Gilliland, Jason. "The Creative Destruction of Montreal: Street
Widenings and Urban (Re) Development in the Nineteenth
Century." *Urban History Review / Revue d'histoire urbaine* 31.1 (Fall
2002): 37–51.

– "Muddy Shore to Modern Port: Redemensioning the Montreal
Waterfront Time-Space." *Canadian Geographer* 48.4 (Winter
2004): 448–70.

Goheen, Peter. "Parading: A Lively Tradition in Early Victorian
Toronto." In *Ideology and Landscape in Historical Perspective*,
edited by Alan Baker and Gideon Biger, 330–51. Cambridge:
Cambridge University Press, 1992.

– "Symbols in the Streets: Parades in Victorian Urban Canada." *Urban
History Review / Revue d'histoire urbaine* 18.3 (February 1990):
237–43.

Greenwood, Frank. *Legacies of Fear: Law and Politics in Quebec in the Era
of the French Revolution*. Toronto: University of Toronto Press, 1993.

– "The Montreal Court Martial 1838–9: Legal and Constitutional
Reflections." In *Canadian State Trials: Rebellion and Invasion in the
Canadas, 1837–1839*, edited by Frank Greenwood and Barry Wright,
325–52. Toronto: University of Toronto Press, 2002.

Greer, Allan. "The Birth of the Police in Canada." In *Colonial
Leviathan: State Formation in Mid-Nineteenth-Century Canada*,
edited by Allan Greer and Ian Radforth, 17–42. Toronto: University
of Toronto Press, 1992.

Greer, Allan, and Ian Radforth, eds. *Colonial Leviathan: State
Formation in Mid-Nineteenth-Century Canada*. Toronto:
University of Toronto Press, 1992.

– *The Patriots and the People: The Rebellion of 1837 in Rural Lower
Canada*. Toronto: University of Toronto Press, 1993.

Grittner, Colin. "Privilege at the Polls: Culture, Citizenship, and the
Electoral Franchise in Mid- Nineteenth-Century British North
America." PhD, McGill University, 2015.

Guildford, Janet, and Suzanne Morton, eds. *Separate Spheres: Women's Worlds in the 19ᵗʰ Century Maritimes*. Fredericton: Acadiensis Press, 1994.

Gunn, Simon. *The Public Culture of the Victorian Middle-Class*. Manchester: Manchester University Press, 2000.

Habermas, Jürgen. *The Structural Transformation of the Public Sphere: An Inquiry into a Category of Bourgeois Society*, 1962. Translated by Thomas Burger. Cambridge: MIT Press, 1989.

Hall, Catherine. "The Rule of Difference: Gender, Class and Empire in the Making of the 1832 Reform Act." In *Gendered Nations: Nationalisms and Gender Order in the Long Nineteenth Century*, edited by Ida Bloom, Karen Hagemann, and Catherine Hall, 107–35. Oxford: Oxford University Press, 2000.

– *White, Male and Middle Class: Explorations in Feminism and History*. New York: Routledge, 1992.

Hall, Catherine, Keith McClelland, and Jane Rendall, eds. *Defining the Victorian Nation: Class, Race, Gender and the British Reform Act of 1867*. Cambridge: Cambridge University Press, 2000.

Hanagan, Michael. "Charles Tilly and Violent France." *French Historical Studies* 33.2 (Spring 2010): 283–97.

Hardy, René. "À propos du réveil religieux dans le Québec du XIXe siècle: Le recours aux tribunaux dans les rapports entre le clergé et les fidèles (district de Trois-Rivières)." *Revue d'histoire de l'Amérique française* 48.2 (Fall 1994): 187–212.

– *Contrôle social et mutation de la culture religieuse au Québec, 1830–1930*. Montréal: Boréal, 1999.

– "Le charivari dans l'espace québécois." In *Espace et Culture*, edited by Serge Courville and Normand Séguin, 175–86. Ste Foy: Les presses de l'université Laval, 1995.

Harring, Sidney. *White Man's Law: Native People in Nineteenth Century Canadian Jurisprudence*. Toronto: University of Toronto Press, 1998.

Harrison, Brian. *Drink and the Victorians: The Temperance Question in England, 1815–1872*. Pittsburgh: University of Pittsburgh Press, 1971.

Harrison, Mark. "The Ordering of the Urban Environment: Time, Work, and the Occurrence of Crowds, 1790–1835." *Past and Present* 110 (February 1986): 134–68.

Harvey, David. *Paris: Capital of Modernity.* New York: Routledge, 2003.

Havard, Gilles. *The Great Peace of Montreal of 1701: French-Native Diplomacy in the Seventeenth Century,* Montreal: McGill-Queen's University Press, 2001.

Henderson, Jarett. "Banishment to Bermuda: Gender, Race, Empire, Independence and the Struggle to Abolish Irresponsible Government in Lower Canada," *Histoire sociale / Social History* 46.92 (November 2013): 321–48.

– "Uncivil Subjects: Metropolitan Meddling, Imperial Interference and Conditional Loyalty in Lower Canada." PhD, York University, 2010.

Heron, Craig. *Booze: A Distilled History.* Toronto: Between the Lines Press, 2003.

Hobsbawm, Eric. *Primitive Rebels: Studies in Archaic Forms of Social Movement in the 19th and 20th Centuries.* Manchester: Manchester University Press, 1959.

Hobsbawm, Eric, and Terence Ranger, eds. *The Invention of Tradition.* Cambridge: Cambridge University Press, 1983.

Hofstra, Warren, ed. *Cultures in Conflict: The Seven Years' War in North America.* Lanham, MD: Rowman and Littlefield, 2007.

Holendahl, Peter. "Jürgen Habermas: 'The Public Sphere' (1962)." Translated by Patricia Russian. *New German Critique* 3 (Fall 1974): 45–8.

Holman, Andrew. *A Sense of Their Duty: Middle-Class Formation in Victorian Ontario Towns.* Montreal: McGill-Queen's University Press, 2000.

Holton, Robert. "The Crowd in History: Some Problems of Theory and Method." *Social History* 3.2 (May 1978): 219–33.

Horner, Dan. "'If the evil now growing around us be not staid': Montreal and Liverpool Confront the Irish Famine Migration as a Transnational Crisis in Urban Governance," *Histoire sociale / Social History* 46.92 (November 2013): 349–66.

– "'Like a Thread of Gold': Tracing Alfred Perry's Lifelong Engagement with Montreal's Politics of Ethnic Confrontation." In *Engaging with Diversity: Multidiscipinary Reflections on Plurality from Quebec,* edited by Stéphan Gervais, Raffaele Iacovino, and Mary Anne Poutanen, 327–46. Brussels: Peter Lang, 2018.

– "'Shame upon you as men!': Contesting Authority in the Aftermath of Montreal's Gavazzi Riot." *Histoire sociale / Social History* 44.87 (November 2011): 29–52.

– "'The Public has the right to be protected from a deadly scourge': Debating Quarantine, Migration and Liberal Governance during the 1847 Typhus Outbreak in Montreal." *Journal of the Canadian Historical Association / Revue de la société historique du Canada* 23.1 (2012): 65–100.

Houston, Cecil, and William Smyth. *The Sash Canada Wore: A Historical Geography of the Orange Order in Canada.* Toronto: University of Toronto Press, 1980.

Hubert, Ollivier. *Sur la terre comme au ciel: La gestion des rites par l'Église catholique du Québec (fin XVIIe-mi-XIXe siècle).* Saint-Nicolas: Les presses de l'Université Laval.

Hudon, Christine. "La sociabilité religieuse à l'ère du vapeur et du rail." *Journal of the Canadian Historical Association / Revue de la société historique du Canada* 10.1 (1999): 129–47.

– "Le renouveau religieux québécois au XIXe siècle: Éléments pour une réinterpretation." *Studies in Religion / Sciences Religieuses* 24.4 (1995): 467–89.

Huggins, Michael. *Social Conflict in Pre-Famine Ireland: The Case of Country Roscommon.* Dublin: Four Courts Press, 2007.

Igartua, José. "A Change in Climate: The Conquest and the *Marchands* of Montreal." *Historical Papers* (1974): 115–34.

Ignatiev, Noel. *How the Irish Became White.* New York: Routledge, 1995.

Inglis, Tom. *Moral Monopoly: The Catholic Church in Modern Irish Society.* Dublin: Gill and Macmillan, 1987.

Ingram, Darcy. "Saving the Union's Jack: The Montreal Sailors' Institute and the Homeless Sailor, 1862–1898." In *Negotiating Identities in 19ᵗʰ and 20ᵗʰ Century Montreal,* edited by Bettina Bradbury and Tamara Myers, 49–72. Vancouver: University of British Columbia Press, 2005.

Ismer, Suen. "Embodying the Nation: Football, Emotions and the Construction of Collective Identity." *Nationalities Papers: The Journal of Nationalism and Ethnicity* 39.4 (2011): 547–65.

Jackson, James. *The Riot that Never Was: The Military Shooting of Three Montrealers in 1832 and the Official Cover-Up.* Montreal: Baraka Books, 2009.

Jenkins, William. *Between Raid and Rebellion: The Irish in Buffalo and*

Toronto, 1867–1916. Montreal: McGill-Queen's University Press, 2013.

Jones, Bradley. *Repubicanism and Responsible Government: The Shaping of Democracy in Australia and Canada*. Montreal: McGill-Queen's University Press, 2014.

Jones, David. *Rebecca's Children: A Study of Rural Society, Crime and Protest*. Oxford: Clarendon Press, 1989.

Joyce, Patrick. *The Rule of Freedom: Liberalism and the Modern City*. London: Verso, 2003.

Kealey, Gregory. "Orangemen and the Corporation: The Politics of Class in Toronto during the Union of the Canadas." In *Forging a Consensus: Historical Essays on Toronto*, edited by Victor Russell, 41–86. Toronto: University of Toronto Press, 1984.

Kenny, Kevin. *Making Sense of the Molly Maguires*. Oxford: Oxford University Press, 1998.

Kenny, Stephen. "'Cahots' and Catcalls: An Episode of Popular Resistance in Lower Canada at the Outset of the Union." *Canadian Historical Review* 65.2 (June 1984): 184–208.

Lamonde, Yves. *Histoire sociale des idées au Québec, 1760–1896*. Montréal: Fides, 2000.

Lawson, Philip. *The Imperial Challenge: Quebec and Britain in the Age of the American Revolution*. Montreal: McGill-Queen's University Press, 1989.

Le Bon, Gustave. *The Crowd: A Study of the Popular Mind*. London: MacMillan, 1896.

Leitch, Gillian. "The Importance of Being English? Social Organization and Ethnic Identity in British Montreal, 1800–1850." PhD, Université de Montréal, 2007.

Lewis, Robert. *Manufacturing Montreal: The Making of an Industrial Landscape, 1850–1930*. Baltimore: Johns Hopkins University Press, 2000.

Macdonald, Amy. "Imagining the City of Festivals: Festivalization and Urban Space in Montreal." Master's thesis, McGill University, 2012.

MacLeod, Roderick. "Salubrious Settings and Fortunate Families: The Making of Montreal's Golden Square Mile, 1840–1895." PhD, McGill University, 1997.

Martin, Scott. *Devil of the Domestic Sphere: Temperance, Gender, and Middle-class Ideology, 1800–1860*. DeKalb: Northern Illinois University Press, 2009.

McCalla, Douglas. *Planting the Province: The Economic History of Upper Canada, 1784–1870*. Toronto: University of Toronto Press, 1993.

McCormack, Matthew. *The Independent Man: Citizenship and Gender Politics in Georgian England*. Manchester: Manchester University Press, 2005.

McKay, Ian. "Canada as a Long Liberal Revolution: On Writing the History of Actually Existing Canadian Liberalisms, 1840s–1940s." In *Liberalism and Hegemony: Debating the Canadian Liberal Revolution*, edited by Michel Ducharme and Jean-François Constant, 347–452. Toronto: University of Toronto Press, 2009.

– "The Liberal Order Framework: A Prospectus for a Reconnaissance of Canadian History." *Canadian Historical Review* 81 (December 2000): 617–45.

McNairn, Jeffrey. *The Capacity to Judge: Public Opinion and Deliberative Democracy in Upper Canada, 1791–1854*. Toronto: University of Toronto Press, 2000.

Monet, Jacques. *The Last Cannon Shot: A Study of French-Canadian Nationalism, 1837–1850*. Toronto: University of Toronto Press, 1969.

Moore, Christopher. *The Loyalists: Revolution, Exile, Settlement*. Toronto: Macmillan, 1984.

Morgan, Cecilia. *Public Men and Virtuous Women: The Gendered Languages of Religion and Politics in Upper Canada, 1791–1850*. Toronto: University of Toronto Press, 1996.

Morton, Adam. *Unravelling Gramsci: Hegemony and Passive Revolution in the Global Political Economy*. London: Pluto Press, 2007.

Mungar, Frank. "Contentious Gatherings in Lancashire, England, 1750–1893." In *Class Conflict and Collective Action*, edited by Charles Tilly and Louise Tilly, 71–89. London: Sage Publications, 1981.

Nelles, H.V. *The Art of Nation-Building: Pageantry and Spectacle at Quebec's Tercentenary*. Toronto: University of Toronto Press, 1998.

Nelson, Wendie. "'Rage against the dying of the light': Interpreting the Guerre des Éteignoirs." *Canadian Historical Review* 81.4 (December 2000): 551–81.

Neuman, Gerald. *Strangers to the Constitution: Immigrants, Borders and Fundamental Law*. Princeton: Princeton University Press, 1996.

Noël, Françoise. *The Christie Seigneuries: Estate Management and Settlement in the Upper Richilieu Valley, 1760–1854*. Montreal: McGill-Queen's University Press, 1992.

Noel, Jan. *Canada Dry: Temperance Crusades Before Confederation.*
Toronto: University of Toronto Press, 1995.
– "Dry Patriotism: The Chiniquy Crusade." *Canadian Historical Review*
71.2 (June 1995): 189–207.
Olson, Sherry, "Research Note: Ethnic Partition of the Work Force in
1840s Montreal." *Labour / Le Travail* 53 (Spring 2004): 159–202.
Olson, Sherry, and Patricia Thornton. "The Challenge of the Irish
Catholic Community in Nineteenth-Century Montreal." *Histoire
sociale / Social History* 35.70 (November 2002): 331–62.
– *Peopling the North American City: Montreal, 1840–1900.* Montreal:
McGill-Queen's University Press, 2011.
Orsi, Robert. *The Madonna of 115th Street: Faith and Community in
Italian Harlem, 1880–1950.* New Haven: Yale University Press, 1988.
Ó Tuathaigh, Gearóid. *Ireland before the Famine: 1798–1848.* Dublin:
Gill and Macmillan, 1972.
Oxx, Katie. *The Nativist Movement in America: Religious Conflict in the
19th Century.* New York: Routledge, 2013.
Palmer, Bryan. *Cultures of Darkness: Night Travels in the Histories of
Transgression.* New York: Monthly Review Press, 2000.
– "Discordant Music: Charivaris and White-Capping in Nineteenth-
Century North America." *Labour / Le Travail* 3 (1978): 3–62.
– *Working Class Experience: Rethinking the History of Canadian Labour.*
2nd ed. Toronto: McClelland and Stewart, 1992.
Pâquet, Martin. *Tracer les marges de la cité: Étranger, immigrant, et état
au Québec, 1627–1981.* Montreal: Boréal, 2005.
Pentland, H. Clare. "The Lachine Strike of 1843." *Canadian Historical
Review* 29.3 (1948): 255–77.
Perin, Roberto. "Elaborating a Public Culture in Nineteenth-Century
Quebec." In *Religion and Public Life in Canada: Historical and
Comparative Perspectives*, edited by Marguerite Van Die, 87–108.
Toronto: University of Toronto Press, 2001.
– *Ignace de Montréal: Artisan d'une identité nationale.* Montréal:
Boréal, 2008.
Perrot, Michelle. *Femmes publiques.* Paris: Les Éditions Textuel, 1997.
Petitclerc, Martin. *"Nous protégeons l'infortune": Les origines populaires
de l'économie sociale au Québec.* Montréal: VLB Éditeur, 2007.
Petitclerc, Martin, et Martin Robert. "La loi spéciale et son contexte

historique: La désinvolture du gouvernement quant au droit de
grève." *Histoire engagée.ca*, 7 juillet 2013.

Podmore, Julie, and Line Chamberland. "Entering the Frame: Early
Lesbian Activism and Public Space in Montreal." *Journal of
Lesbian Studies* 19.2 (2015): 192–211.

Podruchny, Carolyn. *Making the Voyageur World: Travelers and Traders
in the North American Fur Trade*. Lincoln: University of Nebraska
Press, 2006.

Poutanen, Mary Anne. *Beyond Brutal Passions: Prostitution in
Early Nineteenth-Century Montreal*. Montreal: McGill-Queen's
University Press, 2015.

– "Bonds of Friendship, Kinship, and Community: Gender,
Homelessness, and Mutual Aid in Early-Nineteenth-Century
Montreal." In *Negotiating Identities in 19ᵗʰ and 20ᵗʰ Century
Montreal*, edited by Bettina Bradbury and Tamara Myers, 25–48.
Vancouver: University of British Columbia Press, 2005.

– "Regulating Public Space in Early-Nineteenth-Century Montreal:
Vagrancy Laws and Gender in a Colonial Context." *Social History /
Histoire sociale* 35.69 (November 2002): 33–57.

– "To Indulge Their Carnal Appetites: Prostitution in Early Nineteenth-
Century Montreal." PhD, Université de Montréal, 1996.

Radforth, Ian. "Collective Rights, Liberal Discourse, and Public Order:
The Clash over Catholic Processions in Mid-Victorian Toronto."
Canadian Historical Review 95.4 (December 2014): 511–44.

– *Royal Spectacle: The 1860 Visit of the Prince of Wales to Canada and
the United States*. Toronto: University of Toronto Press, 2004.

– "Sydenham and Utilitarian Reform." In *Colonial Leviathan: State
Formation in Mid-Nineteenth-Century Canada*, edited by Allan Greer
and Ian Radforth. Toronto: University of Toronto Press, 1992, 64–102.

Robert, Jean-Claude. "The City of Wealth and Death: Urban Mortality
in Montreal, 1821–1871." In *Essays in the History of Canadian
Medicine*, edited by Wendy Mitchinson and Janice Dickin
McGinnis, 18–38. Toronto: McClelland and Stewart, 1988.

Roberts, Paul. "Caravats and Shanavests: Whiteboyism and Faction
Fighting in East Munster, 1802–1811." In *Irish Peasant: Violence
and Unrest, 1780–1914*, edited by Samuel Clark and James Donnelly,
64–101. Madison: University of Wisconsin Press, 1983.

Roediger, David. *The Wages of Whiteness: Race and the Making of the American Working-Class*. London: Verso, 1991.

Rogers, Nicholas. *Crowds, Culture, and Politics in Georgian Britain*. Oxford: Clarendon Press, 1998.

– "Serving Toronto the Good: The Development of the City Police Force, 1834–1884." In *Forging a Consensus: Historical Essays on Toronto*, edited by Victor Russell, 116–40. Toronto: University of Toronto Press, 1984.

Rogers, Nicholas, and Adrian Shubert. "Introduction: Spectacle, Monument, and Memory." *Social History / Histoire sociale* 29.58 (November 1996): 266–7.

Rorabaugh, W.J. *The Alcoholic Republic: An American Tradition*. Oxford: Oxford University Press, 1979.

Rousseau, Louis. "À l'origine d'une société maintenant perdue: Le réveil religieux montréalais de 1840." In *Religion et culture au Québec: figures contemporaines du sacré*, edited by Yves Desrosiers, 71–92. Montréal: Fides, 1986.

– "Note de Recherche: À propos du 'réveil religieux' dans le Québec du XIXe siècle : Où se loge le vrai débat?" *Revue d'histoire de l'Amérique française* 49.2 (Fall 1995): 223–45.

Rousseau, Louis, et Frank Remiggi. "Le renouveau religieux à Montréal au XIXe siècle: Une analyse spatio-temporelle de la pratique pascale." *Studies in Religion / Sciences religieuses* 21.4 (1992): 431–54.

– eds. *Atlas historique des pratiques religieuses: Le Sud-Ouest du Québec au XIXe siècle*. Ottawa: Les Presses de l'Université d'Ottawa, 1998.

Rudé, George. *The Crowd in the French Revolution*. Oxford: Clarendon Press, 1959.

Ryan, Mary. "The American Parade: Representations of the Nineteenth-Century Social Order." In *The New Cultural History*, edited by Lynn Hunt, 131–53. Berkeley: University of California Press, 1989.

– *Civic Wars: Democracy and Public Life in the American City during the Nineteenth Century*. Berkeley: University of California Press, 1997.

– *Women in Public: Between Banners and Ballots, 1825–1880*. Baltimore: Johns Hopkins University Press, 1990.

Ryerson, Stanley. *Unequal Union: Confederation and the Roots of Conflict in the Canadas, 1815–1873*. New York: International Publishers, 1968.

Sandwell, Ruth. "The Limits of Liberalism: The Liberal Reconnaissance and the History of the Family in Canada." *Canadian Historical Review* 84 (2003): 423–50.

Schlör, Joachim. *Nights in the Big City: Paris, Berlin, London, 1840–1930.* Translated by Pierre Gottfried Imhof and Dafydd Rees Roberts. 1991. Reprint, London: Reaktion Books, 1998.

Scobey, David. "Anatomy of the Promenade: The Politics of Bourgeois Sociability in Nineteenth-Century New York." *Social History* 17.2 (May 1992): 203–27.

– *Empire City: The Making and Meaning of the New York City Landscape.* Philadelphia: Temple University Press, 2002.

Scriven, Tom. *Popular Virtue: Continuity and Change in Radical Moral Politics, 1820–1870.* Oxford: Oxford University Press, 2017.

See, Scott. "Nineteenth-Century Collective Violence: Towards a North American Context." *Labour / Le Travail* 39 (Spring 1997): 1–26.

Séguin, Renaud. "Pour une nouvelle synthèse sur les processus électoraux du XIXe siècle québécois." *Journal of the Canadian Historical Association / Revue de la Société historique du Canada* 16.1 (2005): 75–100.

Senior, Elinor Kyte. *British Regulars in Montreal: An Imperial Garrison, 1832–1854.* Montreal: McGill-Queen's University Press, 1981.

Sennett, Richard. *The Fall of Public Man.* Cambridge: Cambridge University Press, 1974.

Sheito, Christine. "Une Fête contestée: La procession de la Fête-Dieu à Montréal au XIXe siècle." Master's thesis, Université de Montréal, 1983.

Shiman, Lilian Lewis. *Crusade against Drink in Victorian England.* New York: St Martin's Press, 1988.

Shoemaker, Robert. "Using Quarter Sessions Records as Evidence for the Study of Crime and Criminal Justice." *Archives* 20.90 (October 1993):145–57.

Smart, Barry. *Foucault, Marxism and Critique.* London: Routledge, 1983.

Stansell, Christine. *City of Women: Sex and Class in New York, 1789–1860.* Urbana: University of Illinois Press, 1987.

Stewart, Brian. *The Ermatingers: A Nineteenth-Century Ojibwa-Canadian Family.* Vancouver: University of British Columbia Press, 2007.

Sutherland, Neil. "'We always had things to do': The Paid and Unpaid

Work of Anglophone Children between the 1920s and the 1960s." *Labour / Le Travail* 25 (Spring 1990): 105–41.

Sylvain, Philipe. "Quelques aspects de l'antagonisme libéral-ultramontain au Canada français." In *Les idéologies québécoises au 19e siècle*, edited by Jean-Paul Bernard, 127–49. Montréal: Éditions du Boréal Express, 1973.

Sweeny, Robert. *Why Did We Choose to Industrialize? Montreal, 1818–1849.* Montreal: McGill-Queen's University Press, 2015.

Thompson, E.P. *The Making of the English Working Class.* London: Victor Gollancz, 1963.

– "The Moral Economy of the English Crowd in the Eighteenth Century." *Past and Present* 50 (February 1971): 76–136.

Tilly, Charles. "Citizenship, Identity and Social History." *International Review of Social History* Supplement 3 (1996): 1–18.

– *From Mobilization to Revolution.* New York: McGraw-Hill, 1978.

– *The Politics of Collective Violence.* Cambridge: Harvard University Press, 2003.

– *Popular Contention in Great Britain, 1758–1834.* Cambridge: Harvard University Press, 1995.

Tilly, Charles, Louise Tilly, and Richard Tilly. *The Rebellious Century, 1830–1930.* Cambridge: Harvard University Press, 1975.

Toner, Peter. "The Origins of the New Brunswick Irish, 1851." *Journal of Canadian Studies* 23.1–2 (Spring / Summer 1988): 104–19.

Tosh, John. *A Man's Place: Masculinity and the Middle-Class Home in Victorian England.* New Haven: Yale University Press, 1999.

Trigger, Rosalyn. "Irish Politics on Parade: The Clergy, National Societies, and St. Patrick's Day Processions in Nineteenth–Century Montreal and Toronto." *Social History / Histoire sociale* 37.74 (November 2004): 159–99.

Trudel, Marcel. *Chiniquy.* 2nd ed. Montréal: Éditions du bien public, 1955.

Truesdell, Matthew. *Spectacular Politics: Louis-Napoleon Bonaparte and the Fête Impériale, 1849–1870.* Oxford: Oxford University Press, 1997.

Tulchinksy, Gerald. "The First Construction of the Lachine Canal, 1815–1826." Master's thesis, McGill University, 1960.

Turner, Victor. *The Ritual Process: Structure and Anti-Structure.* New York: Aldine de Gryter, 1995.

Vernon, James. *Distant Strangers: How Britain Became Modern.*
Berkeley: University of California Press, 2014.
– *Politics and the People: A Study in English Political Culture, c.1815–1867.*
Cambridge: Cambridge University Press, 1993.
Voisine, Nive. "L'ultramontanisme Canadien-français au XIXe siècle."
In *Les ultramontaines Canadien-français,* edited by Nive Voisine et
Jean Hamelin, 67–104. Montréal: Boréal, 1985.
Waldstreicher, David. *In the Midst of Perpetual Fetes: The Making of*
American Nationalism, 1776–1820. Chapel Hill: University of North
Carolina Press, 1997.
Watt, Steven. "Authoritarianism, Constitutionalism, and the Special
Council of Lower Canada, 1838–1841." Master's thesis, McGill
University, 1997.
– "'Duty bound and ever praying': Collective Petitioning to Central
Authorities in Lower Canada and Maine, 1820–1840." PhD,
Université du Québec à Montréal, 2005.
Way, Peter. *Common Labour: Workers and the Digging of North*
American Canals, 1780–1860. Cambridge: Cambridge University
Press, 1993.
Weinstock, Daniel. *"Occupy, Indignados,* et le printemps érable: Vers un
agenda de recherche." *McGill Law Journal* 58.2 (2012).
Welland, Heather. "Commercial Interest and Political Allegiance: The
Origins of the Quebec Act." In *Revisiting 1759: The Conquest of*
Canada in Historical Perspective, edited by Phillip Buckner and
John Reid, 166–87. Toronto: University of Toronto Press, 2012.
Wilentz, Sean. *Chants Democratic: New York City and the Rise of the*
American Working-Class, 1788–1850. Oxford: Oxford University
Press, 1984.
Wilton, Carol. *Popular Politics and Political Culture in Upper Canada,*
1800–1850. Montreal: McGill-Queen's University Press, 2000.
Winter, James. *London's Teeming Streets, 1830–1914.* London: Routledge,
1993.
Wright, Donald. *Donald Creighton: A Life in History.* Toronto:
University of Toronto Press, 2015.
Young, Brian. *In Its Corporate Capacity: The Seminary of Montreal*
as a Business Institution, 1816–1876. Montreal: McGill-Queen's
University Press, 1986.

– *Patrician Families and the Making of Quebec: The Taschereaus and the McCords*. Montreal: McGill-Queen's University Press, 2014.

– *The Politics of Codification: The Lower Canadian Civil Code of 1866*. Montreal: McGill-Queen's University Press, 1994.

– "The Volunteer Militia in Lower Canada, 1837–1850." In *Power, Place and Identity: Historical Studies of Social and Legal Regulation in Quebec*, edited by Tamara Myers, Kate Boyer, Mary Anne Poutanen, and Steven Watt, 38–54. Montreal: Montreal History Group, 1998.

Zemon Davis, Natalie. "The Reasons of Misrule: Youth Groups and Charivaris in Sixteenth- Century France." *Past and Present* 50 (February 1971): 41–75.

Zubrzycki, Geneviève. *Beheading the Saint: Nationalism, Religion, and Secularism in Quebec*. Chicago: University of Chicago Press, 2016.

Index